I0888266

ECONOMIC HISTORY

THE TWO NATIONS

FINANCE, MONEY AND BANKING

THE TWO NATIONS

A financial study of English history

CHRISTOPHER HOLLIS

Routledge
Taylor & Francis Group
LONDON AND NEW YORK

First published in 1935

Published in 2006 by
Routledge
2 Park Square, Milton Park, Abingdon, Oxfordshire OX14 4RN
711 Third Avenue, New York, NY 10017

First issued in paperback 2014

Routledge is an imprint of the Taylor and Francis Group, an informa business

British Library Cataloguing in Publication Data
A CIP catalogue record for this book
is available from the British Library

The Two Nations
ISBN 0-415-38267-X (volume)
ISBN 0-415-37850-8 (subset)
ISBN 0-415-28619-0 (set)

ISBN13: 978-1-138-86537-2 (pbk)
ISBN13: 978-0-415-38267-0 (hbk)

Routledge Library Editions: Economic History

THE TWO NATIONS

THE TWO NATIONS

A FINANCIAL STUDY OF ENGLISH HISTORY

By

CHRISTOPHER HOLLIS

Author of "*The Breakdown of Money*", etc.

LONDON

GEORGE ROUTLEDGE AND SONS, LTD.

BROADWAY HOUSE: 68–74 CARTER LANE, E.C.

1935

THE TWO NATIONS

" Say what you like, our Queen reigns over the greatest nation that ever existed."

" Which nation ? " asked the young stranger, " for she reigns over two . . . two nations ; between whom there is no intercourse and no sympathy ; who are as ignorant of each other's habits, thoughts and feelings, as if they were dwellers in different zones, or inhabitants of different planets ; who are formed by a different breeding, are fed by a different food, are ordered by different manners and are not governed by the same laws."

" You speak of—" said Egremont hesitatingly.

" THE RICH AND THE POOR."

Disraeli's *Sybil*, Book ii, Chapter 5.

TO R. McNAIR WILSON

My dear Wilson,

Our minds move so much along the same paths, so large is the debt that I owe to you for having brought me to those paths that it is but fitting that I should offer you the dedication of this work.

The footnotes give the authorities for the statistics and for the quotations which appear in the text. From the text, too, it will, I think, be sufficiently clear who are the writers of the past by whose teaching I have been led to my conclusions. Among living writers in this, as in all that I have ever written, I gratefully recognize the debt which I owe to Mr. G. K. Chesterton—a debt so large that, in accordance with the best traditions of international finance, I intend never to repay it. This is a very different book from any book that Mr. Chesterton would himself write. But it will not have been without its value if it serves to show—what Mr. Chesterton's own brilliance and wit have sometimes concealed—that the dullest and driest of statistics are often clamorous upon his side. It is worth while being dull if by doing so one can prove to the British public that Mr. Chesterton, when he is brilliant, is also right.

I am under obligation, too, to many others—to some who had no notion that, when they were talking to me, they were helping me to write a book. But in particular I should like to mention, and to recommend to those who have not come across it, *A Main Cause of Unemployment*, by Mr. P. C. Loftus, M.P. When I consulted Mr. Loftus on a point, his modesty caused him to say that he owed his own theories to Holsinger's *Mystery of the Trade Depression*, but, if it was so, I can only reply as Voltaire replied to the quip that Homer wrote Virgil. If Holsinger wrote Loftus, it was his best work.

Finally I should like to thank Lord Oxford and Mr. Douglas Woodruff for revising the proofs and my wife for performing the thankless task of making an index.

CHRISTOPHER HOLLIS.

CONTENTS

THE TWO NATIONS

CHAPTER I

THE MEDIEVAL MANAGED CURRENCY AND ITS COLLAPSE

There is one central truth running through all history. It is that a steeply falling price-level inflicts such widespread suffering that no attempt drastically to reduce a price-level has ever been permanently successful. Once prices have been allowed to rise, whether by dishonesty, by wise policy, or by miscalculation, experience has invariably proved that there has been no alternative but to accept the new price-level as a *fait accompli*.

A falling price-level inflicts great hardship and injustice—on producers and debtors. A rising price-level also, it may be argued, inflicts hardship and injustice—on creditors and those who live on fixed incomes. The rise may be as unjust as the fall, but those who suffer from the rise are in no position to hit back at the society which has robbed them. Those who suffer from the fall—the producers—can always compel society to suffer with them by refusing to produce if it is not made worth their while to do so. Therefore it has happened throughout the course of centuries that prices have sometimes risen but have never substantially fallen. By consequence they are to-day, in England as in every other country, greater by a very considerable multiple than they were at any date in the distant past.

It is also true that, had the country lived under an automatic monetary system, as that phrase is often understood—that is, had the amount of money in the country been dependent merely on the amount of silver or gold in the country and that amount in its turn been dependent on the accidents of commerce and mining—in many periods of history prices must inevitably have fallen. A country's productivity as a rule increases gradually from generation to generation; the proportion of goods produced that are sold for money on a market tends to increase. On the other hand, throughout a large portion of the world's history—from Roman times, for instance, almost until the discovery of America—there has been no important addition to the world's supply of precious metals at all. Had it been merely England that was short of silver in the Middle Ages, the problem would have righted itself without management. The shortage of silver would have caused low prices in England, and the low prices in England would have caused the owner of silver in, say, France to spend his money in England where he could buy more for it. Thus silver would have flowed into England until the price-level was restored. But in the late medieval Europe there was no country that was possessed of this surplus of silver. It is clear then that, had the currency not been managed then, prices must have fallen. In medieval Europe we lived under a managed currency.

The way in which it was managed was as follows. From time to time the weight of silver in every coin was reduced. Thus the number of coins that could be coined out of a constant amount of silver was increased, and by this means an increased monetary supply was put out to buy the increased quantity of goods and a fall in prices prevented. If we study a list of medieval prices such as that collected by Thorold Rogers,[1] we find that, owing to the poverty and slowness of communications, there were considerable local and seasonal variations of price in the different commodities. Yet at the same time, for the hundred and fifty years before the Black Death—the high period of the Middle Ages—the general price-level was held absolutely steady. Then, with the Black Death and the consequent sudden decrease of productivity, prices jumped up by about 20 per cent. Edward III had the wisdom to accept the new price-level as a *fait accompli* and not to attempt to force it down again to the pre-Black Death level. They

[1] *History of Agriculture and Prices*, vol. ii.

remained steady at the new level until the end of the century. Then came the revolution of 1399 against Richard II, a sort of Catholic dress-rehearsal of 1688, the overthrow of the true English monarchy, and the establishment in its place of the Lancastrian monarchy, which was a cross between a monarchy and a plutocratic republic. For the first time in English history power passed into the hands of men who wished to play tricks with the price-level. As a result it fluctuated about wildly. According to the computation which Mr. Feaveryear[1] has made from Thorold Rogers's figures of a price-index of commodities not dependent on the chance of harvest, if prices were 100 in 1400, by 1402 they had risen to 115·3. Then they fell steadily until by 1446 they were down to 80·4—just about what they had been before the Black Death.

Yet to medieval morals such a policy was so intolerably wicked that no régime could long survive which allowed it to be practised. Both the Yorkists and the Lancastrians learnt their lesson, and throughout the second half of the century, whoever was in power, prices remained remarkably stable. By 1500 they were at 76·8 to 1400's 100 and there they remained until the dissolution of the monasteries and debasement of the coinage by Henry VIII in 1542. Throughout all those hundred years they never moved more than a trifling number of points either way. With the two exceptions of the period of the Black Death and the quite exceptional first forty years of the fifteenth century, prices moved far less in a hundred years in the Middle Ages than they have often moved in a single year in our times.

"From the 25th of Edward III," writes Adam Smith,[2] "to the beginning of the reign of Elizabeth, during the space of more than two hundred years, six shillings and eight pence, it appears from several different statutes, had continued to be considered as what is called the moderate and reasonable, that is the ordinary or average, price of wheat. The quantity of silver, however, contained in that nominal sum was, during the course of this period, continually diminishing in consequence of some alterations which were made in the coins. But the increase in the value

[1] *The Pound Sterling*, A. Feaveryear, p. 60.
[2] *Wealth of Nations* (ed. Routledge), p. 143.

of silver had, it seems, so far compensated the diminution of the quantity of it contained in the same nominal sum, that the legislature did not think it worth while to attend to this circumstance."

It is hard to know just what Adam Smith means by "the legislature did not think it worth while to attend to this circumstance". For it was obviously the threat of falling prices which caused the King and the legislature to "attend to this circumstance" and reduce the silver content of the shilling. It is also true that during the last sixteen years of that period—during, that is to say, the last years of Henry VIII and the reigns of Edward VI and Mary—6*s*. 8*d*. might indeed be spoken of as an ordinary price of wheat, but only in the sense in which some people in the years after the War spoke of the 1914 price-level as a normal price-level to which, when the world was sane again, we should return. It was not in fact the price-level of the moment, and very soon people had to recognize that it never would be possible to return to it. In the same way the price-levels of Edward VI's and Mary's reigns were not the price-level of pre-1542 England and people had in the end to reconcile themselves to the impossibility of returning to that price-level. Nevertheless Adam Smith's words are of importance as evidence of the stability of the price-level for the two hundred years up to 1542.

In 1542 Henry VIII began to debase the coinage. He did it in the hope that thus he would be able to pay his debts for nothing. To begin with, he kept secret what he was doing, collected all the silver and gold that was paid in to him as loans and benevolences, and issued it out again from the Mint, mixed with alloy, and thus he was able to pay out about a quarter as much again as he received. With every £100 of new loan that he received he could pay off £125 of old debt. As was inevitable, the trick was soon discovered. He then frankly raised the price which he was prepared to pay for gold and silver, thus causing all possessors of those metals—there were plenty such owing to the recent loot of the monastic plate—to bring them to the Mint to be recoined into a larger quantity of base metal coins. He himself profited out of the seigniorage which he charged them for minting and also by borrowing the metals for his own uses for the period of some three or four months which elapsed between delivery and reissue.

The difficulty was, as may be imagined, with foreign trade. Foreign merchants were reluctant to take Henry's debased coins. The reason for this was not that in itself it mattered whether the coins were pure or alloyed. The trade between England and the Continent was a trade of goods against goods. Coin was only used to effect a temporary balance if the English did not happen, at a moment when no foreigner wanted any of their goods, to have an export with which to buy back their import. In the long run the English coins returned to England, or at least about as much gold and silver returned to England as left it. The concern then of the foreigners, it is clear enough, was not that the coin should be made of this or that purity of metal but that they should have a guarantee that the English price-level would be kept stable—that the coin would buy as many goods on the day when the debt should be collected as it did on the day when it was incurred. With such a guarantee they would have been perfectly willing to have accepted payment in paper. Owing to the debasement, to the inflationary effect of the first American silver and of the coining of a certain amount of the looted monastic plate, money had in Henry VIII's time increased more rapidly than goods, and therefore there had been a rise in prices. The two hundred year old English tradition of a stable price-level had been broken, and therefore Henry's credit abroad necessarily suffered.

Yet it is vital to the understanding of the story of England that we should grasp clearly the statistics of Henry VIII's experiment. According to Mr. Feaveryear's[1] calculation, between 1542 and his death in 1547, Henry called in £400,000 of pure silver money and reissued it as £526,000 of debased silver money. The inflation of those five years, that is to say, was trivial in comparison with, say, the inflation of the four years of the war of 1914. Comparatively trivial, too, was the effect on prices. According to Thorold Rogers's price-lists, if 100 was the price-level in 1541, then that level rose to 124·6 in 1545 and by Henry's death in 1547 had sunk again to 116·4.

[1] *Pound Sterling*, Feaveryear, p. 57.

A King is not likely to debauch the currency unless he is the veriest simpleton. For, as Lenin pointed out in our own day, such debauchery is the most effective way possible of plunging a country into anarchy. From anarchy it is clear that a King is very likely to lose and cannot possibly gain. For he cannot become more than a King. It is not even to the true interest of a King to raise the price-level for, though such a manœuvre may be immediately convenient to him in enabling him to pay off more cheaply some debt that he has contracted, it is clear that, if he raises the prices of everything, he will raise the cost of his own government. Therefore taxation will have to be increased, and the necessity of increasing it will bring unpopularity, if nothing worse, to the monarch.

Now a King, whether he be a good man or a bad man, has little motive for preferring any other interest before that of the preservation and strength of the monarchy. For a King intends to be a King for life. A regent, on the other hand, knows that his term of office is limited. If he be a good man he will, in spite of this, be conscientious. But if he be a bad man then he is under every temptation, just as any other politician is, to use his term of office to feather his own nest. History can tell us of good regents but it would, I think, be possible to argue without much exaggeration that no ancient monarchy has ever fallen except when it has been previously weakened by a period of unscrupulous regency. For it is obviously to the baser interests of a regent to issue an excess of money and to put the surplus, directly or indirectly, into his own pocket, to sell the Crown lands to himself or his friends at unfairly low prices. It is nothing to him that such conduct will create a monetary problem that will certainly embarrass and may in the end destroy the monarchy, so long only as he behaves with sufficient restraint to postpone the crash until after the conclusion of his own period of office.

So it was during the protectorship of the Duke of Somerset that the English monarchy was destroyed. In contrast with Henry VIII's comparatively trifling £126,000 Somerset by his further debasement increased the monetary supply by £1,000,000 and, as a result, prices rose from 116·4 of 1547 to 202·3 in 1551. Somerset died, leaving behind him

Somerset House, the English currency debauched, and the monarchy fatally weakened.

Somerset left to his successor, Northumberland, a very difficult problem. For, once the currency was thoroughly and admittedly debauched, then no action of the Government was required to cause a steady further inflation. For obviously everybody possessed of an old coin of good silver would turn it into two coins of debased and thus contribute to a yet further inflation. To counteract this process Northumberland hoarded and put out of circulation all the coins on which he could lay his hands. He was thus successful in checking the rise in prices, which fell somewhat so that by Edward's death they were down to 173·6.

Northumberland forced them down, if anything, too far, for he checked production. Therefore Mary at her accession threw a little of Northumberland's hoard back on the market with the result that prices rose again to 199·3. Froude in his *History* [1] accuses Mary of "pouring out a fresh shower of money containing but 3 oz. of silver", but subsequent investigation has shown that for this as for so many of his statements that great writer was indebted wholly to his imagination. Mary was able to keep prices at approximately their new level throughout her reign with the exception of the years 1555 and 1556, when they jumped up to 212·9 and 213·5. Those years were years of exceptionally bad harvest. The effect of a very bad harvest in a country with a metallic currency is always inflationary, for people in their necessity bring out their savings and thus put into circulation money which is not in circulation in normal years. Also, if there are fewer goods, then, unless the monetary supply is also reduced, each particular article will clearly cost more. However, Mary recaptured control of the price-level in 1557 and brought it back again to that level at which she found it at her accession.

Elizabeth on her accession found in circulation some £900,000 of debased silver money. She borrowed from Antwerp 200,000 crowns of pure silver. On 27th September, 1560, she issued a proclamation that henceforth every penny should pass for three farthings, every twopenny bit for a penny halfpenny, and the sixpenny teston for fourpence

[1] vii, 454.

halfpenny. She then announced that anyone who brought in the base money would receive its new value in pure silver with a bonus of 3*d.* in the £. She proclaimed vigorous penalties against anyone who should export the coins in the hope of getting a better price abroad. The new silver she, of course, to begin with coined out of the Antwerp crowns. She fixed a date—9th April, 1561—after which the old base coins would no longer be legal tender. The business was carried through with vigour and ability and was successful. For the base coins that were brought in she had to pay out £638,113 15*s.* 6*d.* But, when she had extracted the silver out of them, she was able to make of it £733,248 of new good money. Her gross profit on the proceeding was thus a little short of £100,000 and her net profit, after all expenses had been deducted, some £14,000.

But the effect of the whole proceeding was, of course, deflationary. For the coins for which she paid out her £600,000 odd had, before the proclamation of 1560 reducing the coins' purchasing power by 25 per cent, a value of £600,000 odd × $\frac{4}{3}$, that is to say, of about £850,000. Elizabeth had therefore taken £850,000 out of circulation and only put back £730,000 in its place. We should therefore expect to find that prices fell, and so they did for the moment. In 1561—the year when the old base coins ceased to be legal tender—they stood at 205. By 1562 they had fallen to 192·9.

Yet immediately afterwards they took a turn upwards again and rose steadily throughout the rest of her reign, at the end of which they stood at about 275 to 1541's 100. They rose because the money in circulation was increasing more rapidly than the goods in circulation. For that there were two reasons. The first reason was that, as always before the invention of milled edges, the clipper was at work, decreasing the *de facto* value of the coins by clipping little bits off the edges of them. Such were his activities that by the end of the reign in 1601 the Government found that it had no alternative but to reduce the silver content of the coins that it itself issued—a measure, of course, of inflation. The second reason was the influx of American gold and silver.

Now the first of these two evils the Government was unable

to remedy, for the method of circumventing the clipper had not as yet been discovered. The second, on the other hand, it could well have remedied. Among the many important services that have been rendered to truth by Professor Soddy, there is none more important than his exposure of the sloppiness with which so many historians and economists at every interesting stage of their narrative try to slip past truth beneath a camouflage of impersonal verbs. Listening to language about gold and silver pouring into England from America, one might think that the precious metals fell like rain from heaven, or that they were a couple of ducks which swam across and landed one morning on English soil without so much as a " by your leave ".

If gold and silver came into England somebody brought them. Who brought them ? and why ? A good deal, of course, came in as result of piracy. But the greater part came in as a result of trade—a new sort of trade—the exchange of goods against gold and silver. The Spaniards, having a surplus of precious metals, developed the habit of purchasing goods with them and of living on foreign imports instead of on the products of their own country. Whether or not this was wisdom in them we need not discuss. But the consequence of it for the English was that they gave the Spaniards consumable goods and received in exchange for them unconsumable metal. If, as Adam Smith truly says, the one object of production is consumption, it is clear that this exchange was pure loss to the English, and it is not surprising that with such a commerce the reign of Elizabeth should be filled loud with the poor's complaints of their desperate poverty.

Why then did Elizabeth tolerate this disadvantageous commerce ? The notion that she did not understand the plain consequence of filling the country with silver and emptying it of goods may be dismissed at once. The woman was not an idiot. The elements of monetary theory had been perfectly understood since the time of the Greeks. As Macaulay records,[1] Gresham's Law is found noted in Aristophanes. In the Middle Ages the quantitative theory was familiar to every educated person, nor was it, as will be later shown, until in the eighteenth century the educational

[1] *History of England*, Macaulay, iv, 621–2, footnote.

machine deliberately imposed confusion on men's minds, that there was any misunderstanding of the ABC of these problems. Both Elizabeth and all other educated people were then well aware that if silver " poured " into England it would cause a rise in prices. It would have been perfectly possible to have forbidden its import and insisted that the Spaniards, if they wanted our goods, must give us goods in exchange. Had she done so there would have been in England both a more adequate supply of goods and a stable price-level—to the great advantage of the country.

Why then did she let the treasure in ? It is true that, as the mercantilists argued, it was an advantage to a Government to possess a reserve of gold and silver which it could use in the event of the emergency of war. And, had Elizabeth been able to capture for herself, as the French Kings were able to do, the new supplies of metals and to hoard them against the day of necessity when she might wish to buy from abroad and be unable to offer goods in exchange for those that she wanted, her policy would then have been most intelligible. But that was not at all what happened. An inconsiderable proportion of the new metal passed into the royal hands. As a result the royal wealth and royal income did not at all keep pace in increase with the increase of the national wealth and national income, while the royal expenditure rose with the rise of prices. Thus according to Professor Neale,[1] Elizabeth's ordinary revenue from Crown lands, Customs, etc., at her accession was £200,000. By her death it had risen to £300,000. From taxation she was able to raise on an average about £50,000 a year at the beginning of her reign and £80,000 at the end. In other words her revenue was increasing less rapidly than prices were rising, while the revenue itself in the first place was a revenue adequate for the expenses of government at the price-level of Henry VII's time rather than that of the latter half of the century. It was by that latter half quite inadequate if ever there was any extraordinary expenditure. How then did she manage ? She raised money by a variety of dodges, as her two successors were to do after her. But, when every dodge was exhausted, Elizabeth again and again had to face the ugly truth that she could only make both ends meet

[1] *Queen Elizabeth*, p. 284.

by selling some of the Crown lands. In one year at the time of the Irish campaigns she had to sell £120,000 worth of these. A temporary relief, these sales by reducing income left the situation more desperate still for the future. By the end of her reign the royal income was beginning to decline not merely in proportion to the national income but absolutely. It is clear enough then that the influx of gold and silver was against Elizabeth's interest because it impoverished her; she would have stopped it had she been free to follow her proper policy and not the servant of the stronger forces that guided her. It was also against the interests of the poor because it caused an artificial scarcity of commodities. But it was to the interests of those who sold goods to the Spaniards in exchange for gold and silver, of those who robbed the Spaniards of their gold and silver, and of all the others who could in any way annex to themselves a share of the new store of precious metals. Such people were indifferent to a rise in prices, for they immediately invested their gains in land and houses whose price rose with the general rise. They were the masters of the State, so that no one could prevent them from passing on the burden of higher prices to the poor by a successful refusal to raise wages, whereas they were strong enough to prevent the Queen from passing on the burden of her increased expenses to them in the form of increased taxation. For at that date there was, of course, no question of the Government acting as it does in modern Parliamentary States and just taking from the subject whatever money it sees fit. The money-lending interest, on the other hand, which likes falling prices, was not yet strong enough to dominate the State.

Chapter II

THE FAILURE OF THE STUARTS

Income falling, expenditure rising—that was the situation which Elizabeth bequeathed to her successor, James I. The price-level stood at about 275 to 1542's 100. There was no possibility of reducing prices by any substantial amount, but at least it should have been the object of James's policy to have prevented a further increase in them. In this he failed. In Elizabeth's reign a high proportion of the silver that had come into the country had been used for domestic and not for monetary purposes. But the effect of her reduction of the silver content of the shilling in 1601 was, of course, to increase the sale price of silver. The result was that for the next ten years the owners of plate were in a steady stream bringing their plate to the Mint and having it turned into coin. Clearly James should have raised the Mint charges so high as to have made it unprofitable for silver to be brought in. He did not do so. The result was that between 1601 and 1611 there was a great increase of money in circulation, a gross inflation, and consequent rise of prices to between 400 and 500.

During the last fourteen years of James's reign there was, it is true, little minting of new silver, but clipping of the old coins was proceeding at a rapid rate. Throughout the whole of English history the clipper had been steadily at work, but, so long as the price-level was kept stable, he preserved some discretion in his activities, knowing that it was he who would be blamed if that stability was upset. At a time when that stability was already notoriously upset by other causes, he felt secure from risk and able to throw all discretion to the winds. In these years and in the first years of Charles I's reign good new silver was coined in large quantities in accordance with an arrangement by which a third of the Spanish silver from America for use in the Netherlands was coined in London. No sooner were the new coins issued than they were clipped. As a result, by James's death the price-level was up to 550.

Thus it is easy to see that Charles I was the inheritor of a situation that was already utterly incapable of solution. By no wriggle of arithmetic is it possible to pay off a debt of $5\frac{1}{2}d.$ when you possess only $1d.$ It was that which Charles spent the last sad half of his life in trying to do. Had the problem been merely a financial problem, Charles would have appealed to the Parliament and said to them, " Gentlemen, the situation has changed from that which existed in my predecessors' time through faults that are neither mine nor yours. We must therefore have a New Deal. If you wish me to be your King, will you please endow me with capital sufficient to give me an income so that I can carry on the government ? " If they refused to do that, the alternative was that the King should be dependent upon annual Parliamentary grant for his income—that is to say, what was later to be known as Parliamentary Government.

Unfortunately the situation was complicated. There was a powerful party which wanted not to solve the difficulties but to take advantage of them in order to prevent the institution of monarchy from working in its historic fashion. Between the King and the Puritan party, which was powerful in Parliament, there was the unbridgeable gulf of religious difference. The King's conscience would not permit him to allow Puritanism to dominate England, nor would the Puritan conscience allow such a domination to the King's Anglo-Catholicism. There was then, after every twist and evasion had been tried, no alternative in honour but to fight the matter out to the death.

Unfortunately, as so often happens, victory in war settled little. The killing of the King did nothing to bring down prices. Cromwell, inheriting the power of Charles, inherited also the expenses of his Government. He had in addition the expense of the upkeep of a large standing army. The dishonesty of the Parliamentarians, who had ascribed to extravagance and tyranny Charles's demand for money instead of explaining that that demand was an inevitable result of circumstances, recoiled on the head of Cromwell, their only important survivor, and made it impossible for him to put forward a demand for high taxes without forfeiting all popularity. He dared not disband the army until he had obtained some popular support for his rule, and, the longer that he continued to rule through the army, the more unpopular his rule became. Caught in an insoluble dilemma, he dragged out his miserable days.

Cromwell's rule was opportunist, and under it no attempt was made to recapture for sovereignty that control of the price-level, without which any plan for the reform of the nation's financial arrangements was foredoomed to failure. The problem now was the problem of the clipper. New supplies of the precious metals from America were no longer coming into the country to any important extent. On the other hand, the busy clipper was increasing the monetary supply too rapidly for productivity to keep pace and was forcing up prices.

The first need for the day was then for a method of circumventing the clipper. In 1649 there arrived in England a Frenchman, Pierre Blondeau, equipped with an invention for coining milled edge coins, which was already in use in France and which would effectually make clipping impossible. A Parliamentary committee examined his plan and reported favourably on it. For seven years, however, the Government on one excuse and another delayed adoption. The reason for this delay Blondeau explained without hesitation in an angry pamphlet which he issued. It was that not only were there clippers abroad throughout the country but that the very officers of the Mint issued the new coins light of weight and pocketed themselves the profits of their roguery. Blondeau's machine would have prevented the possibility of this theft, but the officers of the Mint were strong enough to raise petty difficulties and prevent its adoption. At last in 1656 he was able to get leave to stamp some new coins, but Cromwell, "probably for political reasons," says Mr. Feaveryear,[1] decided at the last moment not to issue them and Blondeau retired in disgust to France.

In 1660 Charles came in and the great issue had at last to be fought out. The situation was as follows. Charles was not brought back to be a king in the sense in which any of his predecessors had been kings. The old theory of the monarchy had been that the King should possess sufficient

[1] *Pound Sterling*, Feaveryear, p. 86.

capital to give him an income which would enable him to carry on the government of the country in normal times. In abnormal times he appealed to the people to help him by the supplement of taxation. The new theory of the monarchy was that the King should have no capital of any importance and should be entirely dependent upon a regular income, voted to him by Parliament who would thus be able to control his conduct. In practice Parliament took care to vote him an insufficient income so as to compel him to contract debts. Charles's policy, on the other hand, was to come back to the throne on what terms he could and then to find some means by which he could trick those who had restored him and escape out of their clutches.

He very nearly succeeded. It was the age of the first rumours of invention. The roads were open for the development of commerce. Once therefore, that the country settled down to peace after the disturbances of the last twenty years, there was an opportunity for a very great expansion of productivity. Obviously then, if the goods in circulation were going to increase, it would be possible to increase the money in circulation in proportion without any change in the price-level. How was that increase to be effected ?

As has been said, the influx of precious metals had by now ceased. The monetary-supply, so far as it was increased, was now being increased by the activities of the clippers. Clearly Charles's first task was to put a check on these activities. Therefore he called back Blondeau from France and made him Engineer of the Mint. In future only milled-edged coins were to be issued. It is true that that was not an immediate and total solution of his problem. To solve the problem he should clearly have called in all the old clipped coins and issued in their place new milled coins of the average *de facto* weight of the old coins, declaring that, after such and such a date, the old coins would no longer be legal tender. He did not do that, with the result that the new coins got melted down by the clippers and made up again into a larger quantity of " fake-antique " coins of short weight. The melting of them was illegal but it was a law which it was impossible to enforce. Yet clearly Charles had discovered the remedy and was only waiting the convenient opportunity of properly applying it.

Having thought of a way of preventing the clipper from increasing the country's monetary-supply, Charles had next to find a way of issuing that increased supply himself and for his own benefit. His remedy was paper-money. Clearly, the more that he could reduce the quantity of gold and silver in the country, the larger the gap which Charles could fill with his paper money without causing that rise in prices, which would of course discredit the experiment. How could he get gold and silver out of the country?

It has been explained how in the sixteenth century the trade between Spain and England was peculiar in that it was a trade not of goods against goods but of goods against money. In Charles's time there was growing up another such trade—peculiar this time in the opposite direction—the trade between England and India. The Indian had not as yet developed any considerable taste for English or European goods; on the other hand, he loved the precious metals simply for their own sake. Therefore the trade between England and India was, to a large extent, one of the exchange of Indian goods against English money. It was estimated, according to Davenant [1] at the end of the seventeenth century, that the gold and silver "carried away and sunk in the East Indies" amounted to £150,000,000.

According to Davenant and to the conventional bullionist opinion, which considered the object of trade to be the acquisition of as large as possible a stock of precious metals, this trade was a loss. Europe, he said, would "be richer by full one third if that trade had never been discovered". But to one who looked on economic problems with a gaze free from confusion the Indian trade was a trade of pure gain to England. We got from the Indians consumable goods which we wanted; we gave them in return useless gold and silver which we did not want and whose place in our internal economy could be supplied by paper money which cost us nothing. Therefore Charles very reasonably removed the restrictions on the export of bullion and encouraged the East India Company by all the means in his power. Throughout his reign it flourished exceedingly,

[1] *Works* (ed. 1771), i, 91.

and the shares which had stood at 100 at his accession had risen by his death to 300.

In that way he made as large as possible the gap which his paper money was to fill. Now let us understand how it was that he issued that paper money. He did not venture merely to issue Treasury notes, as the Government issued them during the late War. Public opinion would not have been prepared for that. His plan was more subtle. In every age of the world's history there has been a certain amount of trading on credit. That is to say, *A* is willing to buy an article from *B* but has not for the moment the cash ready at hand. *B* therefore sells him the article in return for a promise to pay, made out in one form or another, at some future date. Such credit-trading has, I say, existed in every age and in every country and, naturally enough, it always grows more common in a period of disturbance when physical obstacles often separate a man from his cash. Therefore it had been widely used in the years before Charles's accession. People were used to it. The essence of it was that the seller always got paid in real cash *eventually*.[1]

Charles was in debt, and it had been his habit, just as it had been that of his predecessors, to issue to his creditors tallies, or notched pieces of wood, which the creditors re-presented when the taxes came in and in return for which they then received the cash due to them. Charles conceived the plan of making these tallies negotiable and later, since pieces of wood were not convenient for this purpose, he paid his debts in negotiable paper orders instead. That is to say, these paper orders—which, of course, cost him nothing—were to count as money up to such and such a date. They were to be accepted in the shops, to be legal tender for the discharge of a debt and so on. When the given date came, then whoever found himself in possession of them could bring them to the Treasury and exchange them for cash.

"Why was this of such importance," it may be asked, "if the King was going to pay cash in the end? He was

[1] There is, it is true, another sort of credit-transaction in which *B* gives the article to *A* in return for a promise from *A* to supply an article of equal value at some future date. In such a transaction, of course, the promise is cancelled when the second article is delivered and no cash ever changes hands at all. The cash value is merely a measure.

merely postponing the payment of his debt—just like anyone else who gives an IOU for his debt instead of paying cash down." That was, of course, what he wished people to say. The experiment was important for this reason. According to Charles's system each particular holder of a paper order would, it is true, at some future date be able to exchange it for cash and thus have a feeling of security, which, in the temper of the times, a purely paper currency could not perhaps have given him. But at any given moment there would be a considerable amount of paper money in circulation. Thus a creditor, to whom Charles owed money on 1st January, 1667, was given a paper order which could be turned into cash by whoever chanced to be in possession of it on 1st January, 1668. But on 1st January, 1668, the King would issue a new set of paper orders which would run current until 1st January, 1669, and so on. It was not intended that there should ever come a day on which all the outstanding paper orders should be redeemed. The process was like that of emptying a cistern into a bath, to take a metaphor which Professor Soddy has used to illustrate a different point. Every drop of water that leaves the cistern and enters the pipe in time comes out of the cistern into the bath. But at any given moment the quantity of water in the bath is less than the quantity that has left the cistern by the quantity in the pipe.

Doubtless, had the experiment succeeded, Charles would gradually have lengthened the period to elapse before redemption. By lengthening and shortening the period in accordance with the demands of the price-level he could have regulated the monetary supply in exactly the same way as that in which President Roosevelt regulates it to-day by unbalancing his budget. Eventually, no doubt, he would have issued the orders, frankly as paper money, accepting a vague obligation to convert into gold and silver on a demand which he had discovered from experience to be very rarely made. In fact, as Dr. Shaw, the greatest authority on the subject, points out,[1] the orders would have performed all the functions that were in the next century to be performed by the privately issued bank-notes. They would have played in history a part much

[1] Introduction to the *Volume of Treasury Books* in the *State Papers*.

more important than that of temporarily relieving the financial embarrassments of a harassed monarch. For the vastly increased productivity of the next two hundred years were to necessitate a vastly increased monetary supply. By a strange anomaly private persons were to be permitted to invent that money and put it into circulation in the form of loans. Nor is it any paradox to say that that anomaly is the cause of the greater part of the evils that have since afflicted mankind. Had Charles's experiment succeeded, had it come to be recognized that, when new money was required, it was the business of the King to issue it, the whole history not only of England but of the world must necessarily have been changed.

Now why did Charles's experiment fail? Let us first understand who exactly was interested in its failure. It has been said that the proclaimed theory of the Restoration of 1660 was to restore a King dependent upon taxation voted by Parliament for the expenses of government. That was the theory. But in practice from the first year of the Restoration Parliament refused steadily to vote the King a sufficient income, while of the £1,200,000 which it voted he never in fact received more than £800,000.[1] The legend that Charles's extravagance was to any important extent responsible for the insufficiency of his income has been quite exploded by the researches of Mr. Bryant. Parliament refused to vote Charles sufficient taxes—some of its members because they were ill-read squires with a natural dislike of taxation and of an understanding incapable of comprehending the consequences of unbalanced budgets, others because they understood those consequences only too clearly. They were consequences which would be, they reckoned, directly or indirectly to their own advantage.

It was clear that, if Parliament would not vote Charles the necessary money then he must either get that money by some trick or windfall or else he must borrow it from the owners of gold and silver. The price of such loans would be, in the end, the passing of the control of policy away from either King or Parliament into the hands of the money-lenders. It was in an effort to avoid that consummation that Charles made his experiment with paper money,

[1] *Charles II*, Bryant, p. 139.

just as it was for the same purpose that he afterwards accepted the gold and the silver of Louis XIV.

It is hard to form a just judgment of the monetary problems of this reign unless we bear in mind the balance-sheet of it which Dr. Shaw drew up. "With our modern system of annual budgets," writes Dr. Shaw,[1] "estimates and supplementary estimates, we are so far removed from this seventeenth century practice and theory that we cannot conceive it possible. It is this want of proper sense of historical perspective that has produced the accepted Whig view of Charles II's reign—a view which is as mean in its psychology as it is gross and palpable in its ignorance.

ROUGH BALANCE-SHEET AS BETWEEN CHARLES II AND HIS PARLIAMENT

Deficit.		*How the Deficit was made up.*	
In his ordinary revenue (including interest) Charles was cheated by his Parliament on the whole reign roughly . .	£4,432,000	Rendition of Dunkirk	£290,000
In the extraordinary or war revenue Charles was cheated by his Parliament—		Queen Catherine's dowry . . .	180,000
On the 1st Dutch war	1,500,000	French King's money .	742,000
On the 2nd Dutch war	100,000	Bankers' debt . .	2,000,000
On the thirty ships .		Crown lands sold .	1,000,000
On the intended war with the French King and the disbandment . .	180,000	Departmental debts and debts at interest resting on the executive at the death of Charles . .	2,000,000
	£6,212,000		£6,212,000

"Even and quit.

"Requiescant in pace Rex et Parliamentum suum fidelissimum."

It is easy enough to see why the owners of gold and silver are always anxious for it to appear that it is not possible to maintain a stable price-level with a non-metallic currency. But it is important, too, to understand who were at that time the owners of the gold and silver. Doubtless the little clipper was working for Charles's defeat, but the real business of clipping and melting was in the hands of the

[1] *Calendar of Treasury Books*, vol. vii, part i.

big London goldsmiths, now for the first time emerging also as bankers or money-lenders. "The bankers," explains Clarendon,[1] "did not consist of above the number of five or six men, some whereof were aldermen and had been lord mayors of London. . . . They were a tribe that had risen and grown up in Cromwell's time. . . . They were for the most part goldsmiths." They had first gained their riches by supplying Cromwell's "wants of money upon great advantages". The names of the two best known were Viner and Backwell.

Yet they themselves were as yet hardly masters in their own houses. The financial centre of the world at that date was Amsterdam. "I believe there is at this day," writes a correspondent from Amsterdam in 1652,[2] "forty times more gold and silver in the Low Countries than in England." We must not, of course, attach any importance to the figure "forty", but the sentence was substantially true. Seventeenth-century Holland, like nineteenth-century England, was a comparatively high-wage country, whose financiers were anxious to export their capital to lower-wage countries where it would earn a larger dividend. England was, in the circumstances of the time, such a country. The Dutch, wrote Child [3] about this time, "give generally more wages to all their manufacturers by at least twopence in the shilling than the English." As a consequence, interest rates in England were higher than in Holland. There was a difference, says Barbon,[4] of 3 per cent, and right back in James I's time the plea that it would cause a flight of foreign capital was already being used as an argument against the reduction of English interest-rates. "This will draw much money out of the country, the Dutch having much here," was the argument against the reduction of the legal rate to 8 per cent.[5] During the Civil War some of the Dutch capital was withdrawn, but it returned after the Restoration. It was stated that London after the Great Fire was largely rebuilt with Dutch capital.[6] In 1669,

[1] *Life of Edward, Earl of Clarendon* (ed. 1827), iii, 7.
[2] *Calendar of State Papers*, Domestic Series, xxiv, 21.
[3] *A New Discourse of Trade* (4th ed.), pp. x–xi.
[4] *A Discourse of Trade* (1690), 33, 84–5.
[5] *House of Commons Journal*, i, 679.
[6] *Hist. MSS. Comm.*, part i, 134.

the very time when Charles was making his experiments with paper money, a Parliamentary committee was being told[1] that "Alderman Bucknill had above £100,000 in his hands, Mr. Meynell above £30,000, Mr. Vandeput at one time £60,000, Mr. Dericost always near £200,000 of Dutch money lent to merchants at 7, 6 and 5 per cent when money was at 8 per cent". That is to say, the London goldsmiths, who play so large a part in the story of Restoration England, were to a very great extent mere agents, operating with Dutch money.

Now why did Charles's experiment fail? and how did it fail? It was not that the price-level got out of hand. There was no rise in prices. Charles did not issue an excess of paper money, but he did on the other hand make the blunder of only issuing his paper orders for large sums. This meant that the recipient of them naturally, as a rule, wanted to change them. The bankers—the goldsmiths—offered to change them. In return for Charles's orders they gave to their clients their own notes, or "promises to pay" in smaller denominations. These "promises to pay" they professed themselves willing to change into cash on demand, and on the strength of that profession charged a heavy discount on Charles's "promises to pay" in the future. At the same time they did all that they could to persuade their clients that it would in practice be foolish of them to bother to change their notes into cash.

Now by refusing to make the exchange except at a large discount the goldsmiths were able to bring Charles's orders into a certain discredit. Thus in the year 1672—in the middle of the Dutch War—Charles, saddled with heavy expenditure which Parliament refused to meet out of taxation, found his creditors reluctant to accept more of their payments in paper orders. Therefore he said most reasonably that, since it was the goldsmiths who were the cause of that reluctance, it must be they who should be inconvenienced rather than the whole country suffer by defeat in war, by defeat at the hands of those who were in fact the goldsmiths' paymasters. He therefore postponed for a year his repayment of his past debts to the goldsmiths and announced that the taxes as they came in would entirely be devoted

[1] Ibid.

to current needs. An exception was made for the paper orders that were in the possession of contractors, suppliers of stores, or servants; they were to be redeemed. Of those in possession of bankers the redemption was to be postponed. On the other hand the debt was not repudiated. On the contrary the King promised to repay the principal as soon as possible and in the meanwhile to pay 6 per cent interest.

However, the news of the exchequer's stoppage made the holders of the goldsmith's "promises to pay" wonder if the goldsmiths really were in possession of the cash for which they had issued those promises. They went to the goldsmiths and demanded their cash. Of course the goldsmiths had not got it, for they had been promising to pay cash on the King's orders to the extent of ten times what they possessed. According to Sir Dudley North,[1] a banker, then as now, who owed £10,000, seldom kept more than £1,000 in his vaults. Therefore they had, of course, to suspend payment. In 1667, when the Dutch had been up the Medway, there had been talk of a run on the banks, and they had had to postpone payment. Thus Pepys, under the date of 14th June, 1667, "So to the office after dinner; and thither comes Mr. Pierce who tells me his condition, how he cannot get his money, about £500 (which he says is a very great part of what he hath for his family and children) out of Viner's hand; and indeed it is to be feared that this will wholly undo the bankers." However, the King had then come to their rescue by pledging his word to the punctual repayment of their loans. For up to that time they had only lent on to the King cash that had been deposited with them by their clients—or at least so they were able to pretend. By 1672 they had developed quite a new technique. They had lent to their clients "promises to pay" which they knew themselves unable to make good and were taking interest on them as if they were loans of cash.

So in 1672 they smashed. A large number of poor people, of course, suffered as they always do from bankers' inability to perform their promises. But the whole story dealt no murderous blow to the country's prosperity, for immediately afterwards—in 1674—a movement of unexampled trade expansion began. The Customs receipts rose; credit steadily

[1] *Discourses upon Trade* (1691), 21.

improved, and this improvement continued for the rest of the reign. Yet suffering had been caused and there was blame to be awarded. But it was clear to one who properly understood what had happened that the bankers were far more deeply to blame than Charles. Charles, at the worst, was guilty of a somewhat slick exploitation of public stupidity. He did not deceive people about what he was doing; he confessed it frankly, possibly a little hoping that they would be too stupid to follow. But the bankers had been guilty of the far greater fault of giving promises which they knew themselves unable to redeem.

To-day we take it for granted that that is what bankers do, but at that date it was not yet frankly admitted that bankers lent out beyond their cash-holdings. Men like Sir Dudley North, when they let the cat out of the bag, were revealing a trade secret. It was, however, beginning to be widely suspected that they did so. And to allay suspicions the Bank of Amsterdam, then the leading bank of the world, every year allowed its vaults to be examined by municipal officials, who then deposed on oath that they had found there cash equivalent to the bank-notes in circulation. Yet it was so manifestly to the advantage of the shopkeepers and burghers of Amsterdam that the city should keep its position as the world's financial capital that the depositions of the officials were not widely believed. At this very date, 1672, there was therefore in face of the French threat a danger of a run on the bank. To check this the magistrates took any depositors who wished into the bank's vaults and showed them its stores of cash untouched, a florin for every florin bank-note that was on issue. How exactly this clever piece of window-dressing was arranged has never been quite discovered, as it is certain that the Dutch did lend well beyond their cash-holdings. Yet it was effective in strengthening public confidence in bankers. It was vital for them that, at this very moment when the Dutch bankers had bluffed with unhoped-for success, the English bankers should not let the cat out of the bag.[1]

Up till now the English bankers had on the whole been on the King's side in politics. But they could no longer afford the luxury of a preference. Somebody was going to be

[1] *Holland*, Thorold Rogers, pp. 223, 224.

blamed for the crisis of 1672 and, if it was not to be the bankers, the only alternative was that it should be the King. Therefore from now on they had two objects—the first, to weaken the monarchy politically so as to make sure that it did not strengthen itself financially—the second, so to confuse the public over the story of 1672 that they should think that it was the King and not the bankers who was responsible for their sufferings and thus to divert public attention from inquiry into what it was that they were doing.

This is not the place in which to trace through the fascinating but intricate story of the duel between Charles and Shaftesbury with which the rest of Charles's reign was filled. It was a complex multitude of causes which went to build up that Whig mentality which was prepared to use every weapon to prevent a revival of the ancient monarchy. But it is notable that whereas Shaftesbury had been a member of Charles's ministry at the time of the experiment of paper money and whereas in the early years of the reign the bankers had given their support to a King whom they fondly imagined would be as putty in their hands, now that Shaftesbury went into opposition it was from the financial interests and the City of London that he found his support. It was necessary to clip the King lest the King should stop them from clipping the coins.

Whoever was deceived by the confusions of the times, there was one clear mind, among the clearest that has ever given itself to the study of English politics, to whom every move in the game lay patent and exposable. The whole story can be read to-day in the great verse of John Dryden, the first man clearly to comprehend that necessary battle between monarchy and money-power with which all subsequent history has been filled. The object of Shaftesbury and the City of London was, as he wrote in the *Medal*[1] with characteristic wit and truth,

> " Perhaps not wholly to melt down the King
> But clip his legal rights within the ring."

Their desire, as he explains in *Absalom and Achitophel*, was for a disputed succession, for with two claimants to the

[1] 228–9.

throne, the one to be played off against the other, there would be no risk of a revived monarchy ever challenging, as Charles was challenging, the Whigs' right to rule. Dryden explains the reason why Shaftesbury supported the cause of Monmouth.

> " Not that he wished his greatness to create,
> For politicians neither love nor hate,
> But for he knew his title, not allowed,
> Would keep him still depending on the crowd." [1]

Shaftesbury had united behind him a motley following of people who were ready

> " For several ends to serve the same design." [2]

Among them were those who

> " for interest sought to embroil the state
> To sell their duty at a dearer rate
> And make their Jewish markets of the throne,
> Pretending public good to serve their own.
> Others thought kings a useless, heavy load
> Who cost too much and did too little good.
> These were for laying honest David by
> On principles of pure good husbandry." [3]

And in all the incomparable portrait-gallery of that great poem there is no picture more living nor more damning than that of Slingsby Bethell,[4] the sheriff of the City of London,

> " Shimei, whose youth did early promise bring
> Of zeal to God and hatred to his King."

He had spent his youth, said Dryden,

> " heaping wealth by the most ready way
> Among the Jews—which was to cheat and pray,"

and now, even in maturity,

> " If any leisure time he had from power—
> Because 'tis sin to misemploy an hour—
> His business was by writing to persuade
> That kings were useless and a clog to trade."

Bethell had, as it happened, written a treatise on the *Interest of Princes and States*, advocating free trade and attacking monarchies, but it is characteristic of Dryden's

[1] Part i, 222–5. [2] Part i, 494.
[3] Part i, 501–8. [4] Part i, 585–632.

peculiar felicity to bring against Shimei the accusation that is not only true of Bethell in particular but also true of all the tribe of Shimeis in general.

> "Their business was by writing to persuade
> That kings were useless and a clog to trade."

It would be hard to think of any words that could more aptly hit off the whole business of Whig political teaching, then just coming into being and to rule England for a hundred and fifty years.

Yet it was a paradox in Charles II's England, for so far had that King been from proving himself a "clog to trade", that trade had flourished under his rule as it had never flourished before. The Customs duties,[1] for instance, which in 1661 yielded only £260,000, in 1685 had risen to £800,000. It was indeed this very increase in productivity which made possible that increase of money, the issue of which the City interests were scheming to get completely into their own hands. But of that, according to their campaign, nothing must be said. It must instead be put about that a monarchy was of its nature irresponsible and unfit to be trusted with the nation's monetary-supply. No credit must be given to the King for the increase of the country's trade; the whole blame for the temporary crisis of 1672 must be placed upon his shoulders.

[1] *Jacobite Movement*, Petrie, p. 37.

CHAPTER III

THE ORANGE

As everybody knows, the attempt to substitute the Duke of Monmouth for James, as Charles's heir, failed, but the later plan for supplanting James by William of Orange succeeded. Thus for the next sixty years or so England had a disputed succession ; the King on the throne did not dare to pursue a strong policy through the fear that, if he did so, powerful interests would transfer their allegiance to the King over the water. It was not until fifteen years after the final defeat of the Jacobites in 1745 that it was possible for George III even to attempt to strengthen the monarchy.

Now, once more, it was a complexity of interests which was responsible for the Revolution of 1688. It is not the business of such a book as this to attempt to disentangle them. Contemporaries thought of the revolution as a revolution of the large land-owners—the Grandees—against the monarchy. It established, Lord Acton has said, " the divine right of freeholders." It was well understood that the bankers were also of the opposition to James and that their influence in the State was not to be despised. But none at the time thought of them for a moment as of an equal standing with the large landowners. The social relationship between the two classes was that of a master and his agent. Readers of Macaulay[1] will remember how Sir Dudley North found to his disgust that he " could not go on Change without being followed round the Piazza by goldsmiths, who, with low bows, begged to have the honour of serving him ".

Yet, as Napoleon was to tell the world a century later, " the hand that gives is above the hand that takes," whatever social appearances may seem to say. Just as, forty years before, Cromwell had discovered that he had deposed Charles only to inherit his financial problems in an aggravated

[1] *History*, iv, 491.

form, so now with William III. The Parliament which had been unwilling to vote a sufficient income to Charles II was just as unwilling to vote one to his nephew. Yet William almost from the first moment of his accession was at war with Louis XIV—a war of desperate importance to his own country, Holland, but of little real concern to England and acquiesced in by the moneyed classes principally that they might use it as an opportunity for establishing their power over the State. How was William to get his money ?

After a number of tricks in the way of tontines and lotteries had been tried with little success, the following plan was adopted. It was suggested by a curious financial adventurer called Paterson and piloted through Parliament by Montague, then a Lord of the Treasury. The bill was called " A Bill for Granting to Their Majesties Several Rates and Duties upon Tunnages of Ships and Vessels and upon Beer, Ale and other Liquors ; for Securing Certain Recompenses and Advantages, in the said Act mentioned, to such Persons as shall voluntarily advance the Sum of Fifteen Hundred Thousand Pounds towards carrying on the War with France ". The bill was vigorously opposed, especially in the House of Lords, but Camarthen, who was in charge of it there, was able to silence all objectors with the unanswerable answer that, if the bill was rejected, the country would be left without a fleet in the Channel—as indeed it would have been, unless the rich were to consent to tax themselves more heavily, of which of course there was no question.

The plan was that, instead of borrowing from the goldsmiths, the Government should instead borrow £1,200,000, of which it was in need, from a newly formed Corporation called the Bank of England. This corporation promised to collect the required money from the public and to lend it on to the King at 8 per cent plus £4,000 per annum for expenses—a rate considerably lower than that which he would have had to pay to the goldsmiths. In return for lending at this low rate the Bank received a number of privileges of which the most important was that it had the right to issue notes up to the extent of its loan to the Government " under their common seal " on the security of the Government. That is to say, it had the right to issue a £1 note ; the holder of that £1 note had the right to demand that the Bank give him cash for his note, but, if he made that demand, the Bank had the right to demand that the Government raise that £1 by taxation and repay £1 worth of debt to the Bank so that the Bank might repay its £1 to the note-holder. As Disraeli put it, " the principle of that system was to mortgage industry in order to protect property," [1] or, as Paterson, the originator of the Bank, himself explained with charming simplicity, " The bank hath benefit of the interest on all moneys which it creates out of nothing."

The required £1,200,000 was easily subscribed. The Bank, however, did not hand over the whole sum to William in cash. They handed over £720,000 in cash and the remaining £480,000 in notes " under their common seal ". The Government was thus compelled to use the Bank's notes to pay its bills, which gave them prestige. The Bank on its part was left the possessor of £720,000 in notes " under their common seal " and £480,000 in cash.[2] Now William, in the difficulties of the previous years, had been reduced, as Charles had been reduced before him, to issuing tallies in lieu of payment of his debts. The Bank now determined to use its spare notes and cash to buy up these tallies at a considerable discount, usually of 7 per cent, just as the goldsmiths had done in Charles's day.

Before long they had thus issued notes to the full extent of £1,200,000 which the Act of Parliament entitled them to issue " under their common seal ". No one but a special-pleading lawyer doubted that the intention of the Act had been to prevent them from issuing notes beyond that amount at all, but they knew very well that William was now so dependent upon their notes for the carrying on of his business that he would not dare to break with them. He was caught by what was perhaps the cleverest trick of blackmail in history. If he tried to repudiate his debt, his creditors would certainly go over to James and he would lose his throne. On the other hand he could only pay it if Parliament should vote him the money in extra taxation. The sum required would have been an inconvenient, but not an impossible, burden, but the Bank had seen to it

[1] *Sybil*, Bk. i, chap. 3.
[2] *Short Account of the Bank of England*, Michael Godfrey, p. 8.

that their influence in Parliament was sufficient to prevent it being voted. The monarchy was caught in a trap from which it was never to escape.

Therefore they issued the further notes beyond the £1,200,000, guarding themselves against prosecution by issuing them signed by the cashier and without their "common seal". Now, so far is it from it being true that a purely metallic currency is necessary for stable prices that the price-level had been kept exceptionally stable throughout all Charles II's reign. "The great revolution caused by the rise in prices seems to have run its course in England by or somewhat before the middle of the century," writes Professor Clark,[1] "and until the last quarter of the eighteenth century there seems to have been no very great change." It is true that he adds, "though what change there was ran in an upward direction," but, as we shall see, the slight rise which made the price-level of 1789 a little higher than that of 1660 took place not in Charles II's reign, but in that of William III. That was because both Charles and the goldsmiths, divergent as their other interests were, were at least united in their desire that the whole experiment of paper money should not be discredited by a rise in prices. They therefore kept the quantity of it issued strictly proportionate to the increase in productivity. The Bank of England, however, confident that the King was impotent against them and that at the same time it was the King who would be blamed by public opinion for a rise in prices, saw now no necessity for restraint. They lent freely—a proceeding which did not cost them a halfpenny—issuing their notes well beyond the country's productive capacity. As the figures given in the contemporary Houghton's *Collection for the Improvement of Husbandry and Trade* show, prices rose as a result from 100 to 137 between June, 1694, and August, 1695.

The Government, quite mistaking the disease, thought that the rise in prices was due to the clipped money, although English money had been clipped since the beginning of time and prices had remained perfectly stable since Cromwell's death. They therefore determined to call in all the old money and reissue it instead in milled money,

[1] *The Later Stuarts*, Clark, p. 38.

and fixed a date after which unmilled money would no longer be legal tender. This was wise and fair enough, but with incredible folly they made no provision for seeing that the nation had an adequate temporary monetary supply during the time that silver was in the Mint for recoining. The consequence was a most drastic deflation, threatening far greater suffering than had been caused by the inflation. Through the folly of the Government the Bank of England notes were alone available to prevent that disastrous fall in prices. Sir John Houblon, its Governor, was able to explain to the people that he would indeed, if they demanded it, pay them a proportion of their notes' value in cash but that nothing could be less in their interest than that he should pay the full value, as such a demand would compel a drastic calling in of the Bank notes at the very time of the severe restriction of cash. The people agreed ; so did the Government, which had quite lost control of the situation and was only too grateful for any suggestion which might save the country from chaos. It was not until three months later that it occurred to them to issue their own paper money as an expedient.

Therefore as a result the Bank was allowed to make its notes partly inconvertible. They issued these partly inconvertible notes and with them bought up the Government's tallies. So, when in November, 1696, a return of the position of the Bank of England was given to a Parliamentary committee, it was discovered that only £1,500,000 of cash had ever passed out of the hands of the Bank into those of the King or of anybody else—£1,200,000 of its own capital and £300,000 which it had borrowed in Holland. Yet nevertheless by this puerile conjuring trick the King was in debt to the Bank £3,034,576 16*s*. 5*d*.

The effect of the creation of paper money by the Bank of England was totally different from that of its creation by either Charles II or the Caroline goldsmiths. The King, if he issues money, spends it and it becomes merely a part of the general money circulating in the country. The goldsmiths were but individuals, who, if luck favoured them, perhaps made fortunes, but, having made them, retired and spent them on consumable goods. Their paper had no guarantee ; they were always liable to the demands of their depositors and, taking one goldsmith with another, the profit from the interest of one was not perhaps more than sufficient to balance the loss of another. But the paper money of the Bank introduced an entirely new element. In the first place, the Bank was a continuing joint-stock corporation. There was no moment when it died and divided up its fortune among its relatives, no moment when it retired from business and settled down to spend that which it had amassed. It existed to lend and it proposed to go on lending until the end of time. In the second place, so long as it lent only to the Government or against adequate collateral security, it was lending virtually without risk. Its only risk lay in a risk of the general collapse of the régime.

Now, if a corporation lends money at interest and without risk, then re-lends the repaid loan and so on, never distributing more than a trifle of its profits either as wages or dividends, then, however small its original capital, however moderate its rate of interest, it is but a simple proposition in mathematics that in course of time it must necessarily become the possessor of the entire wealth of the country. The only remedy is, it may be said, for the people to refuse to borrow from it. But, if the corporation has itself the privilege of issuing money, then the public has no choice but to borrow from it, for, as we have seen, the consequence of a deflation is a violent fall in the price-level, causing most widespread suffering. And, if the money issued by the corporation as a loan has once established itself as an important part of the country's monetary supply, then it is clear that the public, if they suddenly started to refuse that corporation's loans, would throw the whole of their productive machinery into chaos.

It is then obvious why it was that the Bank inflated in 1695. As a general rule the bias of a bank is towards deflation, for the bank prefers prices low. But in 1695 the incidental consequence of inflation was a rise in prices, its essential consequence was so to increase the proportion of the Bank's money in circulation to King's money as to make the Bank's money an essential part of the nation's economy.

It is perfectly true, of course, as an abstract proposition in financial theory, that the King might have cancelled the privileges of the Bank and have filled the gap by paper money of his own. But by the bargain by which he held his throne, by the Bill of Rights of 1689, he was prevented from doing this without the consent of Parliament—which meant in practice without the consent of the Bank of England. This bill was passed to protect the liberties of Englishmen against such tyrants as James II. As if the maddest of believers in the divine right of kings had ever fashioned in imagination a tyranny one-hundredth part as strong as that which was clamped upon us by the Revolution of 1688!

It is sometimes said that the foundation of the Bank of England was followed by a great increase in productivity and rapid improvement in credit. But, as Mr. Feaveryear [1] has shown, credit had already been improving and productivity increasing ever since Charles II's time, and especially during James II's reign there had been "a remarkable improvement of credit". The Bank was no more responsible for the increased productivity of the seventeenth century than were the acceptance houses responsible for the increased productivity of the nineteenth century. Both the one and the other merely took advantage of it.

[1] *Pound Sterling*, Feaveryear, p. 107.

Chapter IV

THE ORIGIN OF THE PROGRESSIVE LEGEND

It was not possible to write the previous chapters of this book without reflecting upon a curiosity. Of no one of the facts contained in them is there, I think, any serious dispute. I have given the references for them, and they are all the commonplaces of any important books of admitted authority such as, for instance, Mr. Feaveryear's *Pound Sterling* or Mr. Lipson's *Economic History*. They will be all quite tediously familiar to any one who has given a study to these important questions. Such students will be inclined peevishly to ask why it was thought necessary to tell again a tale already so well known.

At the same time, should this book fall into the hands of anyone who learnt his history at school and has not had occasion to study it since, the whole story will seem to him like a wild fairy tale. Scarcely one of these facts which you allege, he will protest, was even mentioned in the textbooks from which I was taught my history. Why, if, as you say, their truth is admitted and their importance is admitted, why then are we not taught a word about them in the schools ?

It is a very reasonable question and shall receive a proper answer.

After the collapse of the South Sea Bubble, Walpole ruled England for more than twenty years. It can be argued that in some ways he ruled England very well. But the method by which he ruled her was the method of frank bribery and blackmail—of blackmail particular in his neglect to prosecute influential persons of whose corruption there was in reality little doubt, of blackmail general in that he was able to present the people of England with the ultimatum, " The alternative to us is anarchy, therefore you had better allow us to remain in power and not ask too many questions about the manner in which we are enriching ourselves."

Now to-day the very frankness of Walpole's cynicism makes his appear a less unattractive character than that of his contemporaries. The modern reader, sickened with the sentimental rhetoric and imperialistic bombast with which, say, a Chatham was afterwards to cover up the tracks of usury, turns with relief to the very brutality of Walpole and finds it hard not to be persuaded by such a writer as Mr. Stirling Taylor[1] into a certain liking for the blackguard. If the things that he did were often dirty things, at least the things that he loved were clean things. At least he spent the money that he made—on building a house, on entertainment, on the pleasures of the country. He did not merely lend out again at usury the profits of usury in a lunatic's lust for accumulation. Whatever he was, he was at least a man and not a bank.

So at a distance we like a man who lets cats out of bags, but it is only reasonable to remember that to those, whom one can only call Walpole's fellow-gangsters, the prime concern was not whether Walpole's character was attractive or unattractive but whether an arrangement which concentrated the wealth and power of the country into the hands of this gang could possibly be made to last. Walpole's urbane and winking jollity—his candid assumption that " We're all on the make together and each one has a skeleton in his cupboard "—might be tolerable round the dinner-table when the servants had withdrawn. It was well enough to denounce the South Sea Company in public as a fraud and then, when the Earl of Pembroke asked him what he ought to do about it, to say,[2] " I will only tell you what I have done myself. I have just sold out at 1,000 per cent and am fully justified "—so long as such remarks were kept for the Earl of Pembroke. But if the poor heard too much talk like that the whole régime must collapse. " The bank hath benefit of the interest of all the moneys which it creates out of nothing," explained Paterson—which again was fair enough and frank enough, but would not perhaps a little something about " service to the community " have been a trifle more discreet?

[1] *Life of Walpole*. [2] *South Sea Bubble*, Erleigh, p. 82.

It was Townshend, Walpole's brother-in-law, who grasped perhaps more clearly than any of the other Whigs of the early eighteenth century that an aristocracy, if it is to retain its privileges, must make some pretence of earning them by some service to its country. Every régime must have its appropriate rhetoric of half-truths—an aristocracy no less than any other. Englishmen are ready with their criticism and their ridicule when they hear of the masters of the State in Russia, in Germany, in Italy, or America using the machinery of education in order to impose upon the minds of its citizens a certain view of history, selected rather for its convenience to the rulers than its truth. They sometimes fail to understand that these later and cruder countries are but doing two hundred years afterwards what the English with their far subtler technique had already done in the eighteenth century. It was not convenient, as Townshend and his colleagues saw, that the methods by which the gentlemen of England had become so should be widely known. Therefore attention must be diverted from the details of that rise, and an official version must be put out to occupy the minds of those whose interest in history it was not possible wholly to suppress.

The first suggestion of the scheme for a permanent national debt came from Burnet, the historian of the Reformation, who had been secretary to William of Orange before the Revolution and after the Revolution was rewarded with the Bishopric of Salisbury. Now, as the war dragged on, Burnet grew to be seriously alarmed at the unpopularity of the debt-system among the gentry who had to pay the taxes to meet its charges. "The gentry are for the most part the worst instructed and least knowing of any of their rank I ever went amongst," was how he put the point. Nor did the educational system do anything at all to correct this fault in them and to reconcile them to acceptance of the principles of the Revolution. Both Universities, and particularly Oxford, were Tory. "In those seats of education instead of being formed to love their country and constitution, the laws and liberties of it, they are rather disposed to love arbitrary government and to become slaves to absolute monarchy." Therefore a Whig history must be written —the *History of Our Own Times*—in order to show them "what are the methods bad princes have taken to enslave us and by what conduct we have been preserved" and to arouse in them, "which ought to be the top of an an English gentleman's ambition, to be an able Parliament man."

So the Whig history was written. The next thing was to get it read, or at least talked about. The important task was to capture the educational machine. Therefore, in 1724, Townshend and Gibson, the Bishop of London, arranged for "24 persons, who are Fellows of Colleges in the two Universities, 12 from Oxford and 12 from Cambridge" to preach a sermon each at Whitehall. For that sermon the preacher was to receive the considerable emolument of £30, and none "must hope for a share of this bounty but they who are staunch Whigs and openly declare themselves to be so".[1] It was a beginning, but there was needed, thought Townshend, "some further encouragement". He wrote to George I of the race of Dons, "As Your Majesty knows I have always had the gaining them over to Your Majesty very much at heart, so I have lately had frequent conversations with the Bishop of London, who is, with me, fully persuaded it would be very practicable to reduce them to a better sense of their duty; and we have already made a rough draft of some things proper to this end."[2]

The "things proper to this end" were "the foundation of a new professorship to teach the modern tongues and modern history, in which George himself is to put in the professor".[3] "No encouragement has hitherto been made in either of the said Universities," it was explained with truth, "for the study of modern history or modern languages," and thus there have been "opportunities frequently lost to the Crown of employing and encouraging members of the two Universities by conferring on them such employment both at home and abroad". The salaries of these new Regius Professors were to be £400 a year, out

[1] *Portland MSS.*, vii, 377.
[2] *Walpole*, Coxe, ii, 297, 299.
[3] *Reliquiae Hearnianae*, ii, 200; May 20, 1724.

of which they had to pay £25 each to two assistant teachers —" an appointment so ample ", said the University of Cambridge in its letter of thanks, " as well nigh to equal the stipends of all our other Professors put together." The duties of the Professor were to deliver one lecture a term and to keep an eye on " twenty scholars nominated by the King to be taught gratis " and every year to send " an attested account of the progress made by each scholar . . . to our principal Secretary of State ". The only work of historical scholarship produced by a University History Professor during the eighteenth century came from the pen of Spence, Regius Professor at Oxford and tutor to the Duke of Newcastle's son. In the year 1745 he wrote *Plain Matter of Fact, or a Short Review of the Reigns of our Popish Princes since the Reformation ; in order to show what we are to expect if another should reign over us.*[1]

There happen to have survived two books of the Duke of Newcastle's secret service accounts.[2] It is not surprising to find from them that a high proportion of that money the Whig noblemen merely put into their own pockets. There are grants to the two Secretaries of State, to the Dukes of Grafton, St. Albans, Somerset, Bolton, Marlborough, and Rutland. But of what could be spared from this primary purpose a very high proportion again went on capturing the educational machine. We find grants to " the Fellows of Eton College, the Fellows and Master of Emmanuel College, Cambridge, the readers of physics and modern history at Oxford and Cambridge ".

Now what was the history which these endowed teachers taught ? It was the progressive theory of history—a theory hitherto unknown, a theory soon, as a result of their activities, accepted uncritically, a theory created in the first place quite cynically and clear-headedly in order to cover up the traces of truth. It was the purpose of that history to create among the public the ambient feeling that, bad as things might be at the moment of writing, yet the lesson of history was a lesson of steady improvement, that each present generation was always, as

[1] The previous pages are based on an article by Professor C. H. Firth in the *English Historical Review* for January, 1917.

[2] *The Structure of Politics at the Accession of George III*, Namier, p. 231.

Macaulay put it [1] of his generation, " the most enlightened generation of the most enlightened people that ever existed." Where there was evil, that evil was the relic of an evil past ; where there was good, that good was the product of the increasing purpose which runs through the ages and which was assuredly leading us to a yet more glorious and more rosy dawn ahead.

This, though it was said, was not very seriously believed in the eighteenth century. It was said to keep quiet those who did not belong to the governing classes. Yet, as always happens with educational reforms, you have to have one generation of conscious lying, and then the second generation, the generation that was pupil when the masters were lying, honestly believes what it was taught. The common belief that schoolboys like to disagree with their masters is unfortunately entirely untrue ; very few masters are stimulating enough to arouse disagreement. So by the end of the eighteenth century the progressive theory of history had received general acceptance among those who claimed for themselves the prestige of educated people. It was, therefore, not necessary specifically to teach it any more. So long as there was no great risk of their believing inconvenient history, it was much safer for the governing class not to learn any history at all. For they believed that they had a divine right to everything as it was. So history could not possibly teach them that they were justified in taking more, and might possibly arouse in them scruples at having so much.

Therefore, as soon as the Hanoverian régime was safely established, the lectures and pupils of the Regius Professors were allowed to lapse. Only their emoluments remained, as a hint to historians that silence was golden. " When I first read my warrant," confessed Nares,[2] who was appointed Professor in the early years of the nineteenth century, " I well remember feeling ashamed of my ignorance of this curious science "—political economy. But, arrived at Oxford, he found his colleagues indifferent and as ignorant as himself, and " the young men too constantly

[1] *Essay on Southey's Colloquies.*
[2] See article of Professor Firth referred to above.

engaged upon higher pursuits" to attend to "a subject comparatively so light and unacademical as modern history". "Things might be better," he reflected as he retired to his private house in Surrey, "if the office were bestowed upon some resident member of the University."

As a consequence it was possible to be certain that all the ablest youths in the country during all their formative years, during the only years perhaps in which they might ever have leisure for study, should never come in contact within any problem that had been a reality since the foundation of Christianity. And yet in this world of unreality they acquired qualifications which they imagined to entitle them to positions of command in the real world. Thus Sir Robert Peel, the first man ever to win an Oxford double first, was allowed without question to take a leading part in his country's government, and neither he nor anyone else ever suspected for a moment his total misunderstanding of the forces that had gone to shape that country. "Now remember what I say," writes Jackson,[1] his Headmaster, to him, "Give the last high finish to all that you now possess by the continual reading of Homer. Let no day pass without your having him in your hands. Elevate your own mind by the continual meditation of the vastness of his comprehension and the unerring accuracy of all his conceptions. If you will but read him four or five times every year, in half a dozen years you will know him by heart." No one yields to the present writer in his admiration for Homer, but to advise a young man whose business is to reform the credit system to read Homer *every day* is clearly the advice of a maniac.

The miseries of the time, miseries to which Peel's absorption in the classics and consequent ignorance of history made no inconsiderable contribution, raised up at length their protest against the privilege of class. There stepped out another perfectly honest man—from Eton and Christ Church—to make himself the mouthpiece of that protest, Gladstone. The Civil Service, which now governed England, was, he agreed, no longer to

[1] *Peel*, Ramsay, pp. 13, 14.

be filled merely by nomination and favouritism. Entrance to it should be by competitive examination—and naturally to such a man it appeared merely as a matter of course that such examinations should be in the subtleties of the Latin and Greek languages, subtleties which could hardly be acquired save by those whose fathers could afford for them the luxuries of public school and University education and the acquisition of which would take up so much of their time and energy that it was very unlikely that they would also give themselves to any serious study of history. Innocent of that study, they complacently accepted the progressive theory of history of whose origin they had no knowledge, and to sceptical speculations they replied, "Well, such things may have been or may not have been, but you cannot deny that out of them there emerged the present society, which offers to everybody a higher standard of living than has been offered by any of its predecessors." Like Hume, even when they deplored the injustices and barbarities of the past, they felt it impossible to deny that they "produced good", because they "led to our present situation".[1] To question the progressive theory came to be looked on almost as a species of disloyalty—of disloyalty to country, to school, to University, to class, to the philosophy of Gilbert and Sullivan and the half a dozen other things whose claims upon him the English gentleman thinks to be superior to those of truth. For, while the educated Englishman is not perhaps the most mendacious of men, there is certainly nobody else who thinks it bad form to tell the truth for so many different reasons.

Now what is the truth? In the fifties of the last century there lived in Oxford a clergyman, called Thorold Rogers, who made for himself a living by coaching in the classics and in philosophy. The only work that he had published up till then was an *Introductory Lecture to the Logic of Aristotle*. In 1860, however, he began serious research into the wages and prices ruling at the various dates in English history, and on the strength of this research in 1862 he was elected Drummond Professor of Political Economy. It was while he held that chair that there

[1] Quoted by Cobbett in his *Rural Rides*.

appeared the first two volumes of his *History of Agriculture and Prices.* He had set himself a task which no man had ever attempted before. He had set himself to collect all the statistics available of wages paid at different dates and in different parts of the country and of the prices ruling at those dates and places. The material collected for his *History of Agriculture and Prices* he subsequently used again for his *Six Centuries of Work and Wages.* The statistics which he collected alone fill a thick volume, and there is no reason to suspect that the conclusions at which he arrives are generalizations from insufficient data. In a smaller work—of extracts from his large *Six Centuries*—called *The History of Work and Wages,* he summarizes these conclusions.[1]

In 1495 the wages of the agricultural labourer were fixed at 2*s.* a week. The price of wheat was 4*s.* 0¾*d.* a quarter, that of malt 2*s.* 4½*d.*, of oatmeal 5*s.* 4*d.* Suppose, argues Rogers, that the labourer's family requires for its year's provisions three quarters of wheat, three of malt, and two of oatmeal, the cost of that will be 12*s.* 2¼*d.* + 7*s.* 1½*d.* + 10*s.* 8*d.*, or 29*s.* 11¾*d.* That is to say, the labourer will be able to earn it by fifteen weeks' work.

In 1564 the labourer got, on the average, 3*s.* 6*d.* a week, but wheat was now 19*s.* 9¾*d.*, oatmeal probably 25*s.*, and malt 10*s.* 8*d.* a quarter. To earn the same store of provisions, the sum proves that the labourer would have had to give forty weeks' work.

By 1610 the earnings of his whole year would have been insufficient to buy that store by 24*s.* 9½*d.* In 1651 things are a trifle better and he could earn his store by forty-three weeks' work. In 1684 his whole year's work would be just insufficient to earn him the store. By 1725, when the labourer could earn from £13 to £15 a year and when the price of the provisions would have worked out at £16 2*s.* 3*d.*, the sum would plainly have been insufficient.

He then, to vary the method of calculation, takes some figures given by Arthur Young in 1772 of the earnings of a family of seven, all in work. The sum total of their yearly earnings comes to £51 8*s.* a year. The same people, working in Henry VII's time, would, he shows, have

[1] pp. 56–66.

earned £24 10*s.*, and, by a comparison of prices, £183 15*s.* would have been required in 1777 to purchase what could be purchased by £24 10*s.* in Henry VII's time. In Young's time the wage of the agricultural labourer was 7*s.* 6*d.* a week. By 1866 it had risen to 13*s.*, but by 1866 prices were twelve times what they had been in Henry VII's time, when the wage had been 2*s.* a week.

Only less striking is the story told by the study of the artisan's wages. Wages in the building trade in 1877 were, Rogers found, 42*s.* 9*d.* a week. In Henry VII's time they were 3*s.* 4*d.*, which multiplied by twelve is 40*s.* Nor in those figures is there even that small improvement which there appears to be. For in Henry VII's time, and indeed right up to the reign of Charles II, rent was a negligible factor. Wages failed to keep pace with the rise in prices in the sixteenth and seventeenth centuries. On the other hand the amount of the rent, where there was rent to pay, was settled by custom. Now the whole strength of the landowners against the Crown was, as has been already argued, that their dues to the Crown were customary dues, and they had been strong enough to prevent those dues being revised with the rise of prices. But, refusing to permit a revision of their dues to the Crown, they could not demand, as long as the issue between them and the Crown was undecided, a revision of the yeoman's rent to them. By Charles II's reign, however, they thought that the cause of monarchy was so wholly beaten that it was no longer necessary to preserve an attitude of logical consistency in their opposition. They therefore abolished their feudal payments to the Crown, while preserving the yeoman's feudal payments to them.

In 1679 they also passed the Statute of Frauds. By that Statute they enacted that everyone must produce written evidence of his claim to his lands. After the confusion of the Civil Wars there was about such an enactment a superficial appearance of justice. But in truth the gentlemen possessed written titles and the peasants did not. The gentlemen possessed such titles, not because their claims were better than those of the peasants but because they were a great deal worse. The gentlemen had acquired their estates at the time of the dissolution of the monasteries and, foreseeing that such titles might well be challenged, had been careful to obtain written evidence of them from the King. The peasantry had inherited their lands by custom dating back to ancestors in the heart of the Middle Ages and had no written title. Thus the gentlemen were able to acquire the land of the peasants and at will to re-let it to them for a fixed term of years and at a greatly increased rent, to seize the land and employ the former peasant as an agricultural labourer, or to seize the land and turn the former peasant loose to fend for himself. There were a few gentlemen scattered about the country who refused for honour's sake to raise their rents, and among them it is pleasant to find the noble name of John Dryden. But the Statute of Frauds marks in general both the destruction of the English peasantry and the imposition upon the poor of rent as one of the major items in their expenditure.

"We owe the fact," Thorold Rogers tells us,[1] "that the great English nation is tenant-at-will to a few thousand landowners, to that device of evil times, a strict settlement. We are informed that the machinery which has gradually changed the whole character of the rural population of England was invented by the subtlety of two lawyers of the Restoration, Palmer and Bridgman. As there have been men whose genius has bestowed lasting benefit on mankind, so there have been from time to time exhibitions of perverted intellectual activity, whose malignant influence has inflicted permanent evils. It may be that the mischief which this practice has induced is too widespread for remedial measures. But no Englishman who has the courage to forecast the destinies of his country can doubt that its greatest danger lies in the present alienation of its people from the soil, and in the future exodus of a disinherited peasantry."

There are probably but few men to-day who would agree with Rogers's diagnosis that the solution for all these evils is to be found only in the application of the full gospel of his friend, Cobden. Concerning one or two details of his statistics there has been controversy. In

[1] *History of Agriculture and Prices*, Thorold Rogers, pp. 693, 694.

their main outline they remain unchallenged and unchallengeable. His careful and exhaustive evidence makes finally certain what the more random evidence of Cobbett had already shown to be highly probable. Broadly he asserts this. Between Henry VII's time and 1850 the population of England multiplied by about five, rising from four million to twenty million. The productivity of the country had multiplied by about four by 1800, and multiplied by another four and a half between 1800 and 1850, making a total of 18. As a result the poor ought to have been between three and four times better-off. They were, however, considerably worse-off. The gentlemen of England, so far from being those leaders of the nation towards a finer and a wider freedom which the progressive history had represented them to be, were revealed as in the heyday of their power the trickiest and most rapacious class ever known among men.

The sweeping rhetoric of Macaulay [1] had in 1830 professed itself " unable to find any satisfactory record of any great nation, past or present, in which the working classes have been in a more comfortable situation than in England in the last thirty years ". Very different was the verdict of one who was himself born in that class and knew their lives. " Experience," wrote Cobbett [2] in the *Political Register*, " daily observation, minute and repeated personal inquiry and examination, have made me familiar with the state of the labouring poor, and, sir, I challenge contradiction when I say, that a labouring man in England with a wife and only three children, though he never lose a day's work, though he and his family be economical, frugal, and industrious in the most extensive sense of those words, is not now able to procure himself by his labour a single meal of meat from one end of the year unto the other."

It was on the side of Cobbett's rhetoric and not of Macaulay's easy learning that the figures gave their verdict. From Rogers's hard arguments and dry statistics emerged the terrible conclusion, " I contend that, from 1563 to 1824, a conspiracy, concocted by the law and

[1] *Essay on Southey's Colloquies.*
[2] *Political Register*, 6th December, 1806.

carried out by parties interested in its success, was entered into to cheat the English workman of his wages, to tie him to the soil, to deprive him of hope and to degrade him into irremediable poverty. . . . For more than two centuries and a half the English law and those who administered the law were engaged in grinding the English workman down to the lowest pittance, in stamping out every expression or act which indicated any organized discontent, and in multiplying penalties upon him when he thought of his natural rights."[1] "The condition of the peasant," he wrote elsewhere in 1869 in one quiet and awful sentence,[2] "is now lower than it was even in Cobbett's time." And yet, if you go round the school libraries of England to-day, how many hundreds of copies of Macaulay will you find for every one of Cobbett ?

It is true that between the middle of the nineteenth century and 1900 the lot of the poor improved greatly. The standard of living of the modern poor man is definitely higher than that of his medieval ancestor, but it is only slightly higher. The modern poor man has a very much wider selection of objects upon which he can spend his money. He can go to the cinema ; he can eat tinned apricots ; he can ride in a charabanc—all of which were impossible to his ancestor. But, except to a trivial extent, he can only do these things by denying himself things which his ancestors used to enjoy. They are not additions to his life. He possesses, so to speak, more alternatives than his ancestor, but he does not possess more goods. Society at large is at an advantage over medieval society in that it has banished the fear of real famine, but in the Middle Ages, if there was a sufficiency of food, the poor man was certain to be able to get his share of it.

Thorold Rogers stood again for his professorship at Oxford when the term of it expired in 1867. They put up against him a certain Bonamy Price, a man who had until recently been off his head, though Professor Hewins in the *Dictionary of National Biography* assures us that by the time of the election he had completely recovered.

[1] *Work and Wages*, pp. 65, 66.
[2] *Historical Gleanings*, Lecture on Cobbett.

Price was elected by a large majority and subsequently re-elected three times. He had had no previous training in economics and, Professor Hewins tells us, " he made no important contribution to economic science." It was a sufficient qualification. Rogers meanwhile had to earn his living by giving lectures at a coaching establishment in Bayswater. It was only in 1888, two years before his death, that Oxford offered to him some reparation by re-electing him to his professorship.

Now does not the story of Thorold Rogers explain why it is that the truths of history sound to the average man's ear as strange and exaggerated paradoxes? There is hardly a scholar in all Europe to-day who would not acclaim Rogers's greatness. But has anyone who has only studied history in the text-books that they dole out in the public schools ever heard either his name or his thesis? Has such a one to-day any notion that solid scholarship has seriously challenged, let alone refuted, the progressive theory of history? And yet a distinguished modern Cambridge scholar, Mr. Butterfield, is able truly to say in his *Whig Interpretation of History*,[1] after having given a list of the main historical controversies of the last four hundred years, " In all the examples given above, as well as in many others, the result of detailed historical research has been to correct very materially what had been accepted Protestant, or Whig, interpretation." Those whose affection for the public schools is deepest should be the first candidly to admit that their system has not been so much a system of education as a system to prevent boys from getting education, their history little more than a prescription for setting the consciences of gentlemen at rest.

The poor in Townshend's day were illiterate. Therefore, so long as they were not educated at all, there was no necessity to educate them wrong. As a result there remained among them a strange and clouded memory that there had been good times in the past before the dissolution of the monasteries. This memory was quite unconnected with any present Catholic sympathies : it came from the fact that it was the coining of the monastic plate that started the rise in prices.

[1] p. 5.

"I'll tell thee what, good fellow,
Before the friars went hence
A bushel of the best wheat
Was sold for fourteen pence,
And forty eggs a penny
That were both good and new,"

sings Ignorance in the Percy Ballad of *Plain Truth and Blind Ignorance.* And, though Truth is made to win the theological debate, he specifically refuses even to try to refute Ignorance's economic history. The Rev. C. L. Marson is his book on Glastonbury [1] tells how the Somerset labourers in the last century still spoke of the Glastonbury monks as a "wonderful good class of people served terrible bad". It has taken but two generations of compulsory education and text-book history to make the poor as ignorant as the rich.

Now how was it that this perversion of history played into the hands of the masters of the credit-system? That was not its original purpose, the purpose for which Townshend and his friends invented it. They invented it to serve their own interests and owing to it they had a very comfortable innings. Yet from the first they suffered from the inevitable weakness of all blackmailers. They were defenceless against double-crossing. As has been argued, the Revolution of 1688 was essentially the work of gentlemen; the bankers were their very subordinate allies. Yet the most important result of that Revolution was the concession to the Bank of England of the extraordinary privilege of inventing money—a privilege which, as Swift demonstrated, by an inevitable mathematical necessity has caused the possessors of it to acquire a lien on the entire wealth of the nation to the loss of the gentlemen and everybody else. Nothing would have been easier than for a system of education to explain to its pupils the nature of this privilege of the bankers; nothing could be more evidently the duty of any proper system of education than to give such an explanation. But Townshend's education did not dare to give it because it was not possible to tell the story of the founding of the Bank of England unless you also told the true story of the Revolution of

[1] p. 56.

1688. The two were inextricably intertwined. Thus, secure against all dangers of publicity, the power of usury was able to extend its control over the state and, by a horrid irony, all the strong forces of conservatism and tradition were used to defend the activities of the most dangerous enemy that those forces have ever had to encounter. It was the discovery of usury that the gentleman's code could be used, if used with skill, for the promotion of injustice as well as for the promotion of justice. The individual gentleman, unless like Townshend he was very rich, would, it is true, be unwilling to " do anything that would let down the school ", or the regiment, or what not. But, if you could trick the whole school into connivance at injustice, then, on the gentleman's code, it would become disloyalty to question the conduct of the school. So Shylock exchanged the Jewish gaberdine for the Old School Tie and was elected with acclamation to the governing body.

Under the system the gradual extrusion of the landed classes by the monied classes was mathematically inevitable. It happened At the time of the Revolution, Gregory King tells us, the income of a merchant prince was " half that of a baronet, little more than an eighth that of a nobleman and little more than a third that of a bishop ". " In 1750 it is probable that the City of London had a larger commercial income than the rents of the whole House of Lords and the episcopal bench."[1] It was the Napoleonic wars which brought the final and complete triumph of the money-lenders. As Mr. Chesterton has justly put it [2] :

" The squire seemed struck in the saddle ; he was foolish as if in pain.
He leaned on a staggering lawyer, he clutched at a cringing Jew.
He was stricken, it may be, after all, he was stricken at Waterloo."

Cobbett saw the whole thing happening in one part of Hampshire. " Let us look back to the place where

[1] *Work and Wages*, Thorold Rogers, p. 111.
[2] *Secret People*.

I started on this present rural Ride. Poor old Baron Maseres, succeeded at Reigate by little Parson Fellowes, and at Betchworth (three miles on my road) by Kendrick, is no bad instance to begin with; for the Baron was nobly descended though from French ancestors. At Albury, fifteen miles on my road, Mr. Drummond (a banker) is in the seat of one of the Howards, and close by he has bought the estate, just pulled down the house and blotted out the memory of the Godschalls. At Chilworth, two miles further down the same vale and close under St. Martha's Hill, Mr. Tinkler, a powder-maker (succeeding Hill, another powder-maker, who had been a breeches-maker at Hounslow) has got the old mansion and estate of the old Duchess of Marlborough, who frequently resided in what was then a large quadrangular mansion, but the remains of which now serve as out farm-buildings and a farm-house, which I found inhabited by a poor labourer and his family, the farm being in the hands of the powder-maker, who does not find the once noble seat good enough for him. Coming on to Waverley Abbey, there is Mr. Thompson, a merchant, succeeding the Orby Hunters and Sir Robert Rich. Close adjoining Mr. Laing, a West India dealer of some sort, has stepped into the place of the lineal descendants of Sir William Temple. . . . Coming on to old Alresford (twenty miles from Farnham) Sheriff, the son of a Sheriff, who was a commissary in the American war, has succeeded the Gages. Two miles further on at Abbotston (down on the side of the Itchen) Alexander Baring has succeeded the heirs and successors of the Duke of Bolton, the remains of whose noble mansion I once saw here. Not above a mile higher up the same Baring has, at the Grange with its noble mansion, park, and estate, succeeded the heirs of Lord Northington; and at only about two miles further Sir Thomas Baring, at Stratton Park, has succeeded the Russells in the ownership of the estates of Stratton and Micheldover, which were once the property of Alfred the Great. . . . The small gentry to about the third rank upwards (considering there to be five ranks from the smallest gentry up to the greatest nobility) are all gone, nearly to a man, and the small farmers along with them. The Barings alone have, I should think, swallowed up thirty or forty of these small gentry without perceiving it. They indeed swallow up the biggest race of all; but innumerable small fry slip down unperceived, like caplins down the throats of the sharks, while these latter feel only the codfish. . . . The big, in order to save themselves from being 'swallowed up quick' (as we used to be taught to say in our Church prayers against Bonaparte) make use of their voices to get, through place, pension or sinecure, something back from the taxers. Others of them fall in love with the daughters and widows of paper-money people, big brewers and the like; and sometimes their daughters fall in love with the paper-money people's sons, or the fathers of those sons; and, whether they be Jews or not seems to be little matter with this all-subduing passion of love. But the small gentry have no resource. While war lasted, 'glorious war,' there was a resource; but now, alas, not only is there no war but there is no hope of war; and not a few of them will actually come to the parish-book." [1]

"To ascribe the whole to contrivance" he wrote [2] in another place "would be to give to Pitt and his followers too much credit for profundity; but . . . if these knaves had said, 'Let us go to work to induce the owners and occupiers of the land to convey their estates and capital into our hands,' and if the Government had corresponded with them in views, the effect could not have been more complete than it has thus far been. . . . It was the sheep rendering up the dogs [3] into the hands of the wolves".

"The gentlemen of England," said George Wyndham at the beginning of the twentieth century, "must not abdicate." But the whole history of England has been little but a history of gentlemen abdicating. The abdications have only not been noticed for the same reason as that for which Sir John Harrington found that treason never prospered—because the people who stepped into power always called themselves gentlemen.

[1] *Rural Rides*, pp. 310–12. [2] Ed. 1853, p. 92.
[3] *Sic.* Does he mean "The dogs rendering up the sheep"?

CHAPTER V

BISHOP BERKELEY

Out of the continuous story of monetary experiment, which is English history, the text-books pick out one or two passing incidents and give us their account of them. Thus, after no word has been said about the management of the currency during the Middle Ages, a paragraph or two is usually devoted to the debasement of the coinage by Henry VIII—for it is one of the few instances in history of an English King mismanaging the currency. After Henry VIII the river of money plunges underground again. The story of the sixteenth and seventeenth centuries is told as if their controversies were entirely political and religious. Take, for instance, such a book as Professor Neale's *Queen Elizabeth,* which has recently been praised to the skies, or the work of Professor Trevelyan. For all that the painful student can understand there might have been no problems of money at all from Henry VIII's day until, a volume later on, he finds that in George I's time there was something called the South Sea Bubble. It seems to be a working rule with writers of School Certificate text-books that one, and not more than one, monetary experiment may be referred to in each volume.

Now the South Sea Bubble, for all its prominence in the text-books, was not, philosophically speaking, of great original importance in English monetary history. All that happened, in the last analysis, was that a number of rich men told a number of lies to induce people to buy shares from them for more than they were worth. The politicians kept their mouths shut because they had been bribed. It was, as Bishop Berkeley put it [1] with characteristic carefulness of language, an "attempt of men, easy in their fortunes and unprovoked by hardships of any sort, in cold blood to ruin their native country".

[1] *An Essay towards Preventing the Ruin of Great Britain, Berkeley's Works* (ed. Fraser), iii, 206.

Unfortunately such attempts are not sufficiently rare in history to deserve extended notice.

A lot of people lost money over the South Sea Bubble and a lot of people gained it. But nobody made money —in the sense in which bankers make money—that is to say, nobody made it up. The South Sea Bubble is only of ultimate importance for three reasons. In the first place Walpole emerged from it, the master both of an immense fortune and of sufficient evidence to blackmail all the other leaders of the Whig party. It was the foundation of his twenty years of power over England. In the second place the proved dishonesty of the politicians made much easier the later task of the bankers in persuading the public to prefer their bank-notes to a direct state-fiduciary issue. In the third place the South Sea Bubble gave the final blow to the prestige of the monarchy.

The Whigs had already made monarchy impotent. It was their next achievement to make it ridiculous. For such a purpose no candidate for the throne could have suited them better than George I. Not only could he not speak English, as the text-books tell us, but he was also guilty of the more serious crime of having procured the murder of his wife's lover and then of having had him baked in an oven. An historian as careful and restrained as Lord Acton has written[1] of him, "Nobody doubted that Konigsmark had been made away with and that the author of the crime was the King of England, whose proper destination, therefore, should have been not St. James's but Newgate, and indeed not Newgate but Tyburn." There was little risk of a monarchical revival under such a monarch.

Walpole was astute enough to see that the best way of making quite certain that monarchy would never again put forward a claim to the control of monetary supply was to make the royal family, in its personal capacity, a beneficiary from the system of usury. He, therefore, saw to it that the Prince and Princess of Wales gained in pocket from the South Sea Bubble. "One of his (Walpole's) great arts," writes Lady Cowper,[2] "to please the

[1] *Lectures on Modern History*, p. 267.
[2] Quoted by Stirling Taylor, *Walpole*, p. 203.

Princess has been by making her a stock-jobber in the South Sea. They bought in for her the very morning before the great debate. . . . They subscribed at a hundred and fifty—he twenty thousand, she ten." Walpole told them the moment to sell—when the stock stood at about 1,000 —and they thus made a large fortune out of the business. Indeed so completely was the future George II captured by the delights of this new life that he condescended to become the Governor of one of the many fraudulent companies which sprang up in this hysterical period—the English Copper Company. The Lords Justices had to write to him, "Their Excellencies sent a compliment to the Prince of Wales, that the Company of English Copper, of which His Royal Highness had been pleased to be chosen Governor, being illegal, they were forced to involve it in the said Order, which compliment His Royal Highness received very graciously," [1] as well he might, as, receiving warning of the coming crash, he had already sold out with a profit of £40,000.[2]

Yet there were others who were able to look upon the catastrophe of the South Sea Bubble with eyes very different from those of Walpole or George II, and to draw from it very different lessons. In 1721, the year after the Bubble, there returned to England from the Continent a young man, as then but little known but who was destined to leave behind him one of the most remarkable names in the history of English letters. Bishop Berkeley is to-day generally recognized as one of the few English metaphysicians of a quite first-rate importance; few would think it an extravagance to call him the greatest of English metaphysicians. But, besides metaphysics, he turned his versatile genius and extraordinary gift for the writing of lucid prose to numerous other topics—to mathematics, to the virtues of tar-water, to the habits of the tides, to the necessity of sending Anglican missionaries to the Red Indians. It would be hard perhaps to name any other English writer possessed of so wide a versatility of interests until we come to the time of Mr. Hilaire Belloc. And it was not strange that the curiosity of such a man

[1] *South Sea Bubble*, Erleigh, p. 109.
[2] Ibid., p. 80.

should have been aroused with desire to discover exactly why the South Sea Bubble had burst.

He, therefore, wrote in 1721 what he called an *Essay Towards Preventing the Ruin of Great Britain.* The essay contains a number of reflections, true but a little trite, such as that it is better for a country's citizens to be honest rather than dishonest and that consumption is not possible until there has first been production. Yet, just as the calamity of 1931 aroused the interest in monetary matters of many people who had not before much attended to them, so did the South Sea Bubble arouse Berkeley's interest. His curiosity was not satisfied by his own essay. Therefore in the years, 1735, 1736, and 1737, Berkeley, by then the Bishop of Cloyne, published in three parts his *Queries Proposed to the Consideration of the Public,* in which he put forward the monetary and economic reforms which were in his opinion necessary to prevent such catastrophes as that of the South Sea Bubble and to bring prosperity to Ireland—for it was with Ireland that he was then concerned. Of this most remarkable work Sir James Mackintosh a hundred years ago wrote [1] that " Perhaps the *Querist* contains more hints, then original, still unapplied, in legislation and political economy than are to be found in any equal space." This could be said with as large a truth to-day as in Mackintosh's time.

The arrangement of the work—consisting of a large number of unrelated questions, some on monetary, some on general social, matters—is not a happy one. But, if one may throw the general lesson of the queries into a coherent narrative, the argument of the *Querist* is as follows :—

The fundamental service which a monetary system can render to a society is to provide a sufficiency of " counters " to enable such goods as the producers wish to sell and buyers to buy to change hands. The business of the Government is to see that the general price-level remains stable. One article, through the demand for it increasing, may go up in price and another come down. But the price of articles in general must neither increase nor decrease. Any such general increase or decrease,

[1] Footnote to Berkeley's *Collected Works*, vol. iii, p. 355.

" such arbitrary changing the denomination of coin," is, he says,[1] " a public cheat."

All monetary systems are then judged by the efficiency with which they perform this function of keeping prices stable. A metallic monetary system, for instance, is chosen not because there is a magic virtue in gold or silver but because it is thought—whether rightly or wrongly—that it is more probable that prices will remain stable when the monetary supply is kept tolerably stable by the fact that money consists of metals that cannot be created at will than when it consists of something intrinsically valueless that can be manufactured at will in unlimited quantities.

The function of a monetary system then being admitted, it remains to consider what system will best perform that function. But first he stops to explain what system performs it worst. The system that performs it worst is the system of double-money, which, with the privileges of the Bank of England, was then in its infancy and by which the affairs of England and of other countries have been ruled ever since Berkeley's day—the system by which a large proportion of the nation's business is done by one sort of money which can at demand be converted into another sort of money—by notes which can be converted into gold as in Berkeley's day, by cheques which can be converted into notes as to-day. Under such a system a violent alternation of slumps and booms was inevitable. For the very conditions that create prosperity are also the conditions that infallibly kill it.

Let us understand his argument.

The bank, he says, issues its bank-notes, and it says, " You need not be afraid to accept these notes. You are quite safe because you can at will convert them into cash." Now, suppose that some trivial rumour, true or false, should get abroad about the integrity of a particular bank. If but a tenth of that bank's depositors hear that rumour and demand their deposits out in cash, it is unable to satisfy those demands. It may indeed stave off disaster for a time by borrowing cash from another bank. But that other bank also has issued ten times as many bank-notes as it can convert into cash. If it lends some of its cash to its

[1] Query 28.

neighbour in distress, it is dangerously, perhaps fatally, weakening its own position. The attempt to save the one bank may easily bring the whole financial system crashing into ruin.

Even if somehow the panic is allayed and major calamity averted, the smallest increased demand for cash, he argues, cannot but have disastrous effects. Suppose that it is only a tenth of the depositors who go to the first bank and the bank is unable to satisfy their demands. It can only satisfy them by calling in all its outstanding loans and refusing to make any new ones. By so doing it reduces the sum total of money in circulation in the country at large. Therefore, since there is less money with which to purchase the same amount of goods, all prices fall. Therefore the producer who has incurred his costs of production and his debts at the higher price-level can only sell his article at the lower price-level. Therefore he loses money, turns off hands, ceases to produce, perhaps goes bankrupt. Poverty, unemployment, stagnation, and all the other familiar symptoms of the slump appear.

It should clearly be the object of any sane monetary system to narrow as far as possible the area within which any loss of confidence has its effect. The double-money system instead insanely and unnecessarily widens that area until to-day, as we know to our cost, the whole world suffers for some trifling miscalculation or act of folly in a single bank. "Whether a few mishaps to particular persons may not throw this nation into the utmost confusion?" asks Berkeley.[1] Indeed, as readers of Dr. McNair Wilson's *Promise to Pay* will agree, not even miscalculation nor an act of folly is necessary to throw the monetary machine out of gear. Mere prosperity is by itself sufficient. In order to create a boom the banks have lent up to their full capacity. But the mere arrival of prosperity causes people in the lightness of their hearts to ask for a slightly larger proportion of their possessions in cash, just as we read every year how there is an increased demand for cash from the banks as the holiday seasons come round. Whereas before they demanded only a tenth of their deposits, they demand in prosperity, say,

[1] Original Edition, part ii, Query 7.

an eighth. The banks can only supply that demand for an eighth by refusing to renew some of their loans, and thus they inevitably reduce the price-level and destroy that very prosperity which created the increased demand. The politicians are for ever telling us that there is a good time coming. But we are like Tantalus. Prosperity comes, but, when we put the cup of it to our lips to enjoy it, it vanishes away.

"You exaggerate," says the objector. "The financial system does not collapse, because the Government steps in with special measures to prevent the final calamity." "Exactly," answered the Bishop, in effect, "and do you not see what that proves? It proves that the bank is lending money to the community not, as is pretended, on the credit of the bank but rather on the credit of the community itself." "Whether the opinion of men, and their industry consequent thereupon, be not the true wealth of Holland," he asks,[1] "and not the silver supposed to be deposited in the bank at Amsterdam?" and "Whether there is in truth any such treasure lying dead? And whether it be of consequence to the public that it be real rather than notional?"[2]

What paper money is to be issued should therefore be frankly issued by public authority. It should be inconvertible. The check on it should be that the public authority should be forbidden to issue any new supplies of it, when it was seen that those new supplies were resulting not in an increased production of goods but merely in rising prices. "Whether counters be not referred to other things, which, so long as they keep pace and proportion with the counters, it must be owned the counters are useful?"[3]

The only argument in favour of a metallic monetary system is that people are accustomed to it. They think that metals have an intrinsic value equal to their monetary value. This is certainly untrue. The industrial demand for gold and silver is small, and, if the demand for them were merely industrial, their price would certainly be very much less than it now is. It is the fact that Governments use the precious metals for monetary purposes that makes

[1] Query 44. [2] Query 45. [3] Query 310.

them precious. Nevertheless people think that the metals have an intrinsic value, so it is not unreasonable to pay some respect to their prejudice and, if it is possible, to have all the country's business transacted in metallic money. But, if that is not possible, if in order to keep prices stable, it is necessary to issue paper-money, then it is madness to let any other than a public authority issue that money, or to make it convertible. It is indeed better to have a sufficient monetary supply, even privately issued, than an insufficient supply. He asks, " Whether without private banks what little business and industry there is would not stagnate ? [1] " but that does not prevent him from also asking, " Whether it be not a mighty privilege for a private person to be able to create a hundred pounds with a dash of his pen ? " [2]

He considered in some detail the experiment of Law which had a little before met with failure in France. The blunder, he insisted, was not that paper-money had been issued but that so much of it had been issued that prices had inevitably risen. Yet, though creditors must necessarily have suffered from that rise, people could in time have adjusted themselves to this new higher price-level. The fatal blow from which Law's experiment could never recover was the alteration by the Regent of the metallic value of the bank-bills, " Whether, notwithstanding all the above-mentioned extraordinary measures, the bank-bills did not still pass at par with gold and silver to May, 1720, when the French king thought fit by a new act of council to make a restriction of their value, which proved a fatal blow ? " [3] Had he kept the bills as inconvertible legal tender money, all would in the end have adjusted itself.

Paper-money was, argued Berkeley, the simplest and most straightforward of all forms of money, for with it all men could see, what is in any event always the truth, that the credit behind the money was the credit of the community. " Whether all circulation be not alike a circulation of credit, whatsoever medium (metal or paper) is employed, and whether gold be any more than credit for so much power ? " he had asked.[4] Nor did he agree

[1] Query 290. [2] Ibid. [3] Query 98. [4] Query 426.

that a stock of gold and silver was necessary even for foreign trade. "Whether it be not evident that we may maintain a much greater inward and outward commerce, and be five times richer than we are, nay, and our bills abroad be of far greater credit, though we had not one ounce of gold or silver in the whole island?"[1] Foreign trade—at the least the only sort of foreign trade that was desirable—was an exchange of goods either against immediate goods or at least against the hope of goods in the future. "Whether trade," he asked,[2] "be not on a right foot when foreign commodities are imported in exchange only for domestic superfluities?" and he followed up this query with a further one which showed that he understood as well as any modern monetary reformer the difference between real and effective demand. "Whether the quantities of beef, butter, wool and leather, exported from this island, can be reckoned the superfluities of a country, where there are so many natives naked and famished?"[3] "Whether we are not in fact the only people what may be said to starve in the midst of plenty?" he asked,[4] anticipating, perhaps creating, a phrase now on the lips of every currency-reformer. Now this exchange of goods, he argued, is not helped by the presence of gold or silver in the exchanging countries. On the contrary it is, as modern experience has taught, greatly hindered if that gold is moved about in quantity from one country to another. It is true that gold is to-day useful for adjusting short-term balances but, if all the gold and silver in the world were thrown into the sea, they could be adjusted just as well by book-entries. So far from being possessed of an intrinsic value, gold is of all the metals, as Thomas More told us in *Utopia*, the one that is most nearly valueless.

In fact the best way, argued Bishop Berkeley, is the simplest way. The convertibility of notes, the use of metallic money, every other monetary dodge—what are they but somewhat clumsy and ill-working schemes for compelling the Government to keep the price-level stable? Why not cut out these dodges and simply put the

[1] Query 450.
[2] Query 172.
[3] Query 173.
[4] Query 446.

Government under direct obligation to keep the price-level stable? Give them authority to issue sufficient money to keep prices up and make it an offence for them to issue either less or more? It is idle to argue that politicians are corrupt. If, he said, politicians are not honest enough to do their duty nor public opinion widely enough awake to compel them to do it, then any monetary system will collapse. Under Berkeley's system doubtless the politician would issue too many or too few notes, but under a metallic system he would debase the coinage; under the double-money system he would play tricks by suspending and resuming cash-payments to suit his convenience or that of his friends. Did the fact that the high prerogative of issuing money had been wrested from the king prevent the South Sea Bubble? "Where," he asks, "is it most reasonable to expect wise and punctual dealing, whether in a secret, impenetrable recess, where credit depends on secrecy, or in a public management regulated and inspected by Parliament?"[1]

With similarly characteristic common sense he tackled the problem of poverty. The first business of a country's economic system is to give to its citizens the necessities of life. Does our system do this? It does not. Why not? Because there are not enough goods? No, but because the poor have not enough money. Then give them more money. So long as there was on the one hand the labour, the raw material, and the skill to produce the new goods, on the other hand the desire to consume them when produced, for so long would the provision of money, sufficient to make that demand effective, do good to everybody and harm to nobody. "Whether to provide plentifully for the poor be not feeding the root, the substance whereof will shoot upwards into the branches and cause the top to flourish?" he asked,[2] and "Whether a country inhabited by a people well fed, clothed, and lodged would not become every day more populous? And whether a numerous stock of people in such circumstances would not constitute a flourishing nation? and how far the product of our own country may suffice for compassing

[1] Original Edition, part iii, Query 32.
[2] Query 59.

this end?"[1] What was the alternative? A congeries of starving nations, exporting the necessities of life and fighting against one another for the export markets.

Berkeley's proposals failed of acceptance, in truth, not because of the openings that they gave to corruption but because of the difficulties that they put in its way. "Whether it were just to insinuate that gentlemen would be against any proposal they could not turn into a job?" he asked.[2] Unfortunately it was perfectly just. His proposal of an Irish national bank, to keep stable the Irish price-level, would have been not to the disadvantage but to the advantage of the Irish gentry. But they were too stupid to see it so—to see that they were now but playing fly to usury's spider and that their petty and short-sighted greed was the bait by which they were taken. "Whether," he asked[3] sadly, "an uneducated gentry be not the greatest of national evils?"

In the seventeenth century, as has been explained, England was an importer of capital from Holland. At the turn of the century London established itself as "all that Amsterdam was", and England became instead an exporter of capital. Or, to put the truth with more exact accuracy, an international gang, which had up till then operated from Amsterdam, found it more convenient to operate from London instead. Thorold Rogers in his *History of Holland*[4] comments on the high proportion of Dutchmen among the early directors of the Bank of England. Among other countries to which capital had been exported was Ireland. It was the necessity of paying rents to absentee landlords, interest on mortgages from English bankers, etc., which caused that export of "beef, butter, wool, and leather"[5] from the starving island, of which Berkeley complained. Now he did not advocate any repudiation of foreign debt, but he did advocate that it should be paid off as quickly as possible. Nor was there any reason to doubt that under his scheme it could have been paid off within quite a short period of time. Had it been so, one of the deepest causes of all the murder and misery of the last two hundred years of

[1] Query 62. [2] Original Edition, part iii, Query 47.
[3] Query 15. [4] p. 223. [5] Query 173.

Anglo-Irish relations would have been removed at a stroke.

The English usurer however, did not want it to be paid off at all. What he wanted was a permanent lien on Irish land. Now, as long as the Irish were dependent upon metallic money, they never could get out of debt. Ireland herself produced neither gold nor silver nor other metals. Therefore, as productivity increased, she had to import them from England. Either she must buy them with goods or else receive them on loan. She could not buy them with goods because the export surplus in those limited articles that she was allowed to produce was already ear-marked for past debts. Yet if she did not increase her monetary supply the effect would be deflationary, prices would fall, and her productivity be destroyed. Therefore inevitably she had to plunge further and further into debt, compelled to accept the English metal at cheat-prices with the brutal threat, as Swift put it in the *Drapier's Letters*, that " we must either take those half-pences or eat our brogues." Berkeley's suggestion was that gold and silver and copper should be allowed to look after themselves and their deficiencies made up by Irish-issued inconvertible paper-money. Along that road lay a chance of emergence from debt.

His project of a national bank was so little understood that he dropped the passages advocating it out of the edition of his collected works, " which it may be time enough to take in hand," he wrote,[1] " when the public shall seem disposed to make use of such an expedient." So completely successful was what Cobbett would have called " the Thing " of eighteenth and nineteenth century England in suppressing this scheme of one of the greatest of English thinkers that, when in the middle of the last century Fraser was preparing his great edition of the collected works of Berkeley, he was unable for a long time to discover a single copy of the original version of the *Querist*. It was only at the last moment that he struck on a copy—just in time to include it in an appendix.

[1] Introduction to the *Querist*.

Chapter VI

THE AMERICANS AND THE WHIGS

It is a commonplace of history, as she appears in popular table-talk, that the Whig inheritors of the great Revolution of 1688 had a natural sympathy with the American demand for freedom and self-government, that, if they had only had their way, those demands would have been satisfied within the framework of the Empire but that the Americans were compelled into independence by the obstinacy of a stupid King. Nothing could be more false. The Whigs had no intention of establishing beyond the seas a land in which " Government of the people for the people and by the people should not perish from the earth ". On the contrary Lord Shaftesbury, the Whig leader, engaged John Locke, the Whig philosopher, shortly before 1688 to draw up a constitution for the new colonies of the Carolinas. Locke proposed that the colony be handed over to eight proprietors, Shaftesbury himself, Monk, Clarendon, and five others, these proprietors to be called palatine, admiral, chamberlain, constable, chief justice, high steward, and treasurer. To these eight gentlemen one fifth of the land of the colonies was to be given. The next concern should be to provide adequate estates for the resident aristocracy, whose land was to be worked by hereditary serfs bound to the soil. What land was left over was to be sold by the proprietors to freeholders. The grand purpose, said Locke, was to avoid " a numerous democracy ".[1]

Locke's scheme was not, it is true, exactly adopted, but the spirit of it was adopted. The essential object of all Whig policy towards America was to keep the cost of labour low. For the Whigs had invested capital in America as in Ireland, and it is an evident and important law that, where wages are low, then there is money to be divided in dividends, and the product of the low-wage country

[1] *Rise of American Civilization*, C. and M. Beard, i, 66.

can also be used to force workers in other countries to accept wages as low or to starve. Now it is important to understand that in the early years of the eighteenth century the Whigs succeeded in their object. America was a low-wage country—or at least certain American industries were carried on with low wages, or rather with low labour-costs. How was that done ? It was done thus. The labour-market was supplied either by African slaves or by white indentured labourers—by criminals shipped out there and compelled to work for the term of their sentence without wages, or, should the supply of criminals run short, by wretches kidnapped in the London streets by creatures of the capitalists known as "spirits", hustled on board a ship and then compelled in America to earn their freedom by a service of from five to seven years on an estate.[1] Bancroft, the American historian most widely recommended at the English universities and schools during the last century, confessed to having collected "a handful of data about the sources from which the American labour market was supplied in those days" and of "having opened his little finger"[2] and said nothing about it.

It was because of the cheapness of its labour that America was able to attract English capital. Now a new colony in its first years cannot keep itself but must live on loans, for its members must consume and they are not yet able to produce. But, if the country be wisely founded, after a short time they will start to produce and, a short time afterwards, they will be able to produce a surplus. Then their first natural concern will be to get themselves out of debt. This was the condition to which the American colonies were beginning to come by the middle of the eighteenth century.

But the Americans, like the Irish, could never get out of debt so long as they were compelled for monetary purposes to import precious metals and to regulate their currency by the strict rule that the amount of money in the country should rise and fall in exact proportion to the amount of gold and silver. Therefore, like Bishop Berkeley in Ireland, they began to agitate for the right to make a fiduciary issue of paper-money. The answer of the British Parliament

[1] Ibid., i, 104. [2] Ibid., i, 103.

was in 1751 to pass an Act prohibiting the issue of paper-money in New York, and this prohibition was afterwards extended to the other colonies. "On the slight complaint of a few Virginia merchants," said Benjamin Franklin,[1] "nine colonies had been restrained from making paper money, become absolutely necessary to their internal commerce, from the constant remittance of their gold and silver to Britain."

There was thus no possibility for the Americans to get out of debt, and the English financiers looked forward to drawing steady and permanent dividends from their American investments. The result, complained Franklin, was that the American "whole wealth centres finally among the merchants and inhabitants of Great Britain". Of the nature of the Americans these "merchants and inhabitants" knew little and cared less.

After the Seven Years' War it was widely felt in England that it would be just that the Americans should make some contribution to Imperial taxation. Whether that feeling was a right one or a wrong one, we need not discuss. It was a general and national one, shared by King and people, Parliament and financiers. The later Whig legend that it was a special project of George III's brain is sheer fabrication. "The shame of the darkest hour of England's history," writes Green [2] of poor George, "lies wholly at his door." It is nonsense.

The first attempt to raise revenue from America was made by the Sugar Act of 1764, putting a duty on American sugar. But, since sugar could be produced as easily and abundantly in the West Indies as in America, that duty proved to be a protective but not a revenue duty. Its effect was but to ruin the American sugar industry and to make the West Indies almost the sole source of England's sugar supplies—an effect which, it is not perhaps unduly cynical to suggest, may possibly have been foreseen by the seventy-four owners of West Indian sugar plantations who sat in the Parliament which voted the Act.[3] The problem was tackled again by the Stamp Act. The Stamp Act was proposed

[1] *Rise of American Civilization*, Beard, i, 195.
[2] *History of the English People*, viii, 17.
[3] Op. cit., Beard, i, 195.

by Grenville, a Whig, a man personally distasteful to George III. It was supported by the whole Whig Parliament and passed both Houses of Parliament " with less opposition than a turnpike bill "—in the House of Commons by 205 votes to 49, in the House of Lords without a division. "I well remember," said Burke,[1] "that Mr. Townshend, in a brilliant harangue on this subject, did dazzle them by playing before their eyes the image of a large revenue to be raised in America." Townshend was a leading Whig. So far indeed was the Act from being the personal policy of George III that it so happened that the poor man was insane at the time, and the royal assent was only given to it by a regency.

Grenville fell from power for reasons entirely unconnected with America and was succeeded by the Government of Rockingham, the very archetype of Whiggery. The Government was formed in July, 1765. For the first six months of its life it had no particular American policy. Conway, the Secretary of State, occupied them with writing feeble letters to the American governors about the disorders. Then at the end of the year it began to discover that the result of the Stamp Act and of the boycott of English goods was that the dividends were not coming in to the English investors. The merchants of London, Liverpool, and Glasgow sent in a petition complaining that £4,000,000 of debts were owing to them in America and that they were unable to collect them.

It was then, and not till then, that the light of divine illumination fell upon the gentlemen of England. At that date about one person in four hundred in England had a vote. Yet the Whig Members of Parliament, representative of of one four-hundredth part of the people of Great Britain, found that the American cry of " No taxation without representation " was a righteous and a freedom-loving cry. Was not the American cause their own cause of 1688 ? The more prosaic truth was that they saw that the Americans would not pay both the Stamp Act's dues and their private debts, just as the financiers of our own day saw that the Germans would not pay both reparations and the interest on the Dawes and Young Loans. Therefore high Christian

[1] Ibid., i, 210.

and Whiggish principles demanded the repeal of the Stamp Act. Chatham, the City of London's man, made a speech in which he said that liberty was too noble a thing for her rights to be settled by the nice precedents of the Statute Book. Rockingham repealed the Stamp Act. " The whole trading interest of this Empire crowded into your lobbies," said Burke. But it was beneath the dignity of Chatham's great rhetoric to advert to the restraint on liberty of a prohibition on the issue of paper-money, a prohibition which had been expressly reaffirmed by the Whig Government of Grenville and which was not removed by the Whig Government of Rockingham. The Americans accepted the repeal of the Stamp Act with gratitude but sent a petition to the House of Commons concerning their other grievances —among them that of the prohibition on paper-money.

Rockingham fell and was succeeded by Chatham who appointed Townshend as his Chancellor of the Exchequer—the hero of the " brilliant harangue " in favour of the Stamp Act. The Whigs, as the Declaratory Act proved, had no principled objection to the taxation of America. If possible, they wanted to get both taxes and dividends out of the Americans. It was only in case of necessity that they were prepared to jettison the taxes in order to keep the dividends. Therefore Townshend attempted to raise by duties on tea, glass, and paper the revenue that Grenville would have raised by the Stamp Act, thinking that the Americans would object less to external than to internal taxes.

He miscalculated. There was indeed nothing at all novel in the principle of taxation of the Americans in one form or another. But Rockingham's repeal of the Stamp Act had proved to them—what they had not previously understood—that they could get out of paying their taxes if only they made sufficient fuss. Hence the riots and acts of protest with whose story every one is conversant. The Whig Government paid no attention to these protests, nor was it till the advent of a Tory Government under North that all the duties except that on tea were repealed.

Then the situation was complicated by an extraneous accident. The East India Company was in financial difficulties because the shareholders had depleted its reserves by paying themselves an excessive dividend. To save it from bankruptcy the Government had come to its rescue with a loan, and, in order to get its money back, the Government was exceedingly anxious to increase the Company's receipts. Most reasonably it occurred to North that, if Indian tea were sent direct to America, there was no reason why the Company's profits should not be increased to the benefit of the American consumer but at the expense of the two sets of middlemen, the English and the American, who up till then had had the handling of it on its journey from the producer to the market. It was the destruction of this tea, organized by the American middlemen afraid that, like Othello, their occupation would be gone, which first caused the British ministry to pay serious attention to American unrest.

Lord North made attempts to compose the quarrel, which, as is known, failed. It came to the arbitrament of war and the Americans in their Declaration of Independence saw fit to ascribe all their grievances to the personal malignity of George III, hoping thus to gain for themselves the support of English Whigs. But the pretence, though perhaps an astute political manœuvre, had no truth behind it. Nor did the manœuvre succeed. In spite of the efforts of Whig historians in the last century, such as May, or Sir George Trevelyan, to collect evidence of the unpopularity of the war with the English people and governing classes, there is no doubt that every section of English society was solidly behind the Government in its ambition to coerce the Americans. It may be convenient politics to pretend that it was not so but it is not good history. "All the worst measures of American coercion that preceded the Declaration," writes Lecky,[1] "were carried by enormous majorities in Parliament." And indeed, so far was George from being the architect of repression, obtaining for his odious policy formal approval from a bribed and servile Parliament, that, where he did bring personal pressure to bear on Members, during North's régime, he did so, in 1775 in order to overcome their strong opposition to the Prime Minister's conciliatory resolutions.

The General Election of 1774, fought, in so far as elections

[1] *History of England*, Lecky, iii, 525.

in those days were fought on any issue, on the American issue, gave to Lord North's Government a strong majority and on divisions it could usually muster about 260 votes against 90. In 1776, when after the capture of New York it looked for the moment as though the British cause might be victorious, the opposition sank to 47. The mercantile classes were also, according to Burke, for the war. "The mercantile interest," he said,[1] "which ought to have supported with efficacy and power the opposition to the fatal cause of all this mischief, was pleaded against us, and we were obliged to stoop under the accumulated weight of all the interests of this kingdom." "The merchants," he said again, "are gone from us and from themselves. . . . The leading men among them are kept full fed with contracts and remittances and jobs of all descriptions and are indefatigable in their endeavours to keep the others quiet. . . . They all, or the greatest number of them, begin to sniff the cadaverous *haut gout* of lucrative war." The generality of the people of England were also, according to Burke, on the same side. Violent measures, said Rockingham, received the support of a majority of the population "of all ranks, professions or occupations in the country".[2] Sir George Saville, an opponent of the war, estimated in a confidential letter to Rockingham, that "ninety-nine in one hundred"[3] were in favour of it. When the war broke out, "the majority both in and out of Parliament," recorded the Duke of Grafton, "continued in a blind support of the measures of administration."[4]

Burke's voice, it is true, was of course raised on the other side, but it was well understood at the time—and has not perhaps been so well understood since—that Burke was a poor man and that since 1771 he had been the salaried English agent of the province of New York.[5] It is not suggested that his advocacy was therefore merely hired advocacy. Human nature does not work so crudely as that. But there is no absolute measure to tell us the relative

[1] *Rise of American Civilization*, Beard, i, 282.
[2] *Political History of England*, Hunt, p. 158.
[3] *Life of Buckingham*, Albemarle, ii, 305.
[4] MS. Autobiography, quoted by Lecky, iv, 66.
[5] *Political History of England*, Hunt, p. 136.

strength of contending arguments, and there are few of us therefore who do not come honestly but easily to believe that in a quarrel the side that butters our bread has a better case than the side that offers us nothing.

It was not until after the surrender of Saratoga and the French intervention that a vigorous pro-American party began to make its appearance, and it was then that the Whigs took advantage of the King's obstinacy to pretend, for party purposes, that they from the first had been against the coercion of the Americans and he alone in favour of it. The truth of the matter was that the City interests would, as has been said, have preferred to have extracted both dividends and taxes from the Americans. But, after the French intervention, as the City saw the American debts to French and Dutch financiers mounting and mounting, it realized that there was no longer any possibility of extracting taxes, and a prolongation of the war, by ruining the dollar, would very likely rob it of its dividends. Therefore they threw the King overboard, turned against North, on his fall gave their support to Rockingham and made a deal with the Americans by which they agreed to recognize the independence of the United States on condition that the new American Government placed no impediment in the way of the collection of English debts in America. In practice the collection of those debts was to prove no easy matter—but that is another story.

But the war had not been without its compensations. For, while in favour of the war, the money interests had not of course been in favour of paying for it. They had played on George III just the same trick that their predecessors had played on William III nearly a hundred years before. They had let him have his war, provided that he borrowed the money for it from them. The war cost £97,599,496. Of that Parliament voted in taxation £3,039,427. The other £94,560,069 was raised by loan.[1] The National Debt was doubled. The American War completed what had been begun in William III's time—the definitive establishment of a considerable class of moneyed men as the permanent pensioners of the State.

It is not argued for one moment that George III was not

[1] *England under the Hanoverians*, Grant Robertson, App. iv.

in favour of coercing the Americans, and, if such coercion was a blunder or a crime, then he was guilty of that blunder or that crime. But it is argued that he was not especially guilty. Every interest in the country shared the guilt with him—the moneyed interest neither more nor less than the rest. Well, it may be asked, what of it ? This of it. The money power did not take its share of the blame when that policy failed. There still lingers among men a vague tradition that the financial world has managed and still manages its affairs with an almost superhuman competence. The whole record of history stands open in refutation of that tradition. But it persists because there is one particular trick that they have learnt how to play with a skill that is almost uncanny. It is the trick, when things go wrong, of leaving somebody else to hold the baby. We have already seen how in 1672 they left the impression that it was Charles II who was entirely to blame for the country's financial breakdown. So now again the monarch was easily degraded into the whipping boy of the nation. And we shall see in the coming chapters the financial system breaking down again and again and the breakdowns ascribed to every cause except that inherent defect in the system which Berkeley had pointed out. We shall see all working up to the final catastrophe of 1931, when the whole of Christian civilization was brought to the very verge of collapse by the financiers' obstinate refusal to understand the laws by which their own system worked and when, after our escape from calamity, those who had led us to the precipice's brink were allowed to pose before us as our saviours in the hour of peril.

CHAPTER VII

THE FIRST BREAKDOWN

The last sentences of the previous chapter will, I am sensible, seem strange and strained to the reader. Just as one unfamiliar with the certain conclusions of Thorold Rogers's research must have been tempted to dismiss the earlier chapters as perversely paradoxical, so, too, many readers will be inclined to say of Bishop Berkeley's warnings concerning double-money that they are unreal and alarmist. "After all," they will object, "the system perhaps was not theoretically the best. Perhaps it might have collapsed, but at least it did not collapse. We muddled through."

The system, let us clearly understand, did collapse. It collapsed again and again and again. There is not a single record of any considerable strain being put upon it and it being found equal to that strain. And, when we boast that we muddled through, let us bear Thorold Rogers's statistics in mind and ponder on the meaning of the phrase. It means that in some way or other the succession of sovereign to sovereign and of Government to Government was indeed maintained, but it means also that every single sovereign from Henry VIII to Victoria died, leaving the poor more miserable, more degraded, more hopeless than he had found them at his accession, that in every single year of all those years between the dissolution of the monasteries and Thorold Rogers's expulsion from Oxford University men and women and children were dying for the lack of food of which there was in truth an abundance.

Let us see the working of this double-money system, the supporters of which prided themselves on their common sense, the critics of which were dismissed as airy triflers. The year 1797 was one of the darkest in the whole history of this country. We were at desperate war with the resurgent French Republic. Our allies, one after the other, were turning wearily to peace. Between Great Britain and destruction there stood only the navy, and in the navy were heard ominous mutterings, soon to break out into open mutiny. There were rumours about of French invasion. In such a national crisis, on Sunday, the 18th of February, some farmers went into Newcastle to the market. For some reason or other—nobody to this day knows what—a rumour of panic got abroad among them. They therefore sold the cattle for knock-down prices and rushed off in a body to the local banks with the notes that they had received, demanding cash. The banks of course were unable to satisfy the demand and on Monday, 20th February, by agreement they all stopped payment.

It was not then popularly understood, it is not even to-day universally understood, that, when banks lend their Promises to Pay, they lend promises which they know themselves unable to perform—that their promises greatly exceed their cash-holdings. Although of course those who understood the system were well aware that a bank always, automatically and inevitably fails whenever it is asked on any serious scale to make good its promises, yet to the general public the failure of the Newcastle banks was a shock. Other provincial bankers foresaw that holders of their paper would grow nervous and that there would be demands on them for cash. Now these bankers themselves banked, directly or indirectly, with the Bank of England. Therefore, to guard their position, their natural policy was to draw out all their deposits from the Bank of England. Throughout all that next week the Bank was receiving demands for cash at the rate of about £100,000 a day.

But the Bank of England had of course in its turn made Promises to Pay far beyond its capacity to perform. There were about £10 million of its notes in circulation; there were about £5 million deposited with it. To meet these demands it had not even the banker's normal tenth part. In 1795 the French Government determined to return to the gold standard. In order to accumulate sufficient gold to do so, it was willing to pay a price for the metal which made it more profitably useable in France than in Great Britain. The two countries were at war and the transference of gold from one to the other was illegal, but the owners of the metal found little difficulty in circumventing such regulations. In face of the temptation of a profitable use of gold in France the Bank of England virtually abandoned any attempt to keep a cash reserve in England, trusting to luck that it would not be found out. In February, 1794, it had held £7 million in cash; by February, 1795, this £7 million had sunk to £6 million, by February, 1796, to £2½ million, to £2 million by August, to £1 million by February, 1797.[1] Clearly in the face of any considerable demand for cash its survival was only a matter of days. As Sir Francis Baring put it,[2] "the Bank had been drained for foreign services"—a pleasant neutral phrase which meant not merely that loans had been made to the country's allies but also that Sir Francis and his friends had been lending money, hand over fist, to the country's enemies in time of war.

On 18th February, then, for reasons unknown a few farmers in Newcastle lost their heads. By 25th February the whole country was on the verge of collapse. On that very day news reached London that 1,200 French troops had landed on the coast of Wales. In calmer and sillier times it was all very well to gull the public with the pretence that the double-money system worked, but it is to the credit of Pitt, City of London's man as he was, that he understood that with an invading army on British soil the time for mere foolery had passed. Without hesitation he suppressed the system and saved the country. He suspended cash payments. *The Times* issued a leading article, calling on the people to show the spirit of their ancestors of Queen Elizabeth's time—and not to embarrass the bankers by asking for their money back. A committee then issued a statement of the Bank's financial position. It had, it claimed, liabilities of £13,770,390 and against them assets of £17,597,280 private loans and £11,686,800 loans to the Government.

As is always the case with bank-statements, there was room for dispute about the accuracy of the figures. But their accuracy or inaccuracy was of little importance. The purpose of them was to persuade the simple holder of

[1] *Pound Sterling*, Feaveryear.
[2] *Observations on the Establishment of the Bank of England.*

bank-notes that, since the Bank's assets exceeded its liabilities, he had, if only he could restrain his impatience a little, no cause for anxiety and would soon be easily able to cash his notes into gold or silver. Its purpose was, as far as possible, to conceal from the public that the Bank had made up money. Now, suppose that I possess £1 of gold and give authority to A to demand that £1 but A, instead of doing so, writes a cheque for £1 to B, who deposits the cheque with me. It is clear enough that if, at the end of this, I, being in possession of £1 of gold and of A's cheque on me to B, yet pretend that, since I have £1 in gold and £1 in deposits, I therefore possess £2, I have created the £1 of those £2 myself. I tell C that I possess £1 in gold and that A owes me £1, which he will soon repay, and therefore I can safely afford to lend C £2—and the books can be made to balance. But it is all a trick. It is clear enough also—and indeed it had at this time just been proved in practice —that, if this manufacture has gone on to any important extent, then it is simply untrue to say that any considerable number of B's can get their paper money changed into gold or draw out their deposits in gold, even if the gold should happen to be lying in the vaults of the bank. For suppose that the Bank of England could have collected £14 million of its £17 million of assets in gold and with them paid off £14 million of notes. The effect would have been to have reduced the sum total of money in circulation by £14 million. For the Bank would not have dared to put the repaid notes out again into circulation in fresh loans, because that would have created fresh claimants on its gold and all its gold was already required to satisfy the present claimants. There would therefore have been a drastic deflation. The mere attempt to work the double-money system would certainly have lost us the war.

It is not possible to argue that the system was elastic and was modified in the face of a crisis. It was not modified; it was abolished. The essence of the double-money system is that all paper-money only acquires its value by virtue of its convertibility on demand into so-called "real" money. A suspension of cash payments is therefore no more a modification of the double-money system than travelling from Stockton to Darlington is a modified way of travelling from Darlington to Stockton.

It is quite true that, even throughout the rest of the war, the country did live in one sense under a double-money system. The Bank of England notes were not convertible into anything, but the notes of other banks were convertible into Bank of England notes. But between gold and silver as an ultimate medium and any form of paper there is clearly this great difference—the paper-money can be multiplied at will. Since it is the public who in fact pay for it through the effect that it has on the price-level, what conceivable argument, you may ask, is there to be urged against the issue of that paper by public rather than by private authority? And echo can only answer "What?" Even the Bullion Committee, while recommending a return to gold and to what it considered an automatic currency, recognized that, if the currency was to be managed, there were no arguments for allowing it to be managed for private profit. "The addition," they wrote,[1] "of between four and five millions sterling to the paper circulation of this country, has doubtless been made at a very small expense to the parties issuing it, only about £100,000 having been paid thereupon in stamps to the Revenue, and probably for the reasons already stated, no corresponding deposits of gold or Bank of England notes being deemed by the country banks necessary to support their additional issues. These parties therefore, it may be fairly stated, have been enabled under the protection of the law, which virtually secures them against such demand, to create within the last year or fifteen months at a very trifling expense and in a manner almost free from all present risk to their respective credit as dealers in paper money, issues of that article to the amount of several millions, operating in the first instance and in their hands as capital for their own benefit and, when used as such by them, falling into and in succession mixing itself with the mass of circulation of which the value in exchange for all other commodities is gradually lowered as that mass is augmented. If your committee could be of opinion that the wisdom of Parliament would not be directed to apply a proper remedy to a state of things so

[1] Section iv, quoted by Canaan, *Paper Pound.*

prejudicial to the public welfare, they would not hesitate to declare an opinion that some mode ought to be devised of enabling the State to participate much more largely in the profits accruing from the present system."

But the sad truth is that whoever had managed the currency at that date would have mismanaged it. For between that world and an understanding of Berkeley's theories or of medieval practice stood the gigantic barrier of Townshend's education. Neither among our bankers nor among our politicians was there any understanding of the importance of the price-level. The metallic monetary system before 1797 was a foolish one and brought the country to the verge of a catastrophe. Less foolish, but only less foolish, was the unregulated paper system after 1797. According to that system every banker was free to issue all the notes that he cared to and to take his chance on it whether he went bankrupt. Now the story of 1797 had made clear one brutal and not very edifying truth. It was this. If you were a forger and forged a £1 note, you got hanged. But to make a Promise to Pay which you know to be mathematically impossible of fulfilment and to take advantage of the fact that the public has not got that knowledge is, ethically, forgery. Yet, if you in this way in time of war forged ten million £1 notes, not only did you not get hanged, but, owing to the effect that discovery would have on prices and consequently on productivity, the Government could not afford to let the public discover that you had forged. So far from prosecuting you they would co-operate with you in preventing public comprehension of your conduct. Therefore throughout the rest of the war all banks issued notes freely, understanding well that, if they only issued them on a moderate scale, the Government might allow them to fail; if they issued them immoderately they were safe. If only they were sufficiently largely in debt they would never have to pay.

It was a grand time for bankers, and, as a result, the number of country banks between 1797 and 1810 increased from 80 to over 700. The money in circulation naturally increased too and prices rose. By 1799 they were up to 114 to 1797's 100. There they stayed for about ten years until in the boom of 1809 they took a further jump up to about 140.[1] It was this second rise which so aroused public opinion that the famous Bullion Committee, of which Huskisson was the most important member, was appointed to inquire into the cause of the instability and to suggest a remedy. Historians have indulged in most extravagant language about the expert nature of this Committee's judgments. "With the exception of Sir Francis Baring," we are told by Mr. Feaveryear [2] who has given his study to it in recent years, "the Bullion Committee called no witnesses who had made any particular study of currency theory. . . . It is not too much to say that the leading members of the Bullion Committee had made up their minds before upon the theoretical question." Like most of the essays of British Government at that date, it was a very amateur affair.

The Committee reported—as was indeed plainly the truth—that prices had risen owing to the excessive issue of notes by the Bank of England and the country banks. The remedy that they proposed was that of a return to cash payments. It is always the most recent grievance that bulks largest in the mind, and it was therefore natural that people were conscious of the grievance of a rise in prices, which to us of the twentieth century seems comparatively trifling. They had forgotten that black day in 1797 with the French in Wales, the awful calamity to the brink of which the folly of double-money had brought the country and in which the immediate return to cash payments would certainly once more involve it. In June, 1810, when the recommendations of the Committee came before the House, there were in circulation £32 million's worth of Bank of England notes. Against them the Bank had cash holdings of £3,200,000. It was clear then that a return to a metallic coinage would only be possible either by a large devaluation of the pound—which the Committee did not recommend—or by a deflation so drastic that it would certainly lose the country the war. The Committee had had little difficulty in exposing the ignorance of many of those, such as the directors of the Bank of England, whom they had examined. Canning had as little difficulty in showing the folly of

[1] Figures from R. G. Hawtrey's *Currency and Credit.*
[2] *Pound Sterling,* Feaveryear, p. 204.

resumption during the continuance of the war, and the motion for resumption was lost by 45 votes to 180. Indeed so strongly convinced were the Government that deflation could not be risked in face of the enemy, that, when in 1811 some bankers in Glasgow and Lancashire failed, the Government instead of allowing the failure of those banks' notes to have its normal and automatic deflationary effect, stopped the gap themselves with Exchequer bills of their own so as to prevent a fall in prices. As a result not only was the fall prevented, but prices rose, to reach in 1814 their peak-level of 143 to 1797's 100.

Once the war was over there was no longer any pressing necessity—as the governing classes saw it—to keep production at a maximum. There was no longer any objection to deflation, provided only that it was so tempered as to preserve society from complete collapse into anarchy. Now it is clear enough that, from any except a monetary point of view, the standard of living of a country in peace ought to be higher than its standard in war-time. In war-time, clearly enough, a large proportion of its labour is engaged on the unproductive work of fighting. A further large proportion is engaged upon the production of munitions of war, to which again a large proportion of its goods are diverted. Yet for all that it has generally happened that a return to peace brings not a rise but a fall in the standard of living. In any particular case—as indeed in this case of the years after 1815—there may of course be particular complicating causes, such as failures of harvests and so on. But there are also certain general causes by which this almost general phenomenon is explained.

We are told that the cessation of war causes a sudden drop in Government expenditure, and that the demobilization of the troops throws an unassimilable horde on to the labour market. It is the obvious comment that neither of these causes in any way lessons the country's productive capacity. On the contrary they both increase it. The man who has been shooting Frenchmen or Germans can, at any rate ideally, be turned to producing goods instead. The money that has been used for producing munitions, can, at any rate ideally, be used for the purchasing of these goods. All that these causes lessen is the country's effective demand. Men no longer have the purchasing power to buy goods.

Nor, less there be a deflation in process, do they lessen even that effective demand as drastically as at first sight appears. The demobilized soldiers, it is true, have, if no provision be made for them, less money in their pockets; so have those who formerly sold munitions. But the tax-payers have more. It is clearly then the business of society to transfer the labour that had previously been used for war to productive purposes of peace and, during the interval of transference, to see to it that the would-be labourers do not suffer from want. Such a problem has doubtless always presented difficulties of detail. But such difficulties in no way justify the statesmen through the ages who have indulged in talk about the inevitability of post-war slumps. Yet it is just this invocation of an inevitable fate in which they always have indulged. "The war had ceased," said Hudson Gurney [1] at this period in the House of Commons, "leaving England, glutted with merchandise, with abundance of all things." From this strange calamity there was but one conclusion for the practical politician to draw. "Managed as best it might be, there must have been a great revulsion." The troubles of the country, bluntly said Lord Liverpool, the Prime Minister, were due to "over-production."

The truth is that such talk has been permitted and has been indulged in because language of inevitability has been very convenient for disguising the real cause of post-war slumps. "Met with a farmer," as he rode away from Weyhill fair on 11th October, 1822, records Cobbett,[2] "who said he must be ruined unless another good war should come." To the masters of the machine nothing is more convenient than this false ascription of cause to effect. For these slumps have been caused not by the comparatively trivial problems of the transfer of labour but by the deliberate action of deflation.

Clearly a fall in prices is to the advantage of anyone who has money on loan, for debts are repayable in money. Therefore, if he lent when prices were high and can so manage it that he can be repaid when they are low, he is clearly

[1] 18th May, 1818. [2] *Rural Rides.*

repaid (quite apart from interest) more in terms of goods than he originally lent. Naturally this would not be so if debts were scaled down in proportion as prices fell, and for such a scaling down Cobbett at this time persistently clamoured in the *Political Register* and the *Paper Against Gold*, but, needless to say, he was not attended to. Clearly also, immediately after a war, many people, who do not think very deeply, will easily be persuaded that the price-level that existed before the war, just like everything else that existed before the war, was a " normal ", as it were God-ordained, price-level, that the higher prices of the war were " abnormal " and that a natural consequence of peace should be a return to the pre-war price-level. Therefore it is not very difficult for creditors to represent their demand for deflation as a mere demand for a return to sanity and thus to obtain the support of those who do not understand that falling prices will inevitably drag down with them their own wages or salaries or profits.

Thus it was that the years after Waterloo were years of steady deflation, of falling prices, of consequent distress. From 1814's 143 index prices came down until in 1816 they were a trifle below the 1797 level. As its total decreased, the country's monetary supply approached that figure at which it would be once more possible to reinstate metallic money. In 1817, the banks tried to put out some gold coins, but the people would not have them, preferring the paper with which they were familiar. With the issue of the new paper prices rose again. In 1819 a Committee was appointed under the Chairmanship of Peel and including Castlereagh, Canning, Tierney, Huskisson, and Vansittart, to advise on the possibility of the resumption of cash payments. It issued its report on 6th May, 1819, advising a gradual resumption over the course of the next few years. Peel, not then a member of the Government, submitted the recommendation of the Committee to the House of Commons in a series of resolutions. The note-issue, he argued, must be contracted until it could be safely covered by gold pounds in the possession of the issuing authority. And to the question, what is a pound ? he answered, " It is a piece of gold of a certain weight and fineness "—to wit, 123·274 troy grains of 22 ct. fineness—123·274, because the pre-1797 guinea weighed 129·4 and 123·274 is $\frac{20}{21}$ of 129·4. If £1 is 123·274 grains troy, then 1 oz. troy (480 grains) is $\frac{£480}{123.274}$, which is as near as may be £3 17*s*. 10½*d*. Therefore the Bank of England was put under obligation to buy for £3 17*s*. 10½*d*. an ounce any gold that was presented to it.

The resolutions were passed without a division. Prices were driven drastically down to well below the 1797 level, and it proved possible to return to convertibility in two years instead of the stipulated four.

Chapter VIII

UNNECESSARY POVERTY

The purpose of the previous chapters has not been to provide an essay on the follies and stupidities of our ancestors, but to demonstrate two propositions of the highest importance, without which an understanding of such a man as Peel or of almost any other of the statesmen of the nineteenth century is quite impossible, without which indeed our own understanding of ourselves is quite impossible. Its purpose has been to show that it was quite unnecessary for anyone in nineteenth century England to have suffered poverty and to show how it was that thousands of perfectly honest men, the victims of a false education and of a question-begging political economy, nevertheless thought that the poverty of vast masses of their fellow countrymen was not only necessary but permanently inevitable.

Not the least among the services rendered to modern thought by the supporters of Major Douglas has been to familiarize the public with the notion that poverty is unnecessary. In doing so they have rightly insisted on the immense increase of productivity which the modern machine has made possible. But some of them have been less happy when they have spoken of the paradox of starvation in the midst of plenty as a paradox but recently arisen and contrasted our age of abundance with previous ages of supposed scarcity. Englishmen have been starving in the midst of plenty for four hundred years. A hundred years ago Cobbett found [1] in his England "starving in the midst of abundance . . . the Law Church parsons putting up in all the churches thanksgiving for a plenteous harvest, and the main mass of the labouring people fed and clothed worse than the felons in the gaols." A hundred years before Cobbett the very phrase, as we found, was on the

[1] *History of the Reformation*, sec. 411.

lips of Bishop Berkeley.[1] Two hundred years before Berkeley, Sir Thomas More was writing of the same phenomenon in his *Utopia.*

" Though the number of sheep increase never so fast, yet the price falleth not one mite, because there be so few sellers. For they be almost all comen into a few rich men's hands, whom no need forceth to sell before they lust. . . . Thus the unreasonable covetousness of a few hath turned that thing to the utter undoing of your island, in the which thing the chief felicity of your realm did consist. . . . To this wretched beggary is joined great wantonness, importunate superfluity and excessive riot. . . . Suffer not these rich men to buy up all, to engross and forestall, and with their monopoly to keep the market alone as they please." We must go back behind Sir Thomas More to find an age where a man could not starve save when there was not enough food to feed him.

By the nineteenth century improvement of communications had quite banished that possibility of occasional famine, which was the one real weakness of the medieval economic system. But for evil communications had been substituted a much more potent enemy of human happiness —an evil educational system. Nothing but an educational system which deliberately kept from him such writings as those of Bishop Berkeley could possibly have induced Peel to imagine that in a return to the double-money system the country could find stability, nor could anything but a deliberate blocking of the mind to all understanding of the middle ages have led a man to neglect the discovery of the medieval kings that prices can be kept stable by altering from time to time the metallic content of the coinage.

It is said that the younger Pitt once greeted Adam Smith with the remark, " We are all your pupils here." It was the tragic truth. No one who reads the strong pages of the *Wealth of Nations* can fail to be captured with delight at their powerful reasoning. The faults of that book are not in its reasoning, but in its premises—in its unproved assumption that a society must necessarily consist of a few capitalists and the propertyless proletariat, who can

[1] Query 446.

only get a living by working for the capitalists for a subsistence wage. To St. Thomas Aquinas property existed to promote the well-being of society, but to Adam Smith society existed to defend the rights of the owners of property. *Cupiditas*, to St. Paul and to all Christian tradition *radix malorum omnium*, to Adam Smith and the Benthamites was *radix bonorum omnium*.

It is no part of the business of this book to draw out a general indictment of the Universities or of the public schools. They have made their contribution both to happiness and to culture, keeping alive the love of scholarship of a sort and of those poets whose theories were not inconvenient to their masters. They have been a bulwark against the cram-shops and the state-schools and the trickeries of vocational education. Yet even the most fervent of their lovers must in fairness admit that in the dark age of the great betrayal, when the poor of England were lashed back to their unnecessary poverty, the strange handful of ill-assorted men who at all understood what had happened to England and who raised their voices in protest, were almost without exception people who by accident had escaped the influence of the educational system. There was Lingard, the Winchester carpenter's son, driven by the happy accident of a Penal Law to learn English history over the seas beyond the reach of Whig bribery. There was Cobbett, the farmer's son, who went to no school and who learnt no history of the past until in middle age, when he had already learnt the history of the present and knew from experience how much truth to expect upon the lips of governors—Sadler, picking up learning's crumbs at his own whim in his father's library—Disraeli, the strange alien exotic, like an orchid in an English green-house, who saw so clearly simply because he saw from outside—later, a Carlyle or a Ruskin.

Meanwhile, Dr. Arnold, the founder of the public-school system, when appointed Regius Professor of History at Oxford, was telling [1] his biographer, Stanley, that he " could not bear to plunge (himself) into the very depths of that noisome cavern ", the Middle Ages, " and to have to toil through centuries of dirt and darkness "—centuries in

[1] *Arnold*, Stanley, ii, 291.

which, as Thorold Rogers was to show, the poor were materially some six times better off than they were in Dr. Arnold's England. In preference to such a painful theme the doctor would prefer to dwell on "the deep calm of the first seventy years of the eighteenth century . . . as containing within itself the seeds of our future destiny."[1] There stands irrefutable the stinging gibe that the battle of Waterloo was won on the playing-fields of Eton—that battle that laid finally in the dust the great hope of the world's freedom from the empire of usury. But the battle *against* Waterloo, the battle for the overthrow of the monstrous "Thing", erected on the ruins of Napoleon, was fought by strange and gallant men from nowhere in particular. There came no help from Eton nor from Oxford for that battle. From Harrow there came only Shaftesbury and Byron.

Let us then bear in mind, while studying the history of the nineteenth century, this first point—that its poverty was unnecessary. Whether it was better for the country to produce as much as possible of her own food or to produce a surplus of manufactured goods and exchange them against the food of other countries was a secondary detail. The important truth was that there was no difficulty at all in procuring a sufficiency of food for all. And, if you ask, how then anyone can have been in favour of preserving this unnecessary poverty, the answer is, that no one could have been in favour of it, had it not been for a system of education, carefully training them in ignorance with its question-begging phrases such as "favourable balance of trade", "sound money", "artificial prosperity", "gold flowing" hither and thither and the like.

Even after the publication of Thorold Rogers's figures, it will, I am sensible, seem to some an exaggeration to say that poverty in the nineteenth century was unnecessary. They will perhaps admit that wealth was, and is, unfairly distributed, but there is in their minds the memory of one of those calculations, in which Dean Inge delights and which from time to time pop out in the correspondence columns of newspapers, according to which, if we divided the national income out equally, there would only be some £150 a year

[1] Ibid., p. 300.

per family. But it is not suggested that the problem could be solved merely by dividing out equally the goods that are at present produced. It is clear that effects of a greatly unequal distribution of wealth are that the country produces less goods than it might produce and produces the wrong sorts of goods. The first business of a society, Aristotle tells us, is to see to it that its members can live. Therefore, the first business of its economic system is to produce a sufficiency of food and clothing, or of goods that can be exchanged for food and clothing, to meet the necessities of the country's inhabitants. The necessities satisfied, then by all means give attention to the luxuries—the problems of "living well". Now it is clear that the effect of an unequal distribution of an income will be that a large proportion of the country's labour will be occupied in the production of luxury goods or the performance of luxury services, even though the necessities of the poor are not satisfied. It is necessary for a high civilization that a proportion of its members, in the various professions from lawyer or doctor down to flunkey or advertising agent, should be occupied in the performance of services rather than in the direct production of goods. But in an unequal society the proportion of the population engaged on such services is excessive. Therefore the result is an insufficiency of necessities, not because the country is incapable of producing them but because, with the given distribution of purchasing power, there cannot be an effective demand for them.

Nor is it possible to hope for a remedy so long as poverty remains the penalty of unemployment. For, with the fear of such a penalty, it is impossible to expect people to give a fair consideration whether their work is socially desirable or not. Where purchasing power is dependent upon a job and bitter poverty the reward of unemployment, it is inevitable that every individual will be only concerned to get a job and will care little whether that job is one for serving or for exploiting the community. It is inevitable, too, that the humane tendency in every profession will be to spin out the jobs as long as possible and to divide them between as many people as possible. Within every profession there is competition, but every profession as a whole is a conspiracy to pilfer the community. Lawyers want to make the law not as simple as possible, but so complicated there will necessarily be work for a lot of lawyers. Working men fight labour-saving devices simply because they do save labour. Every new suggestion is judged not on its merits but by the test whether it will save or will make work. And thus in the past the abolition of torture was no doubt opposed on the ground that it created unemployment among the torturers, and certainly to-day orders for armaments from powers that are but little friendly are welcomed on the ground that even if British workmen are to be blown to pieces by those guns to-morrow, at least they are to be " employed " in the making of them to-day.

We are told that there is a great moral risk in giving people money for doing nothing. And so there is ; you have only to look at the rich to see that. But is there no moral risk in giving them money for doing things that had much better not be done at all ? How many men are there whom the world would have been well advised to have paid all the money that they ever earned on the sole condition that they never did any of the jobs that they were paid for doing ? We are continually reading statistics of the large numbers of the population employed in " services ". What proportion of those " services " are really services to the community at all ? What proportion of the population is not in truth rather engaged in an unholy advertisers' struggle to create discontent among its fellow-citizens and to prevent them from finding satisfaction in the simple pleasures of life ? And yet those " services " use up not only labour but also raw materials and minerals that could much better have been otherwise employed. What proportion again of the goods that we consume—I will not ask what proportion could we do without, for there is no reason why we should live in an utterly Spartan simplicity. But what proportion would we much rather do without ? What proportion make no sort of contribution to our happiness ? We allow ourselves to be persuaded that we want them only because, if we refused to buy them, it would " create unemployment ".

It is therefore not possible to estimate the potential

standard of living of a country—England in Peel's time or any other country—by merely considering its actual productivity. What is necessary is to put aside for the moment all monetary problems of distribution and to try to estimate its productive capacity as a purely technocractic problem. Now Cobbett, who had been a working farmer and who knew well what he was talking about on such matters, in the course of his Rural Rides visited on the 29th August, 1826, the village of Milton, in Wiltshire. He had the curiosity to make an estimate of the productive capacity of that village. The village contained, according to the population returns of the time, 500 people, including women and children. "The land of this parish," he found,[1] "produces annually about 3,000 quarters of wheat, 6,000 quarters of barley, the wool of 7,000 sheep, together with the pigs and poultry . . . leaving green or moist vegetables out of the question . . . and saying nothing at present about milk and butter."

He then drew up what he considered a proper dietary for a family of five. "Such a family would want 5 lb. of bread a day; they would want a pound of mutton a day; they would want 2 lb. of bacon a day; they would want, on an average, winter and summer, a gallon and a half of beer a day." Such a dietary, which he considers reasonable, would cost them, he reckons, £62 6*s.* 8*d.* a year. In fact, with a wage of 9*s.* a week, the labourer at that date only received £23 8*s.* a year. Yet the productivity of the village of 500 was sufficient to provide food at the more generous standard of living for 2,510 people. That is to say, the condition of agricultural science in Cobbett's time was such that every one agricultural family, allowing for non-productive or only partially productive women and children, was able to produce food sufficient to maintain five families at a proper standard of life or fifteen families at the standard at which the poor were compelled to live. Milton was in no way an exceptional village. What was true of it was true of thousands of villages throughout the length and breadth of the country.

To what extent England should have continued to produce her own food, to what extent it would have been

[1] *Rural Rides* (ed. 1853), p. 371.

wise to obtain her food by the exchange of her surplus manufactured goods, were second and secondary controversies. Cobbett's figures make it quite clear that, either way round, whether under free trade or under protection, there need have been no difficulty a hundred years ago in diverting a reasonable proportion of the nation's labour to services and distribution and to the production of non-consumable goods and in still having a quantity of food sufficient to banish all want from the land.

The truth was that the controversy of protection and free trade, like so many of the controversies of the nineteenth century, was unreal. It was a battle, as Matthew Arnold put it, " Where ignorant armies clash by night." [1] It was hotly argued whether it was a good thing or a bad thing to exchange our manufactured goods for foreign food. But we did not, to any important extent, exchange our manufactured goods for food at all. In the year 1720 we imported £6,090,083's worth ; we exported £6,910,899. That is to say, we did at that date, roughly speaking, exchange goods against goods. In 1760 we imported £9,832,802's worth, but we exported £14,694,970's worth. In 1800 we imported £28,257,781's worth and exported £34,381,617's worth. In 1815 we imported £32,987,396's worth and exported £58,624,550.[2] With every year there was a widening surplus of exports over imports. Throughout all the years of distress we were not only giving away goods every year to foreigners for nothing, but every year we were increasing the quantity of goods that we gave away.

It will of course be said that we did not give them away. We lent them, and our foreign investments were there, ready to be called in in time of need. But what is a time of need, if it be not a time of need when working men starve on what they are paid for their labour and when, as Cobbett was continually proving to be the truth during Liverpool's Government, the convict in the gaol is given a better diet than the agricultural labourer could possibly purchase with his wages? In the years after 1815, for instance, Mr. Slater tells us,[3] " The American markets were grievously

[1] *Dover Beach.*
[2] *England under the Hanoverians,* Grant Robertson, pp. 335, 336.
[3] *Growth of Modern England,* p. 150.

overstocked with all sorts of British manufactures. . . . In Belgium riots took place to prevent the sale of British goods. From Germany there arose an outcry that the new British tyranny that was determined to crush out German manufactures by the sale by auction of vast quantities of British goods at rubbish prices was even more dangerous and odious than the tyranny of Napoleon. There can be no doubt that the peculiar phenomena of British export trade at this period paved the way for the subsequent building up of hostile tariffs against England on the Continent of Europe."

At the same time Robert Owen and his son went inspecting the conditions under which the creators of this favourable balance were working. They reported,[1] " Not in exceptional cases but as a rule, we found children of ten years old worked regularly fourteen hours a day with but half an hour's interval for the mid-day meal, which was eaten in the factory. In some cases we found that greed of gain had impelled the mill-owners to still greater extremes of inhumanity, utterly disgraceful indeed to a civilized nation. Their mills were run fifteen, and in exceptional cases, sixteen, hours a day with a single set of hands, and they did not scruple to employ children of both sexes from the age of eight. We actually found a considerable number under that age. It need not be said that such a system could not be maintained without corporal punishment. Most of the overseers openly carried stout leather thongs and we frequently saw even the youngest children severely beaten. We sought out the surgeons who were in the habit of attending these children, noting their names and the facts to which they testified. Their stories haunted my dreams. In some large factories from one-fourth to one-fifth of the children were either cripples or otherwise deformed or permanently injured by excessive toil, sometimes by brutal abuse. The younger children seldom held out more than three or four years without serious illness, often ending in death. When we expressed surprise that parents should voluntarily condemn their sons and daughters to slavery so intolerable, the explanation seemed to be that many of the fathers were out of work themselves and so

[1] *Life of Robert Owen*, G. D. H. Cole.

were in a measure driven to the sacrifice for want of bread."

" The sons of bitches," explained [1] a Manchester merchant to Francis Place, " had eaten up all the stinging nettles for ten miles round Manchester and now they had no greens to their broth." In the Midlands the correspondent of the Government newspaper, the *Courier*, was convinced that things were not so bad. So he went to see and reported, " Some inconvenience exists but certainly not the grievous distress spoken of, unless it be in the manufacturing towns, where the effects of peace after war and imprudent speculation have undoubtedly thrown a great majority of families out of bread." [2] The rugged individualism of the system ! It was not, be it noted, " the great majority of families " who speculated, nor was it because the bread was lacking that they were compelled to suffer " some inconvenience " by going without it.

Is it not a sin crying to Heaven for vengeance that anyone should have had the impudence to speak of "savings" wrung out in such a fashion and from such conditions ? But, beyond that, once that they attained to any important volume, it became entirely untrue that the foreign investments could be called in at will, just as it was untrue that any important proportion of holders of banks' Promises to Pay could in practice convert those Promises into cash. Debts can only be paid in goods. Our foreign debtors can therefore only repay us their debts in some goods or other which they produce and which we are willing to receive. If we did not consider unemployment an evil, it might not be impossible to find such goods of repayment. But, while we do consider unemployment an evil, it is impossible to find in our debtors' countries goods of repayment, which we do not ourselves produce or wish to produce, on a scale sufficient to repay any important proportion of our foreign investments.

In 1931 our foreign debtors threatened to repay us our debts—for that is what " calling in our foreign investments " means. What happened ? We announced that there was a national crisis ; we called on all parties to present a united front before this menace of catastrophe. The Labour

[1] *Francis Place*, Graham Wallas, p. 141. [2] Ibid., p. 253.

Government under Mr. Ramsay MacDonald fell from office and was succeeded by a National Government under Mr. Ramsay MacDonald. We put a tariff on foreign goods to prevent our debtors from paying their debts. We cut our wages and salaries to the bone so as to make certain that, if any foreign goods did sneak into the country, no one would be able to afford to buy them. Not until the balance of trade had been so altered that it was certain that not a penny of foreign debt was being repaid to us, did our statesmen announce that the crisis had been surmounted. Even then, the Chancellor of the Exchequer told us, we could not really congratulate ourselves that all was well until foreign lending had started again.

" But," it is sometimes objected, " while it is a commonplace that the system has broken down to-day, it at any rate served us well for a long time. For a hundred years, for two hundred years perhaps, people in England lived comfortably on their foreign dividends, regularly received." Such an objection, common as it is, betrays a misunderstanding of the whole economic history of the last two hundred years. Had we had a " favourable " balance of trade for half a dozen years and then in the seventh year called in our loans and enjoyed instead an " unfavourable " balance, it would have been fair to argue that the system was working. But that was not what happened. Every year with but few exceptions, if you count in our invisible exports such as shipping and other services, we had a favourable balance of trade ; every year we gave away more than we received. Therefore it is evident that last year's foreign investor, who thought that he was this year receiving his dividend from his foreign investment, was not really doing so at all. He was really living on the savings of this year's foreign investor, who in his turn was to live on the savings of next year's foreign investor, and so on and so on, until the system's final and inevitable collapse. As Mr. Emil Davies has put it,[1] " The cynic who surveys the history of foreign lendings may be pardoned if he comes to the conclusion that, broad and long, the borrowing nations of the world pay interest on loans just about to the extent that their creditors advance them the wherewithal to do

[1] *Investments Abroad*, pp. 20–1.

so. . . . The net result over a period of years is that as much foreign money flows in as goes out, nominally as interest."

" It follows," says Professor Pigou [1] from his description of the process of foreign lending, " that Labour must be less well off in terms of things in general than it would have been if the opening for investing capital abroad had been closed." Why then does it all go on? Because at any given moment the individual who has made a foreign investment has every interest in creating in the public mind a bias in favour of further foreign investments, since it is out of those further investments alone that he can hope to get his dividends.

Again the system which enforces the payment of debts in monetary terms while it permits alterations of the price-level compels a country to produce less than it could produce through its creation of unemployment. Take the situation which caused the Ely riots of 1816. With prices falling the landlords had to repay the debts which they had contracted at the higher price-level. Therefore they could not afford to reduce their rents. With rents high the farmers could not afford to reduce the price of corn. On the other hand, with less money about owing to deflation, there was not sufficient purchasing power to buy corn at the price at which the farmer could produce it. As a result, the landowner was driven into bankruptcy, good corn land was allowed to go fallow, while those who in past years had worked for the farmers as labourers starved for lack of purchasing power. They paraded the countryside, demanding " Bread or blood," and the Government hanged five of them and transported five for life.[2] But their story is only an especially striking example of a story that has been told again and again in England from their day to our own.

The productive capacity of Peel's England was then such that there was no need for anybody in the country to be in poverty. That is the first and capital point. Set beside it the second—that the financial system which Peel imposed upon the country was one which decreed that, however

[1] *Economics of Welfare*, pp. 660–1.
[2] *Growth of Modern England*, Slater, p. 247.

many times that productive capacity might be multiplied, it was mathematically impossible for the poor ever to escape from poverty. " No possible form of society," wrote Peel's master, Malthus,[1] " could prevent the almost constant action of misery upon a great part of mankind, if in a state of inequality, and upon all, if all were equal."

Let us understand why.

Peel spoke of having put the country back upon an " automatic metallic currency " and of a return to " the ancient right standard of England ". The traditional monetary system was one which caused all payments to be actually made in metallic money. Had Peel wished to return to that, his policy must have been to collect all the gold on which he could lay his hands, to call in the bank-notes, private and Bank of England, that were in circulation, to divide the total quantity of gold by the number of pounds that he possessed, to decree that the new sovereigns should consist of the resultant amount of gold, to coin such sovereigns and to hand them out to those who had previously possessed bank-notes. Such a system might have been called an " automatic metallic system ". We need not delay to consider the difficulties which the working of it would have presented, for it was a system entirely unlike that which he did establish. At the time when cash payments were resumed the Bank of England possessed some £11 million odd in cash and bullion. There were in circulation about £60 million of bank-created money—Bank of England notes, private bank-notes, and bank-deposits. It was not proposed to cut down the country's effective monetary supply to £11 million, nor yet so to devalue the pound as to make a stock of gold, which yesterday represented £11 million, represent £60 million to-day. It was proposed to return to the double-money system, which Berkeley had condemned and which had brought the country to catastrophe in 1797—to bid the people do their business with the £60 million of bank-money, telling them for their comfort that they could convert any one of those pounds into a pound of gold if they wanted to. A system less automatic it would be impossible to imagine.

[1] *Essay on Population* (ed. 1926), p. 36.

It is not necessary to follow through the monotonous and dreary story of the breakdown of Peel's system every single time that it was subjected to any strain from 1821 to 1931. That story has been often told—notably in Dr. McNair Wilson's *Monarchy or Money Power* and in Mr. Feaveryear's *Pound Sterling*—but it is important rather to understand why, under it, it is impossible for the vast mass to escape from the tyranny of poverty. The amount of money in circulation, under Peel's system, obviously depends upon the amount of gold in the country. If the banks as a rule lend ten Promises to Pay for every pound of gold that they possess—the proportion which they soon adopted —then if £1 of gold leaves the country, £10 of Promises to Pay have to be withdrawn from circulation by the banks refusing to make new loans when old loans have been repaid. Therefore the possessors of gold will be the dictators of the country's economic life, and, as Dean Swift and Bishop Berkeley had understood in the previous century, gold will inevitably gravitate into the pockets of those who possess this strange privilege of making up money.

Now the proportion of their wealth that these men spend, or can spend, on their own pleasures and necessities is trivial and negligible. They put money into circulation not by spending it but by lending it. You may ask, what is the good of lending unless one day you intend to spend, but we are concerned with a consideration not of what a wholly balanced person would do with his money but of what the men who shaped the nineteenth century did in fact do with it. And we must recognize that to those men there was an almost mystical value in merely saving and piling up with no intention of ever spending what had been saved—the very notion of spending one's capital seemed to them wicked and horrible. Such a philosophy was the price that we had to pay for allowing ourselves to be dominated by Puritanism in the seventeenth century. These men claimed, too, the right to invest their money wherever in the world it best suited them, and it would again have seemed to them wicked and horrible not to invest it in the place whence it would earn the largest immediate interest. "Work all you can, make all you can, give all you can," preached the great Wesley to his disciples. "Work all you can, make all you can, invest all you can," taught their descendants, emancipated from dogma. The wheel had turned full circle and Townshend's education had launched upon the world a race, who claimed not merely that usury should be permitted but that rather there should be accorded to it something of a religious worship.

Now Peel's Act conceded to the owner of gold the right to move his gold into or out of the country at will. Money was to be allowed to " find its own level ". Once that this is understood, it is easy to see how under Peel's system it was mathematically impossible for the poor to escape from their poverty. By Peel's system the Government was prevented from increasing the monetary supply. Now money could only come into circulation in the shape of loans from those who had the privilege of inventing it. The inventors of money issued their loans to those who would pay the best interest. Other things being equal, the less that a producer pays out in wages, the more is he able to pay in interest to the money-lender; the more that he pays in wages, the less can he pay in interest. With money free to find its own level, the lender can place his loans in any quarter of the world that he chooses. Thus it is obvious that any producer who tries to pay more than the lowest wages will be prevented from doing so, because, if he makes such an attempt, he will not receive the loans to pay his wages with and will therefore be driven into bankruptcy.[1]

It is idle to say that humane feelings would prevent the working out of the system in its full ruthlessness. We will later have occasion to consider the causes which led, to some extent, to its modification in the second half of the century. But we must never forget that in the first half of the century it was not modified at all. Productivity, according to the estimate of Sir Charles Morgan-Webb,[2] was increasing by an average of 3 per cent per annum, which means that in 50 years it was multiplied by about $4\frac{1}{2}$. Population was doubled. But not one pennyworth of advantage from the country's increased productivity went into the pockets of the working man. There was no general rise in wages at all in the first half of the century. Higher

[1] *Essay on Currency Depreciation*, Huskisson.
[2] *Rise and Fall of the Gold Standard*, Morgan-Webb, p. 110.

wages in the new industries were balanced by lower wages in the old. Rent increased. The Royal Commission of 1840 gave the following figures of the wages, and food purchasable with those wages at the current prices, of hand-loom weavers.

	s.	*d.*	*lb. of Food.*
1797–1804	26	8	281
1804–1818	14	7	131
1818–1825	8	9	108
1825–1832	6	4	83
1832–1834	5	6	83 [1]

The death-rate increased from 19·98 in 1806–1816 to 20·33 in 1816–1826 and 21·65 in 1826–1836.[2]

Doubtless the employers had their humane feelings, but they were the victims of a system every bit as much as their workpeople. Doubtless the money-lenders had in their private capacities humane feelings, but they were captured by an evil education which led them to think that it would be a disastrous sentimentality to be softened by those humane feelings. They practised usury with all the awful concentration of a religious fanatic. Talk of religious persecution! What religion has ever persecuted as the great religion of Mammon persecuted in early nineteenth century England? Capitalists to-day sometimes complain of the unfairness of communist abuse of them. But there is nothing which the communist of this century says of them by way of abuse which they did not say of themselves in the last century by way of praise.

It is a most important truth that the financial system stands condemned not so much by what its enemies say against it as by what its friends say for it. "Money," they say, "must be allowed to find its own level." "You cannot expect people to extend credit facilities unless they are to be allowed to share in the resultant increased productivity." But there is no other profession on the face of the earth that would not be ashamed to proclaim such maxims as its guides. Why should not soldiers desert in the middle of battle if they are not given higher pay? Why should not doctors put up their fees when there is an epidemic and announce that, if their patients will not pay

[1] Op. cit., Slater, p. 253.

[2] *Population Problems of the Age of Malthus*, G. T. Griffith.

the higher fees, they can be left to die? Perhaps there have been in history doctors and soldiers who have behaved in such fashions. Certainly there have been financiers who have been much better than their professed principles. Our objection is not that all financiers are cads, but that they all boast of being cads. For what is a cad but a man who in principle always takes the fullest advantage that he can of his neighbour's necessity?

People to-day are familiar with the general theories of Ricardo and Malthus, but do they actually read them? Have they any notion of the language in which they wrote? Ricardo recognizes that it is just possible that one day a new standard of subsistence may be attained but he does not explain how or by whose action. The probability was, he thought, that wages would fall below the subsistence level rather than rise above it. But then, he comforted the working men, wages could never remain below it for long, because, if they did, a proportion of them would die of starvation and thus the value of labour would increase through its scarcity and wages rise a little. "After their privations have decreased their number, or the demand for labour has increased . . . the market-price of labour will rise to its natural price." [1] Malthus was in private life an amiable man, a sincere clergyman of the Church of England. Yet he complacently and explicitly advocated starvation of children as a remedy for unemployment. If children were born in excess of the requirements of the labour-market, then both parents and children, he advocated, should be left to starve. The parent should be told that "the laws of nature had doomed him and his family to starve." "They had no claim on society for the smallest portion of food," and that not because there was not a sufficiency of food but because there was not a sufficiency of work, and therefore, as he argued, no purpose to be served in keeping them alive.

Nor was there, according to this prophet of progress, the least hope of amelioration. "No possible form of society could prevent the almost constant action of misery upon a great part of mankind, if in a state of inequality, and upon all, if all were equal." [2] "The whole of that

[1] *Principles of Political Economy and Taxation*, chapter 5.
[2] *Essay on Population*, p. 36.

region (i.e. the East End of London) " wrote *The Times* [1] at the time of the 1866 bank-crash, " is covered with huge docks, shipyards, manufacturies and a wilderness of small houses, all full of life and happiness in brisk times but in dull times withered and lifeless, like the deserts we read of in the East. Now their brief spring is over. There is no one to blame for this; it is the result of Nature's simplest laws." Those who did not like it, argued Cobden, could " accumulate £20 and emigrate ". But how could anybody " accumulate £20 " out of a wage of 15*s*. a week.

[1] Quoted by Matthew Arnold, *Culture and Anarchy*, p. 190.

Chapter IX

CHEQUES AND NOTES

The frightful conditions of misery under the rule of Castlereagh, the savage suppression, the largely unsuccessful attempts to stir the poor into revolt by the use of *agents provocateurs*—all these are generally known and generally condemned. One can read the story of them in such books as those of the Hammonds. Their story is the most disgraceful story in the whole of English history. After Castlereagh's death things took a turn for the better. In 1822 to relieve the distress, the Government with realistic statesmanship deliberately unbalanced the budget, borrowing the money required for the pensions fund scheme. They also passed an Act permitting bank-notes for sums under £5 to continue in circulation until 5th January, 1833, instead of being withdrawn, as had previously been ordered, by 1st May, 1823. They gave to some 530 country banks the right to issue unlimited £1 notes, convertible on demand into Bank of England notes or gold.

The increased monetary supply could easily be answered by an increase of productivity. A boom resulted, and on the strength of it Huskisson was able to repeal the Navigation Act and to reform the tariff. At the same time Peel, the Home Secretary, began the work of revising the barbarous criminal code. Francis Place and Joseph Hume were also able in 1824 to obtain the repeal of the Combination Acts against Trades Unions. It is true that, when people understood the power that they had conceded to the Trades Unions, an agitation arose against their own concession and the Act of 1824 was repealed in 1825. It was however found impossible to withdraw the substance of the concession, and combinations of workmen for the purpose of shortening hours and raising wages remained legal, although an attempt to coerce employers was illegal.

In 1825 there befell exactly the catastrophe that had been

foretold by Bishop Berkeley a century before. The new money, which resulted from the Government's concession to the country banks, had of course been issued in the form of loans—of investments largely in Central and South American enterprises. The money was spent in England on the production of capital goods for export to those markets. It was distributed in wages to the English producers of those goods. Therefore the amount of purchasing power in English pockets was increased, unemployment was lessened, but the quantity of consumable goods in English markets was not increased. There being more money to buy the same quantity of goods, prices rose somewhat. But the primary industries in England were capable of a very great increase of productivity with the increase of effective demand, and with rising wages a further increase of productivity would have been possible The increased prosperity was in fact beginning to show its effect in slightly increased wages.

But higher wages meant increased demands for cash on the banks. The banks had already lent to their full capacity to finance the boom. The country banks' note-issue, which from 1821–3 had been just over £4 million, rose in 1824 to £6 million and in 1825 to more than £8 million. On the other hand the very threat of higher wages in England had caused the owners of gold to withdraw their gold deposits from English banks and to lend them instead in low-wage countries where the dividends were higher. The banks therefore could only satisfy the demands for increased cash by calling in loans and thus destroying the prosperity. Messrs. Pole, Thornton and Co., a London central house, agent for 47 provincial banks, were unable to supply the demands for cash of their provincial clients. On 12th December, 1825, they had to close their doors. Catching the spirit of panic, depositors with other banks came clamouring for cash ; the cash, needless to say, was not there. Within three weeks 61 country banks and 6 London banks stopped payment. The prosperity was dead —killed by prosperity.

The Bank of England itself fell into panic. Its directors begged the Government either to issue exchequer bills to fill up the gap of gold or else to free the Bank from its obligation to pay its debts in gold. The Government refused to do either the one or the other. The situation was only saved by the chance discovery of a packet of old notes, dated 1818, which had never been issued. With these notes the Bank was prepared to meet its obligations and to start lending again, though why the borrower should be expected to put more confidence in notes printed in 1818 than in notes printed in 1825 it might well puzzle the most curious to explain. The fact that they did so was evidence of the complete fog into which the public mind had by now fallen. At the same time the Bank increased its metallic reserve by purchasing gold from abroad at more than the mint-price.

Now it had been—and indeed it still is—argued that the beauty of the nineteenth century financial system was that it was quite automatic. For the moment, it was said, the English happened not to have any goods to offer the French in exchange for their wine. Therefore they pay in gold. The English allow the loss of gold, the French the gain of gold, to have its full monetary effect. So the monetary supply in England is decreased and prices fall, that in France is increased and prices rise. As a result the English are able to sell more goods in France than the French sell in England, the gold flows back again from France to England and the balance is restored.

But in practice, as was proved in 1825 and has been proved a dozen times since, these changes in price-level cause so violent a dislocation of the nation's life that the system has to be interfered with to prevent them. The essence of the system was that gold has a fixed, unvarying price. Once you start offering varying prices for gold, it is clear that the system has ceased in any sense to be automatic. It must occur to the critic to say, "We were told that the one virtue of gold was that it had a fixed, unvarying and intrinsic value. If we cannot always buy it for the same price, what earthly sense is there in buying it at all?" He cannot but ask, as Berkeley had asked[1] a hundred years before, "Whether it be not evident that we may maintain a much greater inward and outward commerce and be five times richer than we are, nay, and our bills

[1] Query 450.

abroad be of far greater credit, though we had not one ounce of gold or silver in the whole island ? "

It was generally felt—and indeed truly enough—that a system which permitted the privilege of issuing money to some 500 unco-ordinated authorities was a system inviting calamity. Therefore in 1826 Lord Liverpool's Government passed two Acts—one making illegal the issue of bank-notes for sums less than £5, the second removing the restrictions by which banks, other than the Bank of England, had up till now been forbidden to have more than six partners.

The end of the 1820's was filled with the controversy of Catholic Emancipation, and with the beginnings of the 1830's and the fall of the Tories came the Reform Act. There were both in Parliament and throughout the country a handful of genuine democratic reformers, but it was not they who influenced the Reform Act. After their victory in the Election the Whigs were strong enough to be indifferent to radical support, and the Act that was passed was in no way democratic. It only gave votes to some one in twenty-two of the population. What it did was to register the transfer of political power from the old rich to the new rich. Even there it rather recognized an altered balance of power than itself altered the balance of power. As the quotations from Cobbett in previous chapters have illustrated, it was the Napoleonic Wars and their debt which in reality snatched the power out of the hands of the old landed classes.

The story of the passage of the Act was perhaps mainly interesting in the light which it threw upon the true virtue of the double-money system in the eyes of its masters. Its virtue was not that it gave the country a stable monetary system but, on the contrary, that it put it within the power of a few determined men to plunge the country into chaos whenever they wanted to. There was after Grey's first resignation a question of the Duke of Wellington forming a Tory Government. The word went out among the reformers, " To stop the Duke, go for gold," and before the threat of a run on the banks the Tory attempt collapsed and the Whigs returned to power.[1]

[1] *Memoirs of Francis Place*, Graham Wallas.

It would be foolish, in reaction against the drab philistinism of the middle-class Victorian, to indulge in sentimental regrets over the old landed classes who ruled England from 1688 until the Napoleonic Wars. They had a long run for their money, and on the whole they used it without scruple. Yet it was in no sort of way to the advantage of the poor, when power passed out of their hands into that of the masters of the financial system. Where the old masters had robbed the poor out of unashamed greed, the new masters robbed them on philosophical principle. As far as savagery of repression goes, the difference between our unreformed and reformed masters was the difference between Peterloo and Tolpuddle—that is to say, nothing at all. Almost the only member of the unreformed Parliament, who challenged the whole philosophy of the economists and fought wholeheartedly the battle of the poor, was Sadler, a Tory. In the election after the Reform Act he lost his seat, being beaten at Leeds by Macaulay, the historian. It is noteworthy that one of the first acts passed by the reformed Parliament was the renewed Bank Charter Act of 1833, by which the Bank of England was exempted from the restrictions of the Usury Law in its discounting of bills.

But the most important act of this Parliament—one of the most important acts in English history—was the Poor Law Amendment Act of 1834. In time of war it was necessary to provide for those who were producing the nation's food a standard of living sufficient to keep them in health. Therefore a system was adopted, known after the magistrates who first adopted it, as the Speenhamland system, according to which, when wages were deficient, they were made up to a subsistence level out of the poor rates. When the war was over, there was no longer the same pressing necessity to keep the poor alive. It was considered more important to reduce the poor rate. Therefore, instead of doling out monetary relief in an easy way, it was determined to grant relief only in absolute necessity and under conditions as harsh as could be devised, and, in particular, wherever possible, to make entrance into a workhouse the condition of reception of relief.

That the Speenhamland system was altogether too casual and needed revision has hardly ever been denied. And there would have been a certain justice, if a harsh justice, in the new system in a society of widely distributed property, in which a man could only be in poverty if through wanton idleness he had neglected to cultivate his own land. But the society of the 1830's was not such a society. The poor had no property of their own. They could only earn a livelihood if some master employed them, and the master in his turn could only offer employment if a financier financed him. It was a regular principle of the system to see to it that there were always fewer jobs than there were candidates for jobs, so that the threat of unemployment might prevent attempts to raise wages above subsistence level. Under such a system it was not justice to treat unemployment as a misdemeanour.

Again, the system was defended on the tacit assumption that the society was one of scarcity—that there was barely enough food to go round. In such a society again there would have been a certain justice, if a harsh justice, in decreeing that he who did not work should receive only as little food as possible. But again, as we have seen, England of the 1830's was not such a society. Wages were low not because the country's productive capacity was small but because the object of statesmanship was to give the country as large a "favourable" balance of trade as possible and therefore, whatever the country's productive capacity, it was necessary to keep wages as low as possible.

A Poor Law Commission was appointed in 1832 immediately after the passage of the Reform Act to report upon the whole working of the Poor Law. It complained of many things, but principally that the food given in the workhouses compared unpleasantly favourably with that obtainable by the half-starved agricultural labourers outside. This contrast was said to be largely responsible for the riots among the labourers which had just taken place and had been suppressed with stern savagery by the Home Secretary, Lord Melbourne. No relief, therefore, said the Commissioners in the first place, should be given merely on account of poverty but only on account of destitution. "The system of poor relief was contrary to the principles of political economy, which even prohibited the exercise of private charity," explained Lord Althorp, the leader of the Government in the House of Commons. In the second place the lot of the recipient of relief should be made definitely less pleasant than that of the worst paid worker.

The latter maxim was more easily enunciated than applied. For, according to the calculation of Edwin Chadwick, the Secretary to the Commissioners, the agricultural labourer at that date only received 17 oz. of bread per day and $\frac{1}{4}$ lb. of bacon per week. He and his family together received, as will be remembered from Cobbett's calculation, $\frac{1}{15}$th part of that which he produced. And, when the six labourers of Tolpuddle attempted to form an organization whose object was to obtain for themselves and for their starving children $\frac{1}{14}$th, or perhaps $\frac{1}{13}$th part, they were treated as dangerous revolutionaries and sentenced to seven years' transportation. How then could you treat the paupers worse, while at the same time not treating the labourers better? That was the nice dilemma with which the Government was faced. If the pauper was to be given an allowance less than that of the labourer, it would be both less troublesome and less hypocritical to leave him frankly to starve. However it was thought a solution to give him the same quantity of food but to serve it in some less appetising fashion. But how? And so, for the first time in the history of mankind, the salaried servants of a government were turned to the strange research of discovering ways in which the inadequate food of the poor could be rendered artificially more nauseous.

The poor were in fact reduced to such a condition that it was not difficult for Calhoun, the great American champion of slavery, to produce facts to prove how enormously better was the material lot of the plantation slave to that of the English pauper. "Compare," he said,[1] "his condition with the tenants of the poor houses in the more civilized portions of Europe—look at the sick, and the old and infirm slave on the one hand, in the midst of his family and friends, under the kind superintending care of his master and mistress and compare it with the forlorn and wretched condition of paupers in the poor house."

[1] *Rise of American Civilization*, Beard, i, 704.

The purpose of the Commissioners was to reduce the poor rate. In that they succeeded. But, succeeding in making the lot of the pauper worse than that of the agricultural labourer, they made it also far worse than that of the criminal, who after Peel's reform of the criminal code, had on the whole a better time than the greater number of the English poor. Therefore, as Louisa Twining discovered in her interesting researches into the life of the poor at that date, it became a regular custom among the unemployed to commit crimes in order to go to prison rather than to the workhouse. The poor rate gained, but whether the taxpayer gained on balance was more doubtful. It is likely that, what he gained on the poor rate, he lost on the police rate.

On the other hand it is certain that the possession in the workhouses of pauper children was a convenience to the masters of the system, as they were able to use these children as a sort of army to introduce into any industry where organized labour seemed likely to win for itself some rise above the subsistence wage-level, as, for instance, into the cotton industry in Lancashire. If employees became too particular, they could always be brought to reason by the threat that then their jobs would be given to pauper orphans, brought by the load from some distant workhouse and made to work without wages on the excuse that they were undergoing an apprenticeship. With the assistance of this army the masters were able to prevent throughout the 1830's that rise in wages which had looked dangerously probable after the repeal of the Combination Acts in 1824 and to see to it that the poor received no benefit whatsoever from the Reform Acts which they had so enthusiastically supported.

By its provision for the segregation of the sexes within the workhouse the poor law marked the first overt legislative attack on the most fundamental of all human institutions—the family—the beginning of the great campaign to dehumanize the poor.

In the 1830's there was the usual boom, in which the poor were employed in producing capital goods for export, followed in 1839 by the breaking of country banks and the usual slump. It was felt—and again truly—that there was not sufficient public control over the private issue of money. Therefore by the Bank Charter Act of 1844 the issue of notes was strictly regulated. The Bank of England was only allowed to issue notes to the value of its cash holdings plus a fiduciary issue of £14 million. Other banks, which had notes in circulation on 6th May, 1844, were permitted to continue to issue up to the average amount of their notes in circulation throughout the twelve weeks prior to 27th April, 1844. No new bank however could acquire the right to issue notes, and, in the event of the note-issue of any bank lapsing, the Bank of England might fill the gap by adding to its fiduciary issue further notes to the value of two-thirds of those that had been previously issued by the lapsed bank. Thus it was hoped, in the course of time, to concentrate the entire business of note-issuing in the hands of the Bank of England, as has indeed happened.

But, though a bad system of issuing money is a calamity, yet the public must have money, and, if it cannot get it in a good way, it will get it in a bad. Berkeley had seen this. " Whether it be not a mighty privilege for a private person to be able to create a hundred pounds with a dash of his pen ? " he had asked.[1] But he had also asked, " Whether without private banks what little business and industry there is would not stagnate ? " The folly of the Bank Charter Act of 1844 was that it was purely negative. It restricted the power of private banks to issue money in the form of notes ; it made no provision of any other way of issuing it. Therefore the banks got round the Act by issuing cheque-money instead of note-money. Where previously they had printed a note and lent it out as money to their client, now instead they made a book-entry, gave him a cheque-book and authority to write cheques to those with whom he did business up to the amount of the book-entry.

Thus at the time of the passage of the Act of 1844 the private bank-note circulation was £11 million, their deposits £50 million. By 1846 the note-circulation had been reduced by £2¼ million to £7,750,000, but the deposits had risen by £5 million to £55 million. By 1928, when the private bank-note was finally extinguished, bank-deposits had risen

[1] Query 490.

to £2,231,000,000. The public quickly developed the habit of doing its business by cheque. It had no alternative. The only alternative was not to do business at all. The Bank Charter Act of 1844, so far from checking the issue of money by private bankers, entrenched their privilege more firmly as an integral part of the country's life.

Chapter X

THE REPEAL OF THE CORN LAWS

Party government, as Cecil Chesterton truly points out in his *History of the United States,*[1] is only tolerable when the two parties agree in their political opinions. Whether socialism be a good thing or a bad thing, there can be no doubt that we must make up our minds either to have it or not to have it. We cannot have socialism for five years; then return to private enterprise for five years, then go back again to socialism and so on. Now this condition of substantial agreement between the parties was admirably fulfilled in the England of the 1830's and 1840's. Wellington and Melbourne, Peel and Lord John Russell—all were most obedient servants of the laws of political economy, and it was a matter of indifference to the masters of those laws which of them might chance to be in nominal power.

Yet the system was, of course, challenged, even though it was not challenged from either front bench. It was challenged by the Trades Unions, who, though as yet they had accomplished but little, were at least important in compelling the governing classes to draw a distinction between the poor and animals. It was challenged by enlightened and intelligent employers, like Fielden and Owen, who maintained, and demonstrated, that to pay less than a subsistence wage was not good but bad economics, because it lessened disastrously the efficiency of the worker. It was challenged by the best and most intelligent of the privileged classes themselves—by noble men, such as Sadler and Lord Shaftesbury, whose keen sense of honour made the possession of privilege intolerable to them unless they could use it for the service rather than for the degradation of their unprivileged fellows. By the combined efforts of such men it had been found possible to put upon the Statute Book a number of Factory Acts, which, if they did

[1] *History of the United States,* Cecil Chesterton, pp. 227, 228.

nothing to raise wages, at least did something to mitigate the horrors of the conditions under which the workers were compelled to earn their inadequate wages.

Yet few, even among those who were shocked at the sufferings of the people, were at all able to diagnose the disease from which they were suffering. The country's productivity was obviously many times greater than it had ever been before. Yet the poor were worse off than they had been in past ages, and even among the rich the captain of industry of the nineteenth century lived with far less extravagance and ostentation than had the aristocrat of the eighteenth century. What had happened to the wealth? Who had got it? The answer was that nobody had got it. The eighteenth century aristocrat had spent his income. To the moral temper of the nineteenth century captain of industry generous spending was a sin. "Private charity," as Lord Althorp put it,[1] was forbidden by "the laws of political economy". Therefore there was nothing to do but to save it. As a result, savings piled up and up. It was only possible to find a market for the investment of them, if a quite inordinate proportion of the country's labour was diverted to the production of capital goods and of still further capital goods, sent out to replace the first lot, not because the first lot was obsolete but because the maker of the second needed a market. The answer to the conundrum, What had happened to the world's wealth? in the 1840's as in 1935, was that the world is stiff with scrap-iron.

Now, bearing all this in mind, we can see how the issue of the great controversy of the Corn Laws both was then and still is falsely posed. The controversy was whether England should grow her own corn or import it more cheaply from abroad. Had the age been one of scarcity, the Free Trader's argument that everything ought to be sacrificed for cheaper bread would have been unanswerable. In an age of abundance there is clearly not the same desperate need to buy in the immediately cheapest market, and those statesmen were probably the wiser who pleaded for the security which we should gain through remaining as nearly self-supporting as possible. The remedy was not to let in the

[1] See chapter 9, p. 109.

cheaper foreign bread but to give the poor the money with which to buy the dearer domestic bread.

However that may be, it was sheerly idle for a disciple of the classical economists to pretend that the poor could gain from cheap bread. For, on the doctrine of the subsistence wage, the whole virtue of cheap bread was that it would make it possible to reduce wages. On this the earlier opponents of the Corn Laws, such as Villiers, were completely frank. In an autobiographic fragment, quoted by Lord Morley in the *Life*,[1] Mr. Gladstone records of his early years in Parliament. "I remember being struck with the essential unsoundness of the argument of Mr. Villiers. It was this. Under the present Corn Law our trade, on which we depend, is doomed, for our manufacturers cannot possibly contend with the manufacturers of the Continent, if they have to pay wages regulated by the protection price of goods while their rivals pay according to the natural, or free trade, price. The answer was obvious. 'Thank you. We quite understand you. Your object is to get down the wages of your work-people.'" "It was," adds Gladstone, "Cobden who really set the argument on its legs," but, to tell the truth, Cobden only differed from Villiers in his greater carefulness not to let the cat out of the bag.

So long as orthodox economists were masters, the working classes could not possibly gain from the Repeal of the Corn Laws. (What gains they made, and why, *after* the Repeal —*post hoc* but not *propter hoc*—will be discussed later.) Nor was that Repeal, as Cobden used to argue, necessary if our manufactures were to find foreign markets. Cobden's argument was based upon the belief that our exports balanced our imports, that the more corn that came in, the more manufactured goods went out to pay for it and that the manufactured goods could not go out unless the corn came in. But there was in truth no such balance. Our exports, visible and invisible, every year considerably exceeded our imports and there was a surplus left over for foreign investment. What in truth regulated the quantity of goods which we sold abroad was the quantity of the loans which our financiers saw fit to make to foreigners to enable them to buy those goods.

[1] Vol. i, p. 249.

Even less true was it that the Irish, in whose interest the Repeal was pretended, could possibly gain from it. On the contrary they were bound to lose. For by the Act of Union there was free trade between England and Ireland. Therefore the Irish corn-grower was up till then able to sell his corn in England with the advantage of protection against his foreign competitor—an advantage of which the Repeal of the Corn Laws would clearly deprive him. As Croker, who had up till then been Peel's confidant, put it in a private letter of protest at the hypocrisy to Graham, the Home Secretary, "Ireland has no more to do with the grand convulsion than Kamschatka." [1] Indeed it was—to put it mildly—hardly honest to pretend that the Corn Laws were repealed out of consideration for the starving Irishman. For such an argument could only begin to have force if the famine in Ireland had been due to a failure of the country's food supply. That was not so. It was only the potato-crop that had failed. According to Mulhall,[2] the most careful statistician, who has investigated the subject, 1,029,000 people out of the total population of something over eight millions died of starvation or under-nourishment in Ireland during the famine. It is interesting to notice the exact statistics of the food that was *exported* from Ireland during 1845. They are 779,000 quarters of wheat and wheat-flour, 93,000 quarters of barley, and 2,353,000 quarters of oats [3]—that is to say, enough to feed for twelve months every person in Ireland who died of starvation, nearly four times over. Lord Althorp's "laws of political economy", which had been so deeply shocked at the very notion of "private charity", could find nothing objectionable in such an export, nor did Sir Robert Peel even refer to it when he argued that the cause of the calamity was that Ireland was "over-populated"—an argument that is repeated in our day, combined with a similar reticence, by such writers as Sir John Marriott in his *England after Waterloo*. A prince of the blood explained to the Irish that bad potatoes made a nourishing food, if mixed with grass.[4]

[1] *Croker Papers*, iii, p. 64.
[2] *Dictionary of Statistics*.
[3] *Growth of Modern England*, Slater, p. 353.
[4] *Peel*, Ramsay, p. 317.

These exports of food from Ireland had, of course, no imports to balance them at all. They went out, to some extent, to pay the rents to absentee landlords, but, mainly, to pay the interest on the mortgages in English-bank-manufactured money, which the Irish landlords, like the English landlords, had raised in order to pay the taxation required to meet the interest on the Napoleonic War Debt. On a previous page there has been quoted the general truth, enunciated by Mr. Emil Davies, that " the borrowing nations of the world pay interest on loans just about to the extent that their creditors advance them the wherewithal to do so." [1] Ireland in the nineteenth century was a solitary exception to that general truth, for in that country the capital wealth was in the hands of people, whose cultural and political sympathies were with their creditors rather than with the country in which they lived.

Private charity, in defiance of Lord Althorp, did make a certain contribution towards Irish relief. But such very inadequate Government relief, as was eventually given, was given in the shape of a loan on the security of that small proportion of Irish land that was not already fully mortgaged. Lord George Bentinck suggested the putting of purchasing power into the pockets of the Irish by a scheme of railway-building, but " the state of the money-market ", pleaded Lord John Russell's Whig Government, did not permit it.[2] There were more profitable investments elsewhere.

Let us never forget, when we abuse the Irish, that our grandfathers were responsible for these things. I do not say that they understood what they were doing. But what are we to say of a system of education that allowed them not to understand? Their purposes were but subconsciously apprehended, and to put them into explicit language is to do them a certain injustice. Yet I do not think it unfair to say that the Irish were an inconvenience to the financial interests owing to their refusal to accept the English progressive interpretation of history. The grandchildren of the eighteenth century were paid out for their refusal to allow education to Catholics; the happy Catholics knew no false

[1] *Investments Abroad*, pp. 20–1.
[2] *Disraeli, the Alien Patriot*, Raymond, p. 166.

history because they knew no history at all. Therefore, as *The Times* frankly confessed at the time, the policy must be to use the calamity of the famine in order to bring about a future in which " a Catholic Celt would be as rare on the banks of the Liffey as a red man on the eastern seaboard of America."

To whose advantage then was the Repeal of the Corn Laws? As has been shown, ever since the Industrial Revolution English financiers had every year been making investments in foreign countries, principally the new countries outside Europe. It was not possible, as has also been argued, that even the interest on these loans, let alone the principle, should ever, properly speaking, be repaid. But, even if the interest was only going to be paid by fresh loans, yet for the system to continue at all it was necessary to arrange that the debtor countries should export to us some substantial quantity of goods. If they gave us nothing, it would become manifest that the system was unworkable, and it would not be possible to raise the new loans with which to pay the interest on the old loans. Now what goods could these new countries export to us? It was manifest that they could not export manufactured goods, for they did not as yet manufacture any. As long as our foreign investments were mainly in the United States, there was no insoluble problem, for they could pay in raw cotton. But with other debtors the problem was more difficult.

They could only pay in food. But how could that food find a market in England? The rich could not eat it all themselves. For many kinds of manufactured goods the demand is almost unlimited ; for food it is by no means so. No one wants more than his bellyfull, however rich he is. It could only find a market on one of two conditions. Only, if either the wages of the poor were raised so that they could buy more than the subsistence quantity of food, or if English domestic agriculture was sabotaged, so as to create a gap which the foreign food could fill. According to the canons of the system, the former alternative, that of raising wages, was inadmissible. Therefore it was necessary to adopt the second and to destroy English agriculture. Hence the necessity for repealing the Corn Laws.

The politicians who advocated Free Trade, such as Cobden

and Bright, were not, of course, consciously insincere. They believed fervently what they said. Who would be such a fool as to use an insincere tool when he could get a sincere one? The sincere one is the cheaper and therefore, on good Ricardian principles, to be preferred; he will work without bribes. But why was it that their arguments received publicity rather than the arguments of other men? Why was it that the glaring fallacies in their arguments were allowed to go unexposed? It was because there was a power behind them to whose advantage it was that they should be victorious. Even in the seats of that power, no doubt, insincerity was not conscious. The men there were not conscious that they were preferring their own private interests to the interests of the country, but they identified the interests of the country with their own private interests, in much the same way as a patriotic old public schoolboy persuades himself, rightly or wrongly but at the least without any very deep ratiocination, that the collapse of the Public Schools would be a disaster for England. The opinions of the children of the money-power were formed in a certain ambient air which they had breathed since earliest infancy. An increase of foreign trade, however obtained, was to them "progressive" and "natural", and "practical men", "men of experience", were agreed that the preservation of agricultural England was a romantic's dream. The sort of stuff that Cobden and Bright talked sounded right. And beneath such a pressure few Englishmen are strong enough of logic to consider first principles or to demand that assumptions be proved.

The effect of the Repeal of the Corn Laws was as follows. The bad harvest in England in 1846 made necessary the charge of a high price for English-grown corn. Therefore advantage was taken of the new freedom to increase the quantity of imported corn not only from Ireland but also from abroad. So far was it from being true that imports balanced exports that on the contrary the foreign corn could only be paid for in gold. Although these food-producing countries all owed us money, yet we did not dare to accept repayment of our debts. Therefore gold left the country, and the Bank of England's reserves dwindled from £9½ million in December, 1846, to £3 million in April, 1847.

The effect was of course deflationary. The money that had thus vanished from circulation was not replaced as it would have been under another system. And, there being less money about, prices had to come down. Prices of primary products fell most steeply as they always do. Corn fell suddenly from 110*s.* a quarter to 60*s.*, and corn merchants, who had bought at a higher price in order to resell, were ruined. They were ruined because in a starving country there was too much corn. From the corn-merchants panic spread to the bill-brokers, from the bill-brokers to the banks. The Bank of England announced that it would not accept public stocks as collateral security for advances, and this in its turn caused selling of the public stocks and a collapse of their prices. On 23rd October the Bank Charter Act was suspended and the Bank of England promised immunity if it issued notes beyond the restrictions imposed upon it by that Act. That is to say, once more, as had happened just fifty years before in 1797, in an hour of crisis double-money was abolished in order to save the country from a wholly unnecessary catastrophe which double-money itself had created.

By the abolition confidence was restored, but it was not until thirty-three important English firms had paid in suffering and bankruptcy their penalty to the monstrous folly of double-money, their members condemned to starvation for the strange crime of possessing too much corn. The politicians who had thrown upon the Bank of England a responsibility which they had no right to throw upon any private shoulders promised to the Bank an indemnity for any illegalities which it might have committed in its abuse of that responsibility. The public was left to suffer for the follies of the bankers and the politicians, and, when the bankrupt firms had been finally wound up, the system of folly which had brought them to their bankruptcy was quietly restored. As Mr. Keynes has fairly and bitterly written,[1] " A sound banker, alas, is not one who foresees danger and avoids it but one who, when he is ruined, is ruined in a conventional and orthodox way along with his fellows, so that no one can really blame him."

It has been already argued that party government is

[1] *Essays in Persuasion*, p. 176.

only possible between two parties who are substantially agreed in their political opinions, and it is common under the parliamentary system, when any large change of policy is thought necessary, to prevent fair discussion upon it by the leaders of the two parties announcing their simultaneous conversions at the eleventh hour, when it is too late for the organization of any effective opposition. Thus in our own day, in 1931, the electorate was asked to approve of a wild and drastic financial policy under the virtual condition that, if they did not approve of it, they could not have a government at all. In the same way just a hundred years before, when it was found that there was a real and deep feeling against the new Poor Law system, it was agreed between the two front benches that it should not be made a party question. And, when Disraeli, the young Tory, criticized this measure of the Whig ministers, it was " quietly and good-naturedly hinted to him by his chiefs ", as he himself said, that, if he wished for any preferment in the future, he had better keep his mouth shut.[1]

There was a good prospect of getting the Repeal of the Corn Laws through in a similar fashion without having in any way to take the opinion of the electorate, or even the real opinion of the House of Commons. In the past both parties had been protectionist without any very serious pretence of understanding the arguments either for protection or against it. " By the by," said Lord Melbourne, the Whig Prime Minister, as his Cabinet was breaking up, " there is one thing we haven't agreed upon, which is, what are we to say ? Is it to make corn dearer or cheaper, or to make the price steady ? I don't care ; but we had better all be in the same story." [2] A similar spirit reigned in the Conservative cabinet. Readers of *Sybil* will remember the coaching which " a gentleman of Downing Street " gave to Mr. Hoaxem on the manner in which he was to deal with deputations. After having demonstrated to a deputation of tenant-farmers that the policy of the Government was to keep up the price of corn, he was then to face a deputation of manufacturers. " Show them how much I have done to promote the revival of trade. First of all,

[1] Speech at Shrewsbury, 27th August, 1844.
[2] *Russell*, Walpole, i, 369.

in making provisions cheaper; cutting off at one blow half the protection on corn, as, for example, at this moment under the old law the duty on foreign wheat would have been 27*s.* a quarter; under the new law it is 13*s.* To be sure, no wheat could come in at either price, but that does not alter the principle."[1]

Within a few days of each other the leaders of the two parties, Sir Robert Peel and Lord John Russell, became converts to Free Trade and, though there was certainly a large opinion in favour of the Corn Laws throughout the country, yet there seemed a very fair prospect of carrying the repeal through the House of Commons with but little opposition and without splitting either of the parties. We have Gladstone's word for it[2] that Peel thought that he could pass the measure without splitting his party. His opponents were but the back-bench squires, grumbling, inarticulate, hating to see the death of rural England, but hating still more to revolt against a Conservative Prime Minister.

His opponents were but the back-bench squires—and one man—one man more wildly unlike an English squire than any man that has ever lived—one man as exuberantly articulate as they were dumbly inarticulate. With this one exception all the political leaders of mid-Victorian England sprang from exactly the origins from which we should have expected such leaders to have sprung. It was not at all surprising that a Grey, a Melbourne, a Russell, and a Palmerston should have led the Whigs, that middle-class Liberalism should have rallied to Gladstone, old Tories to the Duke, and Protectionist squires to a Bentinck. The very probability of these careers but enhances the wild incongruity of the gentlemen of England turning for salvation to an exotic Jewish adventurer. Yet it was almost entirely through the anger and the persistence of Disraeli that the Repeal of the Corn Laws was challenged, that the Conservative party was split, that English politicians were redivided upon entirely new lines instead of being split into a Tweedledum Conservative party, under Peel, and a Tweedledee Liberal party, inspired by Cobden—the consummation to which Peel had looked forward.

[1] Book vi, chapter 1.
[2] *Gladstone*, Morley, i, 209, 210.

It is not the intention of this book even to attempt to find a formula with which to solve the baffling enigma of the character of Benjamin Disraeli. Few, I think, who have studied the story of Peel's refusal of office to him in 1841 can doubt that, among the motives that actuated him in 1846, were both a desire for revenge upon that stiff and arrogant man and a just calculation that, unless Peel could somehow be unseated, there was no future for Disraeli. No one, who has read *Sybil*, can doubt that also among his motives was a genuine compassion for the miseries of the poor. Whatever the true proportion in which these motives were mixed, at any rate let us understand clearly the predominating importance in history of the stand which Disraeli made against Peel. He failed, it is true, to save protection. Indeed a few years later he even abandoned protection himself. Here was failure, but his success was much more important than his failure. He destroyed the old party political life.

Now let us understand what that old life meant. In the year before the Repeal—in 1844—that very noble philanthropist, Lord Shaftesbury (Ashley, as he then still was) had introduced an amendment to Graham's Factory Bill, by which the labour of young persons—boys from thirteen to eighteen, and girls of under twenty-one—should be restricted to ten hours a day. Most independent Conservative opinion was for it. Disraeli and his friends of Young England were strongly for it. The Conservative Government, on the other hand, was bitterly opposed and made the rejection of the amendment a matter of confidence. It was able to obtain that rejection, in spite of the opposition of some of its followers, by support of the Manchester Liberals, led by John Bright, who thought it a sufficient answer to the plea that there was misery and starvation in the towns of England, if he could demonstrate that there was also misery and starvation in the country districts.[1] Cobden prophesied that "men like Graham and Peel will see the necessity of taking anchor upon some sound principles, as a refuge from the socialist doctrine of the fools behind them ".[2]

[1] House of Commons, 15th March, 1844.
[2] *Cobden*, Morley, i, 302.

What did all this mean in plain English? It meant this. The productivity of the country was vastly greater than it had ever been before. At the same time the condition of the people was vastly worse than it had ever been before in recorded time. When James Caird toured England in 1850, he found that agricultural wages, which in Young's time in 1770 had oscillated between 6*s*. and 10*s*. 9*d*. a week, now oscillated between 6*s*. and 15*s*.[3] On the other hand, to counterbalance this increase, cottage-rents had more than doubled. To recall Thorold Rogers's conclusions, the poor were some six times worse off than they had been in Henry VII's time. Now, according to the comfortable vision in Peel's mind, political power was to have rested, turn and turn about, in the hands of two parties, the dominant spirits of both of which flatly denied that, however great the increase in the country's productivity, it was in any way possible for the poor to obtain any share in that increase. It was Disraeli, who, by driving the Peelites over to the Liberals, saved the Conservative party from becoming a second Liberal party. History may yet come to record her verdict that by doing so he saved the world.

[1] *English Agriculture in 1850–1*, Sir James Caird.

Chapter XI

THE FIRST REVOLTS

The verdict of history may be that Disraeli saved the world because it is not to be believed that the poor would have tolerated for ever this exclusion from the benefits of increased productivity. If political economy and the Parliamentary politicians had insisted on imposing this exclusion on them, then in the end it would have been inevitable that they should turn against party politics and the political economists. So there were the Chartists. But these years also saw the first articulate statement of a theory of history, more important than that of the Chartists, which challenged the whole basis upon which existing arrangements were made—or at the least appeared to do so. In 1848 appeared Karl Marx's and Friedrich Engels's *Manifesto on Communism*. In that manifesto, as in all his subsequent writings, Marx swept away with impatience the whole nursery-version of history, the record of the rise and fall of dynasties, or the mock-figures of party politicians. History's one reality, he claimed, was the unceasing struggle between rival economic classes. In every state the Government was necessarily but "an executive committee for managing the affairs of the governing class as a whole". Minor differences within the governing class, such as those between Whigs and Tories, or Liberals and Conservatives, were secondary and negligible.

Eventually, he argued, every economic system collapsed through its own inherent contradictions, and out of the conflict between the exploiting and the exploited classes emerged a new system and a new society. Capitalism had thus emerged out of the societies of the past and would, in its turn, give place to communism, as soon as the proletariat understood capitalism's inherent incapacity to deliver to it the goods which it created. The leaders of the proletariat must then overturn the capitalist state, seize power themselves in the name of the proletariat and establish the dictatorship of the proletariat, to crush out from the memory and from the life of the country all relic of its bourgeois past. That task achieved, the dictatorship can automatically end. The new classless state has then come into being. The apocalyptic vision with which the first volume of *Das Kapital* ends has then at length been realized. The state, as Lenin put it, " withers away." The problem of government is replaced by that of mere administration in a classless society. " Pre-history ends and history begins," as Marx himself put it.

Now there are surely few who would not agree that, while there is much that is sensible and suggestive in Marx's interpretation of the past and while his economic theory of surplus value is substantially true, yet his prophecies concerning the future are without basis in reason and purely mystical in the worst and most popular sense of a much abused word. Though all the facts of the past do not support his historical theories, at least there are facts in the past which do support them. It is true that the clash between rival economic classes has played a large part in shaping history. It is true that the official historical and economic text-books, written for the dominant class by their jackals, do, to a gross extent, simply take the riches of the rich for granted as an evident part of God's plan. It is true that the whole notion of progress only obtained currency because the dominant class, while but a small proportion of the country's population, yet provided almost the whole of the country's literature. The poor, whose standard of living was being forced down and down, were not asked for their opinions upon progress, but the few among them, such as Burns or Cobbett, who insisted on giving their opinions, whether asked or not, knew very well how little progress there had been. Of Marx's interpretation of history then one can fairly say that, as far as it goes, it insists upon a truth—an important truth, a neglected truth—a truth neglected indeed by the academic historians but as clearly understood by the free minds of the times such as Lingard or Cobbett or Disraeli, as it was understood by Marx himself. On the other hand, he quite misunderstood the nature of religion and entirely neglected its enormous power to compose the conflicts of classes.

Of Marx's prophecy of the future, however, we can only say that it is filled with contradictions even more gross than those of the capitalist system itself. Suppose, as has happened in Russia and as might well have happened in England had not Disraeli fought Sir Robert Peel, that the system of society has collapsed and that the dictatorship of the proletariat has been established. What then? What reason at all is there to believe that out of this dictatorship of the proletariat there will emerge a classless society? "Dictatorship of the proletariat" is clearly no more than a phrase. The proletariat cannot dictate; a few people dictate to the proletariat. No one has been more ready than Marx to pour scorn—largely merited scorn—on those bourgeois leaders who have sought to conceal from themselves and from others the essential selfishness of their motives by the pretence that they incarnate the people. Why is there a magic against original sin in the mouthing of the word "proletariat" which there is not in in the mouthing of the word "people"? And what is this classless world to be like—this world, where "pre-history" is no more, and "history" has at last begun—whatever that may mean? "The Marxists' answer is that they do not know," Mr. Cole tells us.[1] "It is enough for Lilith that there is a beyond," says Mr. Bernard Shaw.[2] It may be enough for Lilith, but it is not enough for me. If we are to be asked to suffer the inconveniences of a revolution, at least we demand to be told what we are revolting for. "The King is dead; long live the question-mark," is not an inspiring battle-cry.

Yet I do not think that we need greatly bother ourselves what this classless Marxian society will be like. It is Marx's own contention—a true contention—that class feelings are among the strongest of the feelings of the human soul. Such small unity as the exploited class has ever achieved, it has achieved only because it has been united in opposition to its exploiters. Once the exploiters have been "liquidated", what reason is there to think that the exploited will

[1] *What Marx Really Meant*, p. 290.
[2] *Back to Methuselah*, Epilogue.

not fall out among themselves—miners against railwaymen, town against country, merchant against manufacturer, white against black, black against yellow ? What reason, above all, is there to think that the dictators, using no doubt the Marxian phraseology to cloak their designs, will not form themselves into a new class of exploiters ? The exploiters in each era of Marxian history have always been the leaders of the exploited in the class war of the previous era. Why should that oligarchy, the Communist party, be any exception to this law ? As every day in the experience of Russia proves, it clearly is not. The careful investigation of Mr. Chamberlain in Russia, *Without Benefit of Censor*, brings us to the conclusion that between 4,000,000 and 5,000,000 people in Russia have died of famine—a famine due not to natural causes, but to a " deliberate withholding of food ". Were those 4,000,000 all capitalists ? How can unity come out of such a policy ?

All probability and all experience then unite to prove that the so-called transitional stage of the dictatorship of the proletariat will never pass and that Marx's gospel of hate does not contain within it the stuff out of which can ever emerge the classless society of Marx's apocalyptic vision. The great eschatological mystics have united to tell us how at the last day Almighty God will come riding to us upon clouds of glory. The belief of Marx, that he can get rid of the God and still have the clouds of glory, is really puerile. Mere hate and envy can never of their nature bring unity. Hate cannot create, and envy demands division in order that there may be somebody to be envied,

So clearly is this true that Marx's disciples have been constrained to admit that the living generation, corrupted by its bourgeois ideologies, cannot properly breathe the communist air. It is corrupted by the God-complex ; it has foolish hankerings of respect for its parents. " Give us but time," they say. " With time and education and a few machine-guns we will produce a new generation, a communist generation, which will care nothing for God and its parents and care only for the community." Then the classless society will be born.

Will be born—the new generation—but, if materialistic hedonism is the only sane philosophy, if motherhood carries with it no privileges and sex possesses no mysteries, why should there be a new generation at all ? What motive can you offer to a woman why she should submit herself to the pains of childbirth ? If you produce your new generation, how are you going to induce it in its turn to generate ? It is true that up till now the birth-rate in Russia has not fallen—but then the bearers are still infected with the ideology of their degraded past—with a hankering, horrible, anti-social feeling for the glory of motherhood—a feeling that will soon be ruthlessly stamped out. The communist theory is by no means unanswerable. Indeed it is at some of its most important points so patently untrue that what is surprising is not that it has failed to conquer but that it has at all survived. It has survived because the answer to it is equally an answer to the orthodox theory against which it was erected. We still have communism because we still have capitalism, and communism will continue so long as capitalism survives. Take, for example, the vulgar and popular objections to communism. We are told that nobody will give of his best unless he is allowed himself to reap where he has sown ; if it be true, what a devastating objection to the system of usury which offers as the reward of success the attainment of an "independent income" ! We are told that the threat of poverty is necessary to save men from the demoralization of idleness ; if it be true, what an indictment of a system that permits the inheritance of wealth ! "We communists," Marx was able to say with unanswerable sarcasm, "have been accused of wishing to abolish the property that has been acquired by personal exertion. . . . We do not need to abolish that kind of property, for industrial development has abolished it, or is doing so day by day."[1] Malthus in a famous passage debates "what should be done with that class of people whose only possession is their labour"—a class whose existence he takes for granted, as if he were speaking of the blind, or of men over six feet. It simply does not occur to him that a possible solution might be that of endowing them with some other possessions. Faced with such philosophizings, Marx has only to answer unanswerably, "You are outraged because we wish to abolish private

[1] *Essay on Population* (ed. 1926), p. 86.

K

property. But in extant society private property has been abolished for nine-tenths of the population."

To go a little deeper, all sane thought revolts from the doctrine that the laws of political economy are independent of religious control—but it was not Karl Marx but Lord Althorp who first taught that doctrine. The Communist denies that there is a God whose purposes can be opposed to Communism, but he only does so because the Liberals have already cornered that God and announced that he was " a force not ourselves, making for usury ". As Ruskin put it in bitter anger, the Liberal faith was : " There is a Supreme Ruler, no question of it, only He cannot rule. His orders won't work."[1] Between a God Who is not and a God Who does nothing there is a distinction without a difference. Again the experience of mankind teaches that the family is the fundamental human society and that a policy which attacks the family cannot bring happiness to mankind, but the family was attacked by the Benthamite Poor Law almost a century before it was attacked by Bolshevist free love. Even to-day which is its worse enemy—Mayfair or Moscow ? Admitting the strength of class divisions, we yet cling to the Christian doctrine of the equality of man and revolt from the exaggeration of the Communist teaching that economic differences have divided the human race into wholly different sorts of animals. Yet the class war was practised by eighteenth century noblemen a hundred years before it was preached by nineteenth century communists, and the only difference on this point between Adam Smith and Lenin is that Adam Smith took tacitly for granted what Lenin explicitly recognized. Unless the human race does consist of two sorts of animals, the theories of Adam Smith do not make sense at all. Yet again, we are moved a little to irreverent mirth by Karl Marx's baseless and apocalyptic vision of a rosy dawn ahead, but the myth of progress was popularized among the rich by Lord Macaulay long before it was popularized among the poor by Trotzky. All the technique of trick-education was perfected by Townshend two hundred years before it was invented by Lunacharsky.

It is clear then that the battle between capitalism and communism, so far from being the eternal struggle of our

[1] *Modern Painters*, v. part ix, chap. 12.

race, was in reality little more than a family quarrel between two Jews for the divine right to deceive mankind—between the Dutch Jew Ricardo and the German Jew Marx. And before the menace of a real challenge to the system—the challenge that has come in our day from President Roosevelt—even the family quarrel is forgotten, and the finance-ridden Western European countries and Communist Moscow come easily together. For in a way

> "Marx does more than Malthus can
> To justify Mammon's ways to Man."

For the very determinism of Marx, which sought to prove that the post-capitalist society must necessarily be communist, was compelled equally to argue that the pre-communist society had necessarily to be capitalist. And, therefore, in the *Communist Manifesto of 1848* Marx, so far from underrating the achievements of capitalism, grossly exaggerated them. Its great achievement, according to him, was that "it has rescued a considerable part of the population from the idiocy of rural life".

Now every tradition of our race stands in opposition to the whole insolent plan for rearranging the poor and refuses to take sides either with Ricardo and his claim that the capitalist shall not be interfered with by the commissar, or with Marx and his claim that the commissar shall not be interfered with by the capitalist. To most of us these old bourgeois notions, so drastically to be rooted out, are utterly fundamental to human nature. Even if they be not so, at least men have held them for a very long time—so much so that the possession of them is an integral part of what we mean by a man—so much so that, when the Marxians propose to produce a man who is quite innocent of them they are in reality proposing to produce a new animal. As Mr. Bernard Shaw frankly admits, "Our only hope is in evolution. We must replace the man by the superman"—which is another way of saying that there is no hope at all—at least for us. For, if Man is replaced, we, at any rate, cease to exist. Other reformers in history have sought to change the constitution of society because it is not suited to the nature of man; the Communists seek to change the nature of Man because it is not suited to their proposed constitution of society. It is the belief of the present writer that their attempt is foredoomed to failure and that Man is possessed of a certain nature which in fundamentals cannot be changed. But suppose the Marxians to be right. Is it not clear that they lay themselves open to a devastating answer from the defenders of the old financial system? "Oh," says the ghost of Malthus with a smile, "if we can produce a new race of men, why then is it necessary to have a revolution with all its inconveniences? Instead of producing a communist race which is happy under communism, why not produce a slave race which is happy under capitalism? While we are "conditioning away" God and the family, why not "condition away" the sense of justice and the sense of equality, the love of children, and the yearning for a merry life as well? The only possible objection to my schemes was that the poor would not stand them. Why not breed a race of poor that will stand them?"

No one used to be more ready than the Malthusians with pompous lectures to the poor on the inevitable retribution which would follow upon their enjoyment of temporary and "artificial" prosperity. But the very strength of Malthus's language used to rob his followers of the right to use such language. If there had been a chance of enduring happiness, it might have been wise to have restrained oneself in order to enjoy it. But, if "the almost constant action of misery" is our inevitable lot, we might as well make hay while the sun shines, being very certain that it will never shine again; break into the lord's cellar and rob and rape and get gloriously drunk to-night, since it is the only night that we shall have. And now at the eleventh hour Marx has come along and set Malthus's argument on its legs again. He will breed Malthus a race that will not be miserable in misery.

Where then did hope lie? There was no hope save in an inquiry into "the mystery of things" by far more fundamental than any that either Ricardo or Marx ever contemplated. What was "creation's final law"? There are but two motives which have ever led anybody to invent or to make anything—necessity and love. God, a self-sufficient being, cannot have needed the world. Therefore

He must have loved it and created it out of love. Love must have been before the world in order that the world might be created. But before the world nothing was save God. Therefore it must be that " God is love ". If that argument be sound, then there is a foundation on which the new society can be built ; if it be not sound, there is no such foundation. For it is useless to preach of love if love be not the law of the world.

Now with such an argument Marx's mind never came to wrestle at all. For, whereas Marx was always pointing out with considerable truth how everybody else was a product of environment, he did not clearly see how he himself was also such a product. Yet, as Mr. Bernard Wall truly says [1] in an admirable article in the *Colosseum*, his " data and theory are the product of a particular and unique period of human history which is already passing away ". And, in particular, he judged religion not by its claims nor by the general record of its adherents through the ages, but by the record—or what he, with no very deep understanding, thought to be the record—of its adherents in his own particular day.

Now it was true that through unhappy accidents the Christian bodies had by no means played the part that they should have played in the battle against usury in the first half of the nineteenth century. The Church of England, which had boasted so splendid a record in the reign of Charles I, had been captured in 1688 by those very forces against which it existed to protest. It was now, in these matters, little more than the support of English nationalism. It was not Herr Hitler nor Signor Mussolini but Queen Victoria who wrote,[2] " It is natural that every one should have their own opinion, especially on religion, but, when the policy of Great Britain comes into consideration . . . *all* private feelings should be overruled." The Nonconformists had in their blood no traditions against usury. The Catholic Church was in a yet sadder and more curious case.

The Emperor Napoleon was by no means a model Christian. Yet the force which he challenged was the

[1] Art., "Marxism and Man," September, 1934.
[2] *Disraeli*, Buckle, vol. vi.

force of usury; the society for which he fought was a Christian society; the society which conquered him, if ever such a word may be used of any society, anti-Christian. It was a society, whose very fundament was usury, the eternal enemy of the Christian faith. The memory of Napoleon lived on as a dream in the minds of the poor.

> "Long, long will they tell of him under the thatched roof.
> In fifty years the humble dwelling will know no other history.
> Children, through this village I saw him ride,
> And Kings followed him." [1]

That dream was in truth the immemorial dream of Christian freedom. Yet most unfortunately in the course of the struggle Napoleon fell into a quarrel with Pope Pius VII concerning the Papal States and treated him with great lack of proper respect and personal consideration. It is the unfortunate but clearly all but inevitable weakness of priests when they come into contact with the affairs of laymen, that their lack of experience is likely to cause them to judge these affairs in a simple-minded fashion. From time to time one comes across a Father Brown among priests, but Mr. Chesterton, I am sure, would be the first to agree that priests are not shrewd as a general rule. It is better that they should not be; it is better that they should be holy. Thus it was that the blunder of Napoleon gave to his enemies the opportunity of posing before the Papacy as the defender of the ancient traditions of Christendom. They were able to persuade it that after 1815 they were restoring the old world of 1789, and because Kings and Emperors sat once more apparently upon their thrones, the Papacy was persuaded that the old order had been re-established. Metternich and Stadion, it thought, were the rulers of Austria because they were called the rulers of Austria. But in reality, as Cobbett ceaselessly preached, what had been restored was the personnel of the *ancien régime*, weighed down by a burden of debt which made their creditors the effectual masters of policy. The Papacy saw Metternich and Stadion in their seats of office. They did not see Stadion pocketing the loans of the Rothschilds and Metternich creeping down into the Frankfort ghetto

[1] Béranger.

to learn their latest will.[1] For fifty years after Waterloo Papal policy was directed by pious and simple men. They preached sincerely the Church's doctrine against usury, but they did nothing to oppose the usurers, because in their innocence of the world they did not know that they were usurers.

Deluded by the trick of the new masters, who cleverly used the phrase "private property", they thought that in defending property in the Ricardian sense they were defending it in the Thomistic sense. But in truth the two doctrines of property had nothing at all in common. "Man should not consider his outward possessions as his own," St. Thomas had taught, "but as common to all, so as to share them without difficulty when others are in need." "All that the rich men hath," taught the author of the medieval *Dives et Pauper*, "passing his honest living after the degree of his dispensation, it is other men's, not his, and he shall give full hard reckoning thereof at the day of doom, when God shall say to him, 'Yield account of your bailywick.'"[2] "Every man has a right to do what he will with his own," answered Malthus[3]—in flat contradiction. And to Althorp the exercise of charity was not only not obligatory; it was not possible.

Later in the century, after the happy loss of the Temporal Power, there came with Leo XIII a régime capable of penetrating these earlier misunderstandings and in our own day with the present Pope the battle has been happily joined where it should be joined. But it was not so at first.

Both Marx and Ricardo, children of their day, could not see beyond their day. Owing to his own insensibility to beauty and the weakness of his powers of observation of nature, Marx found life in the country boring. He therefore erected his own taste into a dogma and proclaimed the town to be the superior of the country. In the same way, finding that for accidental reasons the voice of religion was temporarily not raised loud against social wrong, he

[1] See *Rise and the Reign of the House of Rothschild*, by Count Corti, and *Metternich*, by Algernon Cecil.

[2] Quoted by Cardinal Gasquet, *Eve of the Reformation*, p. 312.

[3] *Essays*, p. 445.

dismissed religion contemptuously as the mere handmaid of the governing class—"the opium of the poor." Yet even such a phrase contained, as Mr. Chesterton has acutely pointed out, the refutation of his whole theory of economic determinism. For it means, if it means anything, that the proletariat refrains from revolt because it has been taught a lot of foolish tales about morality. Whether the tales be foolish or not is nothing to this immediate argument. What is important is Marx's admission that their conduct is influenced by such tales—by motives, that is, that are not at all economic.

Thus it came about that, allowing no place for that part of Man's nature that makes him mostly truly Man, both the Liberal and the Communist made of their disciples stunted, uncertain creatures, doomed for ever to proclaim a lack of faith that it is not truly within human capacity to feel. Every Benthamite and every Marxian, insecurely poised upon a half-belief, is therefore, like Mr. Bernard Shaw's atheist, always in danger of losing his faith. To them, as to poor Gigadibs,

> "Just when we are safest, there's a sunset touch,
> A fancy from a flower-bell, someone's death,
> A chorus ending from Euripides—
> And that's enough for fifty hopes and fears
> As old and new at once as Nature's self,
> To rap and knock and enter in our soul . . .
> The grand Perhaps! We look on helplessly." [1]

Now, if it was two Jews, their minds confused with bogus Whig history, who were most largely responsible for imposing this desiccation upon mankind, it was a third Jew who saw most clearly the folly of it. Disraeli had the gift, more than any of his contemporaries, of putting himself outside the accidents of his age and of the country in which he lived. As the second title of his great work, *Sybil*, shows, he saw, as clearly as Marx saw it, that society had as a fact fallen apart into two nations. Disraeli, alive in the world, knew much better than Marx, shut up in the British Museum, the gulf between Alfred Mountchesney,[2] who "rather likes bad wine because one gets so bored with

[1] *Bishop Blougram's Apology*, Browning.
[2] *Sybil*, book i, chapter 1.

good" and the villagers of Marney, paid 7*s.* a week, because "people without cares do not require so much food as those whose life entails anxieties."[1] But he saw, too, that the gulf between these two nations could only be abridged by some great force utterly challenging the liberal laws of political economy and the communist doctrine of the class war. That great force was the gigantic, explosive force of real Christian faith.

We often tell one another that the Jew, as an alien, stands outside our Christian culture. And so he does. But he stands, too, outside all those elements in our culture that are most flagrantly opposed to Christianity. To a Jew the whole conception of a gentleman is unintelligible—a conception, comic if he be of a comedic turn, and, if he be serious-minded, almost blasphemous. To a Jew the very stuff of life is the binding force of a common faith and a common race. That a man should think himself to be of a different kind from others of his own race is to a Jew but the plainest nonsense.

I do not think that Disraeli was ever himself a Christian. But even where he had not the faith to believe he had not the folly to despise. He was a a highly intelligent man, and he did understand one simple and all-important historical truth, which even to-day is not sufficiently understood. He did understand that for three hundred years the poor of England had been driven down and down and down, that in his own day the rot had at last been stopped and that the force that had stopped it was the force of Christianity. There were, of course, then, as there still are, millions of professing Christians, who, through ignorance or indolence or bemusement at the sophistries of the economists, had played no part in the battle against Christianity's enemy. That was a deplorable truth, but it did not alter the counter-truth that the only effective blows that had been dealt to the system had been dealt by Christians, fighting for the sake of Christ. "Profiting by dissensions among the bourgeoisie, it compels legislative recognition of some of the specifically working class interests. That is how the Ten Hours Bill was secured in England," wrote Marx. Disraeli knew better. He knew that the Ten Hours Bill was

[1] Ibid., book iii, chapter 2.

secured by a handful of Christians who thought it wicked that their fellow-men should be treated as animals.

If words had any meaning at all, there stood this blazing truth that it was impossible to believe both in Malthus and in the God whom Malthus worshipped, in what Carlyle called " pig philosophy " and in Christian philosophy.

> " Our God hath blessed creation,
> Calling it good." [1]

is the ringing challenge of the Christian faith. The two philosophies were, as Ruskin used truly to say, the direct opposite each of the other, the one saying black wherever the other said white. " I know," he added [2] truly, " no previous instance in history of a nation's establishing a systematic disobedience to the first principles of its professed religion." There were a few men who were clear-headed enough and courageous enough to see the contrast and to prefer the latter faith. It was they who saved us.

The first effective attacks on the system had come from that noble and grossly underpraised man, Thomas Michael Sadler; his motive in attacking the system was purely religious. After Sadler, who was a Tory, had been defeated for Parliament owing to the Reform Bill by Macaulay, his work was taken up by the great Lord Shaftesbury (Ashley, as he then was)—inheritor of the title of that man who did more, perhaps, than any other to stamp an anti-Christian character upon the face of England—himself to do more than any other to break that anti-Christian character. His motive, too, was a purely religious one. It is by a paradox the very sovereign greatness of these two great men, the one a Methodist, the other a narrow Evangelical, that they were neither of them men of supreme intelligence. In Sadler's controversies with Macaulay, Macaulay sometimes had the better of it. In face of the sophistries of the economists, " the pests of society and the persecutors of the poor," as Sadler called them, they were not always able clearly to understand nor wholly to explain how it was that society could survive if the poor were raised above the level of starvation. It was their glory that this inability

[1] *Ballad of the White Horse*, G. K. Chesterton, part iii.
[2] *Unto this Last.*

did not cause them to hesitate for an instant. They were Christians, and they saw clearly that the acceptance of Christianity as true in its nature implied also its acceptance as of overriding importance. A Christian world could not be a world of the Two Nations; it was a world in which "barbarian and Scythian, bond and free" were united in the transcendent unity of Christ and, if political economy knew nothing of such a world, so much, they said, with all simplicity and all humility, the worse for political economy. "The Son of God," said Lord Shaftesbury in a quaint meditation at the end of his battered life, "took upon Him all human sufferings save only that of being in debt." It was Sadler who saw that the law of charity must be reintroduced as the law of life, even though it destroy society. It was Disraeli who saw that it would not destroy society but would save it from destruction.

There is a great similarity between the historical opinions of Cobbett and of Disraeli. Both knew the official praise of the Reformation and of 1688, of "Dutch finance and French wars", and both had for that praise the contempt which it deserved. But there could not well be a wider difference than the difference between the natures of the two men. Cobbett was first and foremost a great lover, the lover of England. Like Dante,

> "he loved well because he hated,
> Hated wickedness that hinders loving."[1]

Every turn of an English lane, every English flower, every English country sport was a thing of loveliness to this great man, who was essential England. And it was because he loved that he hated—hated the Wen and the Thing and the Botley Parson, and the whole machinery of greed that was crushing out so much loveliness from the world.

Disraeli could not feel like that. He saw it but he did not feel it. The accidents of his origin compelled detachment. He could not love. But deep down in his soul there was the immemorial teaching of his ancient race against usury—the teaching of Moses and the teaching which the traditions of the race take back beyond Moses to the identification of usury with the serpent's bite of Eden.

[1] *One Word More*, Browning.

There stirred in him the spirit of the great Golconda Jew of Ruskin's *Unto This Last.* Jews have been the world's usurers, but they have only practised usury when, like the Rothschilds and the Ricardos, they have been aliens in a society which they wished to destroy. They have always known that usury does certainly destroy a society. No Jew has ever fallen into the foolish carelessness of so many silly Christians who think that it does not greatly matter whether usury be tolerated or not. Where a Jew is a friend of a society, he will wish to save it from that which will eat it up. And Disraeli, though not an Englishman, was yet the friend of England, her grateful guest.

CHAPTER XII

THE TURN OF THE TIDE

Elderly people sometimes find it difficult to accept a full denunciation of the iniquity of the financial system, because in their own lifetime they have seen so great an improvement in the standard of living of the poor. It is true that there has been such an improvement, though it is also true that the rise in the standard of living has by no means kept pace with the increase in productivity. But it is necessary to remember how great was the depth from which improvement had to be won, how miserable was the condition of the poor in the 1840's, how wretched was the share which they were allowed to enjoy of the country's vast productivity.

There was no immediate recovery from the calamity of 1847. 1848 was indeed the year of European revolution, of Smith O'Brien in Ireland, and of the Chartists in England. It was with the new decade that the great increase in productivity began. That increase was mainly due to the discoveries of gold in California and Australia. As has been shown, the Bank Charter Act of 1844, had restricted the private banks' power to issue bank-notes. The result, as has been said, was to give a great impulse to the cheque habit. Yet the public cannot develop new habits overnight and therefore, until that habit was developed, it was not safe for the banks to lend widely beyond their cash holdings.

The bank deposits—which are merely the bank-loans in another form—did indeed increase somewhat but not nearly rapidly enough. As a result, it was not possible to finance the new production which science had made possible and the last five years of the 1840's were years of gross under-production and consequent unemployment.

Then with the Californian and Australian discoveries the world's gold supply jumped suddenly forward. The world's output of gold, which had been £5½ million in 1847, had risen by 1857 to over £30 million. The English, along with other banks elsewhere and especially those of France, became masters of larger cash-holdings and could lend more freely to finance production. Their loans and deposits jumped up, and the total bank-deposits of British banks, which in 1846 were £55 million, had by 1856 risen to £120 million. This increased monetary supply was to some extent, it is true, answered by a rise in prices. The price of the 4 lb. loaf rose from 6·8*d.* in 1852 to 8·3*d.* in 1853 and to 10·5*d.* in 1854. According to the *Encyclopædia Britannica* index, collated so as to make 1913 100, wholesale prices, which in 1852 were 92, rose in 1853 to 106, and in 1854 to 119. But that was but a small rise. For the most part increased monetary supply was answered by an increase of goods—of consumable goods within the country in addition to the capital goods that were exported from it.

Now, according to the Ricardian gospel, the working-classes, living at their subsistence wage, could have had no share in that increased productivity. All that could have happened would have been that there would have been an increase of foreign loans, an increased production of capital goods, an increase of exports and a still larger favourable balance of trade. There was indeed a great—not to say a gross—increase of exports which jumped from about £50 million per annum in the late 1840's to nearly £120 million in the late 1850's. Wages rose, according to G. H. Wood's figures, taking one industry with another, from 50 in 1852 to 55 in 1853 and 57 in 1854—that is to say, they rose substantially less than prices. The result of the boom of the 1850's was therefore to reduce unemployment but also to make the standard of the living of the worker in employment slightly lower than it was before.

Then in 1857, after the conclusion of the Crimean War, the boom came to its usual slump. The cessation of the war had caused dislocation among firms engaged upon the supply of war material. On top of that came the break in the American railway market. There had been a rage of railway investment in America. More than half of all the capital of that investment came, it is said, from Great Britain and one-fifth of all the goods exported from the

United Kingdom went to the United States.[1] It became evident that there was no prospect of the railways paying any dividends in the near future. The American banks which had lent money to the railways, found that they could not get repaid. They thus had not the cash to meet the demands of their other creditors and all but one of the banks of New York, Boston, Philadelphia, and Baltimore had to close their doors.

English houses, which had accepted the bills of exporters to America, now in their turn found it impossible to collect their debts. But they had developed the habit of borrowing, mostly at call, from the English banks. The banks called in the money—and it was not there. The English banks, therefore, deprived of cash upon which they reckoned, called for cash from the Bank of England without which they could not feel safe. But the gold was not in the Bank of England either. By raising the bank rate to 10 per cent the bank vainly tried to attract it from abroad. But it was too late for such a manœuvre. The acceptance houses had not got the money with which they professed to discount the bills. The joint-stock banks had not got the money with which they professed to lend to the acceptance houses. The Bank of England had not got the money which it professed to lend to the joint-stock banks. And now down, tumbling down, came the whole fantastic pack of cards. On 11th November, 1857, the Bank Charter Act was once more suspended, and the failure of double money once more confessed.

The whole effect of the catastrophe was of course deflationary, and therefore naturally down came prices. Wholesale prices fell from 121 in 1857 to 109 in 1858. The 4 lb. loaf, which had already fallen from 1856's 10·8*d.* to 1857's 9·0*d.*, came down in 1858 to 7·5*d.* But—and this is the interesting point—it was not found possible to get wages down in proportion. According to G. H. Wood's index wages, which were 56 in 1857, were still 55 in 1858. The poor were able to gain on the slump what they had lost on the boom. 50 is to 55 exactly what 6·8 is to 7·5, and therefore the wages of the poor, reckoned in terms of bread, were in 1858 exactly what they had been in 1852. In the

[1] *Pound Sterling*, Feaveryear, p. 271.

intervening years they had been worse. The moral to be drawn was an important one. It was that, for any workman who held a job in which he had any reasonable security against unemployment, it was a positive advantage for trade to be bad. However that was an intolerable paradox, as intelligent employers were quick to see.

With the 1860's employment got better again ; wholesale prices rose to the high level of 120 in 1866, the 4 lb. loaf to 8·8*d.*, but wages were allowed to rise from 55 in 1858 to 66 in 1868—that is to say, for the first time they rose substantially more than prices. To some extent this rise was due to the new, growing Trades Unions. Most of their great strikes, as, for instance, the strike in the London building trades in 1859–60, and the Sheffield strikes made famous by Charles Reade's *Put Yourself in his Place,* ended in failure. Indeed, in all but quite exceptional circumstances, such as those of war in which the governing class cannot afford even a temporary check to productivity, the weapon of the strike usually does do more harm to those who use it than to those against whom it is used. The capitalist has his fat on which to live while the workman has nothing. Strike pay empties the coffers of the Trades Union and in more cases than not the men are eventually defeated and forced back to work on the old conditions and with the situation unchanged save that they have now a bankrupt instead of a solvent Trades Union behind them. The working man is also a consumer. He cannot possibly starve anybody else without also starving himself.

The Trades Union can then almost always be beaten so long as the united opinion of the masters wants to beat it. But that is by no means always so. It was not so in the early 1860's. The work of Shaftesbury had begun to have its effect. Palmerston, his father-in-law, was Prime Minister. Disraeli, his disciple, was the leader of the opposition in the House of Commons. The folly of the paradox of the slump of 1857 had had its effect on those of the employers who were capable of learning from experience and had converted them not indeed to what could with any reason be called high wages but yet at least to the wisdom of giving the working man some share in the country's increased productivity. Those wiser employers, who understood the mutual advantage of good relations with the employees, were glad to use the Trades Unions as weapons with which to break their own stupider colleagues.

The new marginal school of economists had begun to criticize Ricardo, and, though their criticisms were in reality no challenge at all to his fundamental philosophy, yet the effect of them was to shake a little men's faith in the full infallibility of the laws of political economy. The Northern blockade of the South in the American Civil War caused some people to wonder whether there was wisdom in a system which made the poor of Lancashire suffer for the quarrel of other men an ocean away, in which they had no concern, and which, making the reduction of purchasing power the punishment of unemployment, punished the poverty of one man in such a way as inevitably to impose poverty on his neighbour as well.

The employers and the politicians could do a little. It was soon proved that it was only a little that they could do. Under the system money only came into existence by invented loans. The employers, with all the goodwill in the world, could only pay on as wages what money the banks lent either to them to produce their goods or to their customers to buy from them. It is merely useless to promise that you will pay £3 a week, if the banks have determined to put only £2 10*s*. into circulation. And over all there reigned the great law that money was to be allowed to find its own level. If English wages rose high, it ceased to be profitable to lend to English producers at all. The banks would not even put the £2 10*s*. into circulation. The Argentinian borrower would draw his loan out in gold and spend it by buying the capital goods he needed in Germany.

The very prosperity of British industry was used to destroy it. People had developed the habit of depositing their savings with institutions known as finance companies. These institutions invested the money deposited with them, paying an interest to their depositors for the use of it. For the most part and in spite of the lesson of the previous decade they invested the money in new countries of the world and in enterprises such as railway building, which could not in the nature of things make any true profit for some years. Exports rose still further from £120 million a year to £138 million. The finance companies had however to pay their depositors immediately. It was clear then, once that these enterprises were financed on any considerable scale, that an appearance of dividends from, say, Canada or the Argentine could only be produced if somebody else in England could be induced, as he fondly imagined, to invest some more money in Canada and the Argentine—in reality, to give the finance companies the money with which to pay their depositor's interest. For the Canadians and the Argentinians themselves, so far from having an excess of exports over imports with which to pay dividends, on the contrary still needed an excess of imports over exports in order to live, and the people who travelled on the Canadian railways bought their tickets with money that came originally from the savings or creation of a British investor. Without those savings the Canadian railways could never have been made to appear to be earning a profit.

Now the effect of raising wages was to put money into the pockets of people who spent it on consumable goods and keep it out of the pockets of those who saved it and gave it to the finance companies. The finance companies, unable to collect new subscriptions, could only pay their dividends by selling their foreign investments. But who was there to buy them? There was nobody. The price of them collapsed. The companies went bankrupt. The depositors lost their money. Once more the cry was raised—the perfectly true cry—that the whole banking system was unsound. There was a rush for gold to the banks. The banks had not got the gold and demanded it from the Bank of England. The Bank of England had not got it. Once again the system of double-money collapsed, and for the third time the Bank Charter Act was suspended on 12th May, 1866. "Now their brief spring is over," wrote *The Times* [1] of the inhabitants of the East End of London. "There is no one to blame for this; it is the result of Nature's simplest laws."

There was, however, no important fall either in wholesale prices, in the price of bread, or in wages. Wholesale prices for 1865, 1866, and 1867 were 119, 120, 118. The 4 lb. loaf

[1] Quoted by Matthew Arnold, *Culture and Anarchy*, ed. Dover Wilson p. 190.

was 7·5*d.*, 8·8*d.*, and 10·3*d.* Wages were 66, 65, 65. The price of bread therefore immediately after the collapse was very high. It was indeed never again to be so high until the middle of the late War, 1917. The reason was that the harvest had failed. In spite of the Repeal of the Corn Laws there had been as yet no large reduction in the acreage in England under the plough, because owing to the Crimean War and the American Civil War there had been artificial obstacles to prevent the development of a large foreign supply of corn. As late as 1874 there were still 3,821,655 acres under wheat in comparison with about 4,000,000 before Repeal.[1] The price of corn was therefore still dependent on the British harvest, and the bad harvest of 1866 had sent that price up from just under 50*s.* a quarter to almost 64*s.* 6*d.* On top of the failure of the harvest came an outburst of rinderpest among cattle. Therefore in spite of deflation there was no fall in prices, because, since there was a reduction both of money and of goods, price, the proportion between them, was preserved. The working man in employment also was able to keep his wage—sometimes, as in the Sheffield murders, only by the aid of very desperate tactics. But there was less distributed in wages in sum total owing to the great increase of unemployment, which rose from 3 per cent to 7 per cent of the Trades Union membership.[2]

In 1868 began the first Prime Ministership of Gladstone, which lasted until 1874. At the time of his accession he found a country exporting indeed vastly more commodities than had been exported twenty years before but a country in which, in spite of that increase in productivity, the improvement in the working man's lot had been but trivial. If wages had been 50 in 1850, they were 65 in 1868—that is to say, they had multiplied by $\frac{13}{10}$. Prices, which were 92 in 1850, were 116 in 1868. Now $92 \times \frac{13}{10} = 119{\cdot}6$. On the other hand by the time that Gladstone left office in 1874, wages had risen to 78 and prices only to 130. Now $92 \times \frac{78}{50} = 143{\cdot}5$. Therefore during Gladstone's administration there was a substantial rise in real wages.

What was the cause of it? The cause was this. When

[1] See Sir John Russell's *The Farm and the Nation.*

[2] *Short History of the British Working Class Movement*, G. D. H. Cole, Appendix.

the Corn Laws had been repealed, Cobden, a man of high sincerity but of small foresight, had prophesied that their Repeal would be followed by the abolition of tariffs in all the European countries. An era of peace would be ushered in, and for the future Great Britain would live by exchanging her manufactured goods for the food of Europe. His mind, obsessed with the notion that international trade was in fact an exchange of goods against goods, confused by the appearance that Britain imported more than she exported because a high proportion of her imports were paid for by the vast invisible export of shipping and financial and insurance services, revolved in orbits remote from reality. He neglected the influence of loans.

The countries of Europe would have been mad had they thrown down their barriers. The awful experience of the years after Waterloo and the wisdom of List, the great German economist, were united to show to them what would necessarily be the result of such madness. Indeed, even had they wished to throw down their tariff barriers, it is doubtful if British manufacturing interests would have allowed them to do so. For there was an inherent contradiction in Cobdenite policy which from the first made it certain that it would be wrecked by its adherents if it was not first wrecked by its opponents. The object of British policy, said the Cobdenites, must be to export as much as possible. And, if Britain was to export as much as possible, then she had to export not only manufactured goods but also machines. But, however cheaply the machine was put on the market, no foreigner could be found to buy it, unless he could use it profitably, nor could he use it profitably unless he had tariff protection against Great Britain. Thus the Nottingham lace-manufacturer wanted France to have free trade in order that he might sell his lace there, but the Leeds machine-manufacturer wanted France to have protection in order that she might build up her own industries by the use of his machines.

No European country except Russia had any large surplus of food to export, nor had Great Britain at that date any large need for their food. It was not possible for them to procure a surplus by the depression of the standard of living of the producers of food, for that food was produced not, as in England, by a wage-paid propertyless labourer but by peasants who were themselves the owners of what they produced and who would not produce unless they were allowed to keep sufficient for themselves and their families. It was to the interest both of Cobden and of Marx, the prophets of industrialism, to argue from the wage-statistics that the Continental peasant was less well-off than the English working man. But the Continental peasant did not live on wages, and the conclusion was false, as Cobbett who judged by bellies and not by purses had demonstrated a generation before. For these reasons there was no possibility of any immediate large increase of food imports into Great Britain. There was indeed a possibility of a considerable increase in the imports of raw materials. But, on the other hand, if tariffs were brought down, there would, to answer it, be an immediate and proportionately much larger increase in British exports to the Continent—dumped goods exported on loan. The effect of the abolition of the tariffs would have been the capture of Europe by the English acceptance houses. For this the Continental powers were unwilling.

Thus the development of English life took a turn which Cobden had not at all foreseen. Great Britain had to make her investments and look for her markets outside Europe altogether. Some invested, as has already been said, in American railways, others in the low-wage countries of native labour—it was the age of Dalhousie and western improvements in India. But, profitable as investments in these non-European countries were, they were not worth making unless there was in power in London a Government that was willing to use force in order to compel the observance of contracts. Thus it came about that the effect of the Repeal of the Corn Laws was not at all to usher in an era of universal peace but to establish for his life as Prime Minister of Great Britain Lord Palmerston, ready to chastise at will Persians and Indians, Chinamen and Greeks. There was a mutiny in India, and there was also a Government ready to suppress the mutiny. "What had been an embarrassment to Castlereagh, a subject to be virtuously shunned for Canning, was appearing to Palmerston as an opportunity and as a right to be employed with discretion and was foreshadowed as a possible national duty." [1]

After the death of Palmerston and the resignation of his successor, Russell, the leadership of the new Liberal Party passed into the hands of Gladstone. Gladstone was in no way the inheritor of any liberal anti-imperialist tradition. The Conservatives rather than the Liberals were then the pacific party. Of the tradition of liberal anti-imperialism Gladstone was the creator rather than the creature. But Gladstone, like Shaftesbury, was a sincere Christian. And, just as Shaftesbury on Christian grounds had insisted on pressing for factory reform, even though he could not clearly show how it was reconcilable with the dogmas of the financial system, so Gladstone on Christian grounds insisted on breaking with the Palmerstonian policy of *Civis Romanus sum*, even though he too could not clearly show how such a breach was reconcilable with the dogmas of the system.

Gladstone breathed entirely the ambient air around him. This creature of the Victorian compromise had no talent at all for putting himself outside his time and clime and viewing it objectively. So there was no dramatic breach. There was no public recantation of the faith that the children must be sacrified to the great Moloch of the favourable balance of trade. There was no general understanding that the continuance of foreign investment was impossible unless a vigorously Imperialistic Government was to rule in London. Throughout these six years of his rule the balance was indeed still favourable. Foreign investments continued to mount up at an average rate of £61 million a year.[2] Our exports jumped up from some £180 million to £230 million—an increase, though not so large an increase as it seems when we remember that prices rose from 116 to 130.

But imports at the same time increased from £238 million to £291 million. Our so-called new foreign investments, large as they appeared, were not really doing much more than paying the dividends on our old foreign investments. They did not increase more rapidly because the investors could no longer feel that, whatever they did, the British navy

[1] *The Migration of British Capital to 1875*, L. H. Jenks, p. 125.
[2] *Europe, the World's Banker*, Feis, p. 11.

would be lent them for nothing to fetch in their dividends. And, without such a knowledge, the number of safe foreign investments was severely limited. Thus foreign investments, while increasing, were not able to increase as rapidly as productivity. Therefore an increased quantity of goods was thrown on to the home market. These goods could only be sold if wages were allowed to rise. When the market is in a different country to the factory, it pays the manufacturer to give low wages. But, when the market is in the same country as the factory, it pays the manufacturer at least to see to it that all other manufacturers give high wages. Therefore the result of Gladstone's pacific foreign policy was the growth of a public opinion in favour of higher wages. The Trades Unions were able to take advantage of this in order to improve the workers' standard of life.

Nevertheless in typically English fashion the foreign investing continued side by side with the pacific foreign policy and the attempt to combine the two was an attempt foredoomed to failure and clamouring for catastrophe. In 1873 the catastrophe came. A financial panic in America caused the New York Stock Exchange to be closed for ten days. The firm of Bischoffsheim and Goldschmidt—an English firm—underwrote a loan of £32 million for the Khedive of Egypt, and to their surprise were unable to unload it on the public. "The clever sponsors managed to get rid of the remainder in other ways."[1] Nevertheless the effect of the two incidents and of other similar incidents was to destroy at a blow any willingness in the public to invest its savings abroad.

In 1874 Gladstone fell from power and Disraeli succeeded to it. It is a commonplace that the life of late-nineteenth century England was dominated by the great figures of Gladstone and Disraeli, and many pages and many books have been filled with the pointing of the contrast between them. To our purpose it is enough to note this. Both of them were great men. A fool indeed may be pushed into a position of power by others or stumble into it. But a fool cannot impose himself on the minds of a nation as these two men did. The minds of both of them, as we can see from every line almost of Gladstone's diary and equally from all the

[1] *Short History of Investment*, Ripley, p. 105.

most pregnant passages of *Sybil* and *Coningsby* and *Tancred*, were filled full with realization of the uniqueness of the greatest of all forces in history—the religion of Christianity. In that they stood together and stood against all those shallow creatures of a day who dismissed, or who dismiss, it carelessly as a man-made thing or have not the curiosity even to inquire what it may be. Grossly untheological as it is, yet the English nation is never permanently and deeply influenced by anyone whose primary interest is not in theology. But in their attitudes to that unique force these two men differed radically.

Gladstone quite lacked the talent for scepticism. He accepted the faith which he had learnt in childhood. He obeyed its teaching fearlessly, conscientiously, and without regard to consequences, when he saw that teaching overtly challenged. But his very incapacity for scepticism prevented him from recognizing as such a challenge that was not overt. Of usury's unending challenge to Christianity he had but little comprehension. Disraeli's was a deeper mind. If Gladstone was the better Christian, Disraeli had the clearer understanding what Christianity was. He saw clearly that, if this message was true at all, it was explosive. The consequences of its truth must be to destroy the whole cosy Victorian compromise, Liberals and Conservatives, the financial system, the division of the Two Nations. He saw with astounding clearness that the whole revolution of 1688 was an anti-Christian revolution. But then was Christianity true? It was not in his blood to believe it so. If it was true, then all must go. But if it was not quite certain whether it was true or not—well, fighting the rich was very exhausting work. Would it not perhaps be more fun just to be Conservative Prime Minister? Speculation on the Christian faith remained a fascinating exercise to him; the practice of it was never an overmastering compulsion.

Thirty years before he had confided to old Lord Melbourne his "wild ambition" that one day he might be Prime Minister of England. Lord Melbourne was at the time himself Prime Minister. To him the Premiership was "a damned bore", which could not decently be avoided if one happened to belong to one of the governing families and not to be a congenital idiot—qualities but rarely coincidental. To the old cynic the prizes of life came too inevitably to be at all highly valued. To the young Jew from nowhere, to the flaming fighter of *Sybil* the battle of life presented itself with a different aspect, and in 1874 his hour had at last come. But a certain price had been paid for the victory. It was not the Disraeli of the 1840's who was Prime Minister; if it had been the Disraeli of the 1840's, he would not have been Prime Minister.

Chapter XIII

THE EXCEPTIONAL AUXILIARY

It was in that strange and powerful third chapter of *Sybil* that the Disraeli of the 1840's gave to the world his confession of faith. He showed himself there to have an understanding of the trick-history of the textbooks as deep as that of any man save perhaps Cobbett and Lingard alone. "If the history of England," he wrote, "be ever written by one who has the knowledge and the courage, and both qualities are equally requisite for the undertaking, the world would be more astonished than when reading the Roman annals by Niebuhr. Generally speaking, all the great events have been distorted, most of the important causes concealed, some of the principal characters never appear and all who figure are so misunderstood and misrepresented that the result is a complete mystification." The true story, he agreed with Cobbett, was that of "a mortgaged aristocracy, a gambling foreign commerce, a home trade founded on a morbid competition and a degraded people".

It was from 1688 that he traced the degradation. "If it be a salutary principle in the investigation of historical transactions to be careful in discriminating the cause from the pretext, there is scarcely any instance in which the application of this principle is more salutary than in that of the Dutch invasion of 1688. The real cause of this invasion was financial. . . . The prince came; he used our constitution for his purpose; he introduced into England the system of Dutch finance. The principle of that system was to mortgage industry in order to protect property; abstractedly nothing can be conceived more unjust; its practice in England has been equally injurious. . . . The system of Dutch finance, pursued more or less for nearly a century and a half, has ended in the degradation of a fettered and burthened multitude. Nor have the demoralizing consequences of the funding system on the more favoured classes been less decided. It has made debt a national habit ; it has made credit the ruling power, not the exceptional auxiliary, of all transactions ; it has introduced a loose, inexact, haphazard and dishonest spirit in the conduct of both public and private life ; a spirit dazzling and yet dastardly ; reckless of consequences and yet shrinking from responsibility."

Now what did Disraeli mean by saying that credit had become the "ruling power" and by his all-important phrase that it ought rather to be only the "exceptional auxiliary"?

It is clear enough what he meant by saying that it had become the "ruling power". In order that the world may do its business a certain supply of money is required. Now the system of "Dutch finance" has given to a handful of private individuals the right to invent by far the larger part of that supply and issue it out to producers as loans to be repaid after a certain time.

What is the consequence?

The consequence is this. Let us take this fountain-pen with which I am now writing. In order to produce this pen, as to produce any other article, the manufacturer has had to incur certain costs, and it is manifest that he cannot continue in business unless he can sell the pen for a sum at least equal to those costs. Now people do not really pay *for things*. Things are free. They pay money to *people*. The manufacturer indeed paid out some of his costs in wages to his employees ; he paid out others of them, it is true, for the purchase of his raw material or his machinery. But such payments, however many the stages through which we trace them back, were all made in the first place not for things but to people. Therefore, at first sight, it might appear that whatever the cost of manufacturing the pen, that money is somewhere circulating about in society, sufficient to buy the pen back.

However, this, as Major Douglas and his followers have truly shown, is by no means necessarily so. For in every process of production it is always necessary to spend before you can sell and to sow before you can reap. Where is the money for this preliminary spending to come from? Directly or indirectly it must, in the system of "Dutch finance", come out of the invention of a bank. Either the manufacturer borrows it directly from a bank, or he uses for his manufacturing some of his own or somebody else's savings. If he uses, say, £100 of his own savings, then he has £100 less to spend on other goods, and either goods to that value must go unsold, or else, somewhere or other in society, a bank must create £100 and issue it as a loan to someone who can buy them. For, by buying a machine, he has increased by one machine the quantity of goods on the market, but, unless a bank invents it, there is no increased monetary supply to buy that increased quantity.[1] Therefore every stage in the production of my pen was only made possible by the invention of money by a bank and its issue as a loan. But these loans have all to be repaid. The producer's costs consist not only of the payment of wages and salaries but also of the repayment of bank loans. And, when the loans are repaid, the money is simply cancelled from existence. The greater part of the loans are repaid long before the pen comes on the market. The new money is not created, as it should be, at the time that the article is thrown on to the market and cancelled at the time that the article, owing to the consumer's purchase, is taken off the market. It is created and cancelled at quite a different time. The whole system is, as Disraeli justly said, " loose, inexact, haphazard and dishonest."

Under a just and exact system anyone would be allowed to lend money that he possessed but no private person would be allowed to invent money. The Government would

[1] The objector may say : " But all that happens is that the £100 is transferred from the pen-maker to the machine-maker. The machine-maker can spend the £100 on consumable goods." That is to say, there is nothing to stop the same £100 being used twice in the period in which it had previously only been used once. The answer to that is that it is perfectly true that, with a greatly increased velocity of circulation, we could do our business with a much smaller monetary supply than we now use. But people have certain habits, and therefore in practice the velocity of circulation does not in fact greatly vary. It does not vary so long as the monetary system is working. It only varies when that system is already breaking down. That is to say, if prices are threatening to rise very rapidly then money begins to circulate much more rapidly because people are only anxious to turn their money into goods whether they want the goods or not. If prices look like falling then money circulates more slowly because people refrain from purchasing, thinking that they will get articles more cheaply to-morrow. But so long as the price-level is kept stable then they buy goods as they really want them, and the velocity of their real desires does not vary.

be under obligation to keep the price-level stable. When an increased quantity of goods was actually thrown on to the market and its presence was shown by the tendency of prices to fall, then the duty of the Government would be to put an increased monetary supply into the pockets of consumers in order to prevent that fall. It would be essential that that increased supply should be a gift and not a loan to be repaid. How it should be issued would depend on circumstances; the only necessity is that, to solve a problem of under-consumption, the money must be put into the pockets of the under-consumers. The simplest way is merely to unbalance the budget. In the same way, if for any reason there was a decrease in the quantity of goods on the market and prices were showing a tendency to rise, then the Government would call in money by raising more out of taxation than it required for its expenses.

Very different from that, however, was the system which Disraeli found. And it is clear that in that system, the system which still survives to-day, so far from there being an automatic sufficiency of money to buy the pen, the money in the public's pocket would, if matters were left so, automatically be insufficient by the amount of bank-loan repaid to the bank. It is only possible to sell the pen, if indeed it be possible, because the bank has, by the time that it comes on to the market, issued out again further money in the shape of new loans for the financing of new productive processes.

Little purpose can be served by embarking upon the sterile debate whether such a process can properly be described as one of a necessary deficiency of purchasing power. If the banks create new money sufficiently rapidly to buy the products as they come on to the market, there is indeed no deficiency of purchasing power, and it is true enough that a banker who understands his business understands that—at any rate under normal circumstances—it is against his interest to allow such a deficiency. But the debate about the mere quantity of purchasing power obscures the truth which Disraeli saw so clearly—the truth that the banker can freely choose *which pockets* he will fill with that purchasing power. The producer dare not raise a finger in protest against him, for to all protests he can answer, " Very well, then I will not issue the loans at all. I will make your goods unsaleable and thus drive you into bankruptcy." By consequence the banker, able to control the pockets of the purchasers, is able to dictate the sort of goods that a country must produce. It was this that Disraeli saw and, seeing it, saw how foolish and remote from reality was the Cobdenite rhetoric about each country producing those goods which it was best suited to produce. Each country produced those goods which its bankers told it to produce. And the bankers had told England to stop producing food and instead to produce capital goods for export.

Now let us try and see what degree of reality there is behind this façade of unreality, which is the credit system. Let us forget for the moment all about money, the ticket, and consider the metaphysics of debt in terms of real goods. The traditions of mankind have approved the institution of private property on the ground that men are in general happier and work more efficiently if, as far as possible, they are allowed to own the land on which they work, the raw materials and tools with which they work, and the product of their labour. If that tradition be not a sound one, then there is no reason in private property at all. If on the other hand it be a sound one, then clearly it is necessary not only that private property should exist but also that it should be widely distributed. There are no arguments for private property which are not also arguments for widely distributed private property. For clearly, if property is concentrated in a few hands, then neither is the majority able to own the property which it uses nor the minority to use the property which it owns. Private property ceases to be something which the owner uses and becomes instead something which the owner charges somebody else for using.

Now, so long as the credit system survives, it is folly to waste time on debating the secondary issue whether the institution of landlordism or the private ownership of factories is beneficial. For, so long as a few people have the privilege of inventing money, no one in the country except those few people can really possess private property at all. The rest of us in our fancied property are but tenants-at-will of the bankers in the sense that the bankers can at any time that they wish force us to surrender it. It is idle to say that in practice this does not happen. In practice it happens every day. Two hundred years ago Berkeley prophesied that it would happen. One hundred years ago Cobbett showed that it was happening. To-day we can see it happening around us. Crushed down by the burden of rates and taxes, raised to pay the interest on a debt to fundholders who are themselves in debt to the banks, the old landowners one after another give up the struggle. "The last sad squire rides slowly towards the sea,"[1] little understanding perhaps even in the hour of eviction whose was the strong and secret power that snapped the history of his ancient race. A few only struggle on by themselves taking to usury. If there be a Conservative cause it is the cause of the battle against this power, nor indeed was there any dispute about that, until in this century the Conservative party was invaded by the battalions of big business. "In democracies," wrote [2] Lord Salisbury, Disraeli's successor, "the capitalist seems to have a crushing power—so long as he is content to leave political distinctions to other people." It was to prevent that crushing power that Conservatism existed.

Now consider what would be the nature of debt, if instead of the credit system we had a property system. Under such a system men would as a general rule own a little property—the land on which they lived and the land on which they worked or, if they worked in a co-operative enterprise, then they would own a share in the enterprise. They would start life with a certain stock of money. After all what is money but a ticket, the surrender of which entitles us to become possessors of the appropriate quantity of such goods of our fellow-citizens as they choose to throw upon the market? And how can we play at that game of exchange and barter unless we start with sufficient counters to play it with? that is to say, unless the normal family is the unencumbered possessor of a sum of money neither wildly more nor wildly less than its fair, mathematical share of the national income? "Riches," said the great Lord Bacon, "are like muck, which stink in a heap but, spread abroad, make the earth fruitful." It is not necessary that our stocks

[1] *The Secret People*, G. K. Chesterton.
[2] *Salisbury*, Cecil, iv, 93.

of money should be equal to one another to a sixpence; what is necessary is that all of us together, all consumers, should between us have sufficient money to buy the consumable goods which the producers among us are offering for sale.

When we play at *vingt-et-un*, we are each, as we sit down at the table, given a certain number of counters. If at the end of the evening we have more than our original number, we say that we have won; if less, that we have lost. But we do not go into debt unless by misfortune we have lost all our counters. We are not such fools as to think that we are in debt to the bank for the original counters that were given us to play the game with. We can see that, if that were so, the game would be an idiot's game, for then the bank could not possibly lose nor anybody else possibly win. Yet that is precisely the system by which the business of the world is conducted under the credit-system.

Under the property system then the average man will be the possessor of sufficient property and money to enable him to perform the normal business of life without going into debt. It is true that on occasion men would embark on some enterprise that would not of its nature produce its results in marketable goods for a long period—for a period so long that those engaged on it could not keep themselves on their own money. During the interval then, in whatever monetary language we choose to describe the business, they would have to live on the consumable goods produced by others and for which they were at the moment giving nothing in return. They would have, that is to say, to go into debt. That is what Disraeli meant by saying that real credit is an " exceptional auxiliary ". Monetary debt under the credit system is universal, inevitable, and irrepayable; real debt is comparatively rarely incurred and soon liquidated. Establish a true monetary system which only reckons people to be in debt when they really are in debt, and the problem shrinks from its present dominating proportions to proportions proper and manageable.

So far Disraeli went, but there was a necessary consequence to his teaching which he never had the courage to preach, though it is not to be believed that he did not have the intelligence to see it. The life of society is a continuing life.

Therefore we do not apply all our labour to the production of consumable goods to-day. We divert a proportion of our labour to the production of capital goods, to-day useless but necessary because without them it would be impossible to maintain and perhaps increase the supply of consumable goods to-morrow. Those who work on these capital goods and immediately produce nothing must nevertheless consume. Whatever our economic system, those who produce directly, or indirectly, consumable goods must somehow be compelled or persuaded to surrender a proportion of their product for the consumption of the producers of capital goods.

How is that surrender to be arranged?

The Socialist would do it by compulsion. He would take from the producer by force and by taxation a proportion of his product, and with that proportion feed the worker on the capital goods. The capitalist system professes to do it by persuasion. By the device of interest it offers to the possessor of claims on consumable goods that, if he will allow the producers of capital goods to-day to consume in his place, he will in return be allowed to consume somewhat more to-morrow.

The plan is not in itself an unreasonable one. It is indeed unreasonable that a man should be allowed merely to lend money—to lend £100 to-day and to be repaid £105 next year, irrespective of what has happened to the value of the pound in the interval or of what use has been made of that particular £100. But there is no injustice in his allowing another to work on his surplus goods with the understanding that, if, as a result of that work, the number of consumable goods is increased, the surplus shall be divided between the original abstainer and the worker. There is no objection, that is, to benefiting from breeding where there really has been breeding. It is indeed wise and healthy policy for the working partners to buy out the sleeping partners as soon as they are able to do so, but there is no essential injustice in partnership as such. To-day, it is true, with a fluctuating price-level, it is so little possible to tell what will sell, that people dare not risk their savings in ordinary shares and have to have recourse to the usurious dodges of gilt-edged securities and debentures. But with a stable price-level, with a sufficiency of purchasing power to buy the goods that come on to the market, an article would only be unsellable because it was really so unattractive that people would rather not possess it than possess it. Under such circumstances there would be no difficulty in finding securities that really were secure.

Yet, though the right to invest is not an unreasonable right, out of the concession of that right there has arisen the wholly unreasonable notion that all money saved has, as it were, a natural right to interest and that, where there is not an augmentation of savings, there has been a violation of the rights of property—a notion that has only to be stated in its nakedness to be seen to be clearly untrue. A gentleman of independent means, living on the dividends of inherited money, sometimes talks as if he were living on his grandfather's savings. Monetarily he is, but in fact he is eating not the surplus corn produced by his grandfather sixty years ago, but corn annexed from the producers of this year's crop. The system may be right or it may be wrong, but at least that is the system—a system as little respectful of the maxim, " Let him that soweth also reap," as is that of the Communists. Indeed the very phrase " independent means " is a phrase of folly. How can anyone except the chameleon have means that depend on nobody?

Real, and not merely monetary, considerations clearly dictate that, at any given moment in a society's history, such and such a proportion of its labour should be given to capital, such and such a proportion to consumable goods, the particular proportion of course being dependent upon particular circumstances. The first business of an economic system is to produce the necessities of life for all a country's citizens. That business accomplished, it is for the citizens themselves to decide what proportion of their surplus labour they will devote to the production of luxuries and what proportion to capital goods with their promise of benefit in the future. A just monetary system is a system of voting which ensures that that division is made in accordance with the wishes of the inhabitants.

Now, if it is reasonable to reward those who save more when more saving is required, it is obviously equally reasonable to penalize those who save more when less saving is required. At a time, when the great need is not the production of new capital goods but the consumption of the consumable goods that have been produced already, further saving is not a service but a disservice to the community. There is no opening for investment of the money saved and therefore no possibility of transferring it to the pockets of those who will spend it on consumable goods. As Mr. Keynes has so well shown,[1] the money is in fact not invested but hoarded, whether it be put physically into a stocking or be put into a bank which cannot profitably use it. The money is for practical purposes put out of circulation, and consequently the volume of purchasing power available to purchase the consumable goods that have already been produced, already insufficient, is still further decreased. Under such circumstances, so far from rewarding further savings, a wise government would penalize them, taxing them on some such plan as that of Sylvio Gesell, so that, if their first possessor did not spend them on consumable goods, they would at any rate pass into the hands of somebody who would. If it did not tax the hoarded money, it would at the least replace it by new purchasing power sufficient to keep up the price-level.

Private property has its rights. It would be immoral to take from a man his real possession. But money is not a real possession; it is a claim on goods. He can exercise that claim, if he wants to, but he cannot both retain the claim and refuse to exercise it—which is what he does when he hoards. The man who refuses to buy and yet keeps the money prevents anybody else from buying either—or at any rate—what is essentially the same thing at one further remove—he compels the producer to sell at a loss and thus in his turn to buy less. In monetary affairs, as in every other affair of life, a right that is never exercised must after the passage of a certain time necessarily lapse. Credit should be the "exceptional auxiliary". If nobody happens to want to borrow, then there must be no lending. To make it a grievance that you cannot lend your money at usury is an absurdity. If you won't spend it and can't lend it, you ought to give it away to others of richer personality. What happens in fact is that you crowd to buy shares with

[1] *Treatise on Money* and *Essays in Persuasion.*

it and shares therefore rise to an absurd height. You lose your money in the end. You do in fact give it away—to the speculator who is shrewd enough to sell just before the market breaks. How much more sensible, what much better economics, to have put it all in the poor-box in the first place !

There are times when thrift is a virtue. There are other times when it is a grievous vice, nor is there any single habit of human nature which has so large a share of the responsibility for bringing us to the verge of catastrophe as has that of excessive thrift. The harm that has been done by spendthrifts is in comparison small, for bankruptcy soon puts an end to their riot. But the miser goes on saving until society collapses. The financial system has, as Mr. Keynes fairly claims,[1] " exalted some of the most distasteful of human qualities into the position of the highest virtues." " The love of money as a possession " is in reality " a somewhat disgusting morbidity, one of those semi-criminal, semi-pathological propensities which one hands over with a shudder to the specialists in mental diseases."[2] Or, as another and even greater economist put it in language even more outspoken, it is " the root of *all* evil ".

[1] *Essays in Persuasion*, p. 369.
[2] Ibid.

Chapter XIV

DISRAELI'S RULE

In 1874 there came to Disraeli his true opportunity of power. Perhaps, when history has had time to settle her final verdict, she will decide that his chief contribution to British life was the renewed prestige which he gave to the monarchy. In our day even the strongest enemies of the established order, such as Sir Stafford Cripps and Mr. Lansbury, have, in defiance of consistent principles, to go out of their way to express their esteem for the institution of monarchy. And those who are not read in the journalism of the time can hardly form a picture of the disrepute into which the monarchy had fallen in the early years of the 1870's, owing to Victoria's prolonged seclusion after the death of the Prince Consort. As Lord Morley truly records, " A deep and universal feeling of discontent at the Queen's seclusion found voice in the journals of the country." [1] An offensive pamphlet, entitled *What Does She Do With It?* criticized the alleged vastness of her fortune. The creed of republicanism was growing rapidly.

Disraeli truly saw that the monarchy was the one institution in England which transcended the barriers of class and that the revival of its popularity was necessary to break down the division of the Two Nations. In this, as in so much else that he did, it is difficult to assign the exact proportion in his motive between cynicism and conviction. Certainly he was shrewd enough to see that it was a practical advantage to have cordial personal relations with the occupant of the throne, and such relations, he is alleged to have confessed in a moment of unusual frankness, were more easily established if one " laid on flattery with a trowel ". At the same time, while it would perhaps be an exaggeration to say that the monarchy in the last fifty years has had a predominating influence over the life of England, it would certainly be true to say that our life has been predominatingly influenced by the fact that England is a monarchical

[1] *Gladstone*, Morley, ii, 425.

country. Of the importance in the history of India of the proclamation of the Queen as Empress of India the present writer is hardly qualified to speak; of its importance in the history of England there can be no question.

But the largest immediate contribution of Disraeli to English life was the contribution of the new gospel of Imperialism. As was said in a previous chapter, Gladstone had attempted to pursue Palmerston's methods of foreign lending while abandoning Palmerston's methods of debt-collection and the result had been catastrophe. Disraeli had succeeded to power to find the foreign investment market in ruins. The average annual export of British capital, which from 1870 to 1874 was £61 million a year, from 1875 to 1879 was £1·7 million a year.[1] It was calculated in 1878 that of the British loans to foreign governments, which amounted to £613,988,000, £332,160,000, or 54 per cent, were in default.[2] The proportion of private loans in default was far higher.

Disraeli had a choice of alternatives. The Cobdenite dream of free trade and peace lay irretrievably in ruins. The first alternative was to follow a pacific policy and to refuse to allow British arms to be used for what was in effect the forcing of loans down the throats of unwilling borrowers, to follow a policy which would result in the export of capital, if it should be exported at all, only to such countries as the United States, who genuinely desired it and who would honour their obligations not because they were compelled to do so by the big stick, but because they appreciated the importance of good credit in order to enable them to borrow again in the future. The second alternative was to encourage the forcing of loans on the low-wage countries by making it clear that the British army and navy would always be available as debt-collectors and debt-protectors.

It is hard not to believe that in Disraeli's preference of the second to the first of these alternatives there was more than a touch of cynicism. There had been no trace of Imperialism in the old Disraeli of the repeal days. He had voted in the majority with Cobden and Gladstone to

[1] *Europe, the World's Banker*, Feis, p. 11.
[2] *Short History of Investment*, Ripley, p. 102.

defeat Palmerston over his bullying of the Chinese in 1857. He had protested against the severity with which the Indian mutiny had been suppressed. There had been no Conservative tradition of Imperialism. On the other hand he was shrewd enough to see that, unless a policy was adopted which gave a promise of further loans in the future, it would not be possible to induce the present debtors to pay their dividends on the past loans. True enough, to the eyes of an ultimate observer this policy of lending more in order that you can pretend to yourself that you have been paid past debts was a fool's policy, inevitably destined for eventual catastrophe. But Disraeli in 1874 was not an ultimate observer. He was a tired old man, anxious to cut a splash before he died. His eyes were set, as he himself had said of Peel thirty years before, "not on posterity but on the coming quarter-day."[1]

He knew that the money power had been caught napping by the collapse of 1873 and it needed the revived confidence in foreign lending which Imperialism would give in order to unload its holdings. Eventual catastrophe was indeed highly probable, but the system would last his life-time and a little longer. There were "ancestral voices prophesying war", but only war in the time of his grandchildren. If he worked within the system, he might achieve something before he died. If he challenged it, it would break him and he would go down to history a failure. If he worked within it, he would perhaps leave behind him a record of solid achievement and at last cause society to pay back to the poor a little bit of that gigantic debt which it owed to them. If he challenged it, he would accomplish nothing and leave the world a lonely voice. Would any other that came after him do for the poor even what he could do for them? And, as for the distant catastrophe, who could tell what the shape of the future would be? Let the teeth that are set on edge themselves invent a way of sweetening the grapes!

As a political tactician, he was quick to see that Gladstone's repudiation of Palmerston's jingoism gave to an astute Conservative an opportunity to take advantage of a mood which Liberals had aroused but were no longer willing to satisfy. As early as 1866 he had laid down the

[1] *Disraeli, the Alien Patriot*, Raymond, p. 136.

doctrine that Great Britain had " outgrown the European Continent. . . . Her position," he said,[1] " is no longer that of a mere European power. England is the metropolis of a great maritime Empire, extending to the boundaries of the furthest ocean. . . . She is as ready, and as willing even, to interfere as in the old days, when the necessity of her position requires it. There is no power indeed which interferes more than England. She interferes in Asia because she is really more of an Asiatic than a European power." And it was, it seems, after the defeat of the Conservative Government, which had just passed the Reform Bill of the previous year, in the general election of 1868 that he took a deliberate and a somewhat cynical decision. There was perhaps a certain cynicism in his opposition to a Reform Bill when proposed by the Liberal party; there was no cynicism in his carrying a Reform Bill himself. To a Tennysonian Liberal a second Reform Bill was to be supported on the somewhat muzzy grounds, that, with freedom slowly broadening down, Reform Bills were the kind of things that ought to get passed from time to time. But to a Disraelian Conservative a second Reform Bill was to be supported not to complement but to counteract the first Reform Bill. To Disraeli the first Reform Bill had not been merely a vaguely progressive measure; it had been the definitive establishment in power of a particular class—the plutocracy—whose influence over the state he thought pernicious. To him it was wise statesmanship to call in democracy to redress the balance of plutocracy.

And it was precisely because he did pass the second Reform Bill in that spirit that it was a grave disappointment to him, when he found that the democracy, so far from sharing his ambition for its emancipation, on the contrary voted sheepishly liberal, for the continuance of that very system from which he offered to emancipate it. It was then, I think, that he decided, as Townshend had decided a hundred and fifty years before, that it was not possible to capture the British public except by offering them some sort of " bunk " or other. He therefore wrote the preposterous *Lothair*, which must be judged as an electioneering dodge rather than as a literary production—as a kind of pledge that he would

[1] Speech at Aylesbury, 13th July, 1866.

never again show himself so lacking in good taste as to talk sense about religion—and gave himself to the trumpeting of the most convenient "bunk", which was that of Imperialism.

Therefore he inaugurated the policy of vigorous adventure —the Suez Canal shares, "peace with honour" in Berlin, war without it in Zululand and Afghanistan. There was a Turkish public debt, owed mainly to London investors, and, when in April, 1876, the British Government joined with the other powers in urging on the Sultan reform in the Government of his Christian subjects, the Sultan replied by withholding the current dividend. It was the beginning of the troubles which led to the murder of Sultan Abdul Aziz and the substitution for him of his brother, Abdul Hamid, pledged to punctual payment, who, presuming on the support which that pledge would win for him, proceeded to insult the Russians and to goad them into war.[1]

The immediate advantage of a revival of foreign lending would have been, of course, that it would have caused a diminution of unemployment. But owing to the rumours of war with which his policy was attended Disraeli was unable to secure such a revival. Investors like to know that the overwhelming force of the British navy will be used to coerce recalcitrant and helpless "natives", but they do not like rumours of wars with Great Powers on both sides. It is therefore the paradox of Disraeli's policy that during all the nineteenth century there was in no period so little foreign lending as in that of his Premiership. As a result unemployment did not decrease; it steadily increased. Its percentages were 1·7 in 1874, 2·4 in 1875, 3·7 in 1876, 4·7 in 1877, 6·8 in 1878, and 11·4 in 1879.[2]

But, on the other hand, it can fairly be claimed for Disraeli's policy that it did show to the would-be borrowers that London was unwilling to lend, not from any radical change of policy but because of their own disturbed conditions. Hoping therefore for favours to come, they were willing to discharge fairly satisfactorily their obligations on past loans. As a result, while exports remained steady, imports greatly increased. Exports from 1870 to 1874 averaged £234·8

[1] *Political History of England*, Low and Sanders, p. 181.
[2] *Introduction to the Study of Prices*, W. T. Layton.

million a year and from 1875 to 1879 £201·5 million—which was not a diminution at all if we remember that prices fell during that period from 130 to 98. On the other hand imports rose from an average of £290·6 million in 1870–4 to £319·5 million in 1875–9—a very considerable rise on a falling price-level.

Disraeli was far too intelligent a man to think it important to have a favourable balance of trade. All that was important was to pretend that you were going to have a favourable balance one day—to pretend that one day you would start lending again. For the moment an unfavourable balance was an advantage, because it meant that there were more goods to be distributed. How were those goods distributed under Disraeli's rule ? The common opinion was that the years were years of distress, but common opinion is sometimes more apt to notice its grievances than its windfalls. It grumbles at a fall in wages and does nor notice a fall in prices ; it grumbles at a rise in prices and does not notice a rise in wages. Thus there is no doubt that wages did fall during Disraeli's rule. They fell from 78 in 1874 to 73 in 1879. On the other hand, prices fell a great deal more steeply. General wholesale prices fell from 130 in 1874 to 98 in 1879 ; the price of the 4 lb. loaf had already fallen, before Disraeli's accession, from 9·8*d*. in 1872 to 8·9*d*. in 1873, and 7·3*d*. in 1874. By 1879 it had fallen further to 7·1*d*. Therefore, though Gladstone's era was one of rising nominal wages and Disraeli's one of falling nominal wages, the workmen in employment gained a much more substantial advance in real wages during Disraeli's period than during that of Gladstone. On top of that it must be remembered that Disraeli's rule saw the beginning of a vigorous policy of social reform. The provision of services to the poor, though indeed an inadequate, and even a dangerous, substitute for the provision of decent wages, sufficient to enable them to buy the necessities of life for themselves, is at any rate better than a policy which provides for them neither the wages nor the services. Whatever may be said against Disraeli, there is this to be said for him. His cynicism never went so far as to teach him either that poverty was irremediable or that it ought to be called so for the sake of political advantage.

Another reason for the continuance of unemployment, besides that of the absence of foreign investments, was the falling price-level. For with a falling price-level it is no advantage to the manufacturer to produce, even though all the markets of the world be offered to him for his goods. For he must sell at a loss, and therefore to increase his sales is but to increase his losses. But why, it will be asked, was there a falling price-level? Obviously, with imports increasing, there were more goods in the country. More money was required if the price-level was to be kept stable. But in fact there was less money, since the financiers could not put out new money by lending to foreign borrowers and would not put it out by lending to domestic borrowers, having become accustomed through their experience of foreign lending to a swollen notion of what was a proper rate of interest and being unable to get such a rate from the domestic borrower. It is true that the deflation itself caused a shrinkage of the production of manufactured goods but the primary producer is not able quickly to adjust his supply to effective demand and has therefore to suffer in a fall of his prices.

There was a further reason for deflation. The country was on gold. For more money more gold was required. But there was not more gold but less. On the one hand, the supplies from the new Californian and Australian mines were beginning to dry up. In 1875 production for the first time for twenty-five years fell below £20 million. On the other hand, the sudden adoption of the gold standard by Germany, France, and the United States, the three most important industrial countries in the world after Great Britain, diverted the flow of new gold from London. After the Franco-Prussian War the new German Empire found that Holland and the Scandinavian countries, alone in Europe, were their companions in the maintenance of a purely silver monetary standard. The rest of Eastern Europe had gone on to inconvertible paper. Such a standard therefore imposed on Germany all the disadvantages of the double-money system without giving her even the advantage of stable exchange rates with the most important countries of the world. She therefore determined to transfer herself to a gold standard in order to obtain the advantage of a stable exchange with England. The gold received from France in payment of the indemnity for the War of 1870 provided her with a stock sufficient to encourage her to the experiment of a withdrawal of silver money and an issue of gold in its place. Yet, in order to effect the exchange, it was necessary for her to buy—that is to say, to exchange for silver—£50,000,000 more of gold—an exchange which she made during the years 1872–4. The total world's stock of monetary gold was at that date only about £500,000,000.[1]

Now the effect of Germany selling silver and buying gold on this scale was, of course, to make silver enormously more common and gold enormously more scarce in every other country of Europe. The countries of the Latin Union—France, Italy, Belgium, and Switzerland—had up till then been on a bimetallic standard, under which gold was valued as 15½ times more valuable than silver. The effect of the German policy was to make silver in France less valuable in terms of gold. Therefore, naturally enough, it was no longer to anyone's interest to bring in any gold to be coined, for, by turning his gold into coin, he would be robbing himself, for, as coin, he only got 15½ times its weight in silver. If he sold it by weight he could get about 25 times. Therefore, with the relative values of the two metals shifting so rapidly, bimetallism was impossible and the Latin countries, if they were to stick to metallic money, had to choose between a gold standard and a silver standard. A gold standard gave stable exchange-rates with Great Britain. It meant deflation and favoured the creditor; a silver standard meant inflation and favoured the debtor. The creditor won and the Latin countries, too, went on to the gold standard. So, too, did Holland and the Scandinavian countries, countries hitherto on silver but unwilling now to face the large inflation which German policy would impose upon them. Each of these actions contributed to send up the price of gold. Yet in Great Britain, so long as she adhered to the gold standard, the price of gold in terms of money could not go up. Therefore the price of money in terms of goods had to go up. Or, in other words, prices came down.

At the same time the United States, in order to fight the Civil War, had had to resort to an inconvertible paper

[1] *The Gold Standard in Theory and Practice*, R. G. Hawtrey, p. 75.

currency. But so weak was the credit of the Northern Government that it had only been able to borrow its War loans from its own citizens on the promise that it would repay in gold. Therefore after the war it had not the normal debtor's interest in preventing deflation. On the contrary, if it had to pay in gold anyway, it was to its advantage to get the country back to gold. But it was also to its advantage to get or keep as much gold as possible, in order to make the price of gold in terms of goods as small as possible. Therefore, while the German Government was collecting gold for one reason, the French for a second, the American was collecting it for a third. There was little left to come to England. It was impossible to cure the slump—not because there was not the productive capacity to produce more goods, but because there was not sufficient gold at the apex of the inverted pyramid of credit to finance the increased productivity. Whether the Germans, the French, and the Americans were wise or unwise, it is beyond our thesis to inquire. But what a system—a system that punished with atrophy the whole productive life of England because of other policies that were no more connected with that life than were the activities of the man in the moon !

Disraeli's years brought up a further problem. Our debtors, we have said, were anxious to fulfil their obligations ; they therefore sent us goods. Imports increased. So they did. But imports of what ? In what goods could they pay ? They could only pay in food. Therefore British agriculture must be destroyed. When the payment of dividends is at stake, then, as Byron truly put it,

> " corn, like every mortal thing, must fall,
> Kings, conquerors, and markets most of all."

The cheap corn began to pour in from America. English plough land went out of cultivation ; the agricultural labourers drifted off into the towns. For five years—from 1874 to 1879—the strength of habit was sufficient to keep up rents. Then with the disastrous harvest of that latter year they, too, collapsed. Agriculturalists, remembering Disraeli's protectionist past, appealed to him for reciprocity, or fair trade, as protection was then called. But he answered them with a snub. "The fact is," he said,[1] "speaking generally, that reciprocity, whatever its merits, is dead," and declined to argue the point. The fact also was that the towns now returned more members to Parliament than the country and that the landed classes were but tepid in their demand for a remedy. For the movement of which Disraeli had shrewdly noted the beginnings thirty years before in *Sybil* had now developed and the landed classes had themselves for the most part gone over to usury. Dependent now upon their foreign investments for their living, they had come to look on farming as the background rather than the business of life. It is true that they resisted the reduction of rents as long as possible. Yet, when reduction came, they almost prided themselves on losing money out of their lands. It gave them an amateur status. Their minds closed to reality by the educational system, they did not see how on every article they bought they paid a tribute to the inventors of money nor did they understand that what the credit system did with its bank-loans and their investments was secretly to rob them of sixpence and then to give them back twopence with a great palaver of publicity. Disraeli took advantage of their stupidity.

The other sufferers from Disraeli's policy were the Trades Unions, as always the sufferers from unemployment and even the appearance of falling wages. Under his rule the Trades Unions gained in privileges but they lost in numbers. At the time of his accession to power they had raised themselves to a strength wholly unprecedented. In 1872 they had a membership of 1,191,822. By 1880 they had sunk to 494,222.

It was the breaking of English agriculture that really for the first time showed the necessary consequences of Imperialism and foreign lending. That such a policy is in a purely arithmetical sense immediately a loss to the mother country hardly admits of dispute, as the quotation from Professor Pigou[2] on a previous page has shown. That is to say, in its first years the mother country will have to send out to the colony more £'s worth of goods than it will receive in return. Suppose, however, that

[1] House of Lords, 29th April, 1879.
[2] See Chapter viii, p. 96.

the colony possesses some raw material, necessary for the mother country's manufactures and unobtainable elsewhere; it may be wise for the mother country to submit to this arithmetical loss. Thus, even though it should prove impossible to repatriate some of the money invested in it, it has probably been a wise policy of ours to develop jute-growing in India. So, too, with the previously uninhabited countries of the Empire which are suitable for colonization. Once we understand that the productive capacity even of the old European world was quite sufficient to make it a world of abundance, it is clearly folly to treat the problem of the development of the new world merely as an economic one. It is most arguable that the unhappiness that has been caused by emigration has been so great as not to justify its increase of productivity. But there can be no question that the development of the new lands has increased the productivity of the world and that that development would not have been possible had not the old lands in the early years given the new lands the goods with which to start their lives.

If then we had decided in favour of spreading out our English population through the countries of the Empire, it was necessary that we should export to those countries a quantity of capital goods in return for which we could immediately receive no equivalent import. But was it wise to make a loan of those goods? Where there was no prospect of a liquidation of the debt within a few years, would it not have been better to have sent them frankly as gifts? Immediately, it makes no difference whether you give away £1 or lend it, nor, if it is not possible properly to be repaid the loan, does it make any difference even in the long run. And, as has been already argued, on balance we have not been repaid our loans by Dominion borrowers and it is hardly conceivable that we ever shall be repaid. On the other hand, the necessity of keeping up an illusion of repayment in order to persuade new lenders to lend the money to pay the dividends to old lenders has had a most disastrous effect on the freedom of our own productive life. If we had sent out to Canada with our early emigrants a free gift of the capital necessary to set the country going, we could then to-day decide on the merits of the question whether we preferred to grow our own corn or to import Canadian corn in exchange for our manufactured goods. As long as international trade is a goods trade, we do not export unless we want to import. But, when it is a loan trade, our conduct is dictated by no such balance of reason ; it is irresponsible. The capitalists make their investments in Canada or the Argentine with little consideration whether in twenty years' time those countries will be producing any goods that we require or not. And therefore, when the time for dividends comes, we have to take Canadian corn or Argentinian beef, whether we want it or not.

For we must, even at the expense, if necessary, of our own industry and agriculture, bring it about that there is some article which we import in large quantities from each of our creditors. Or at least we must see to it that we have large imports and each of our debtors large exports. Theoretically, it is true, the dividends could have been paid through trade with a third country. But practically there was no solution that way. For our debtors only exported food, and all the countries which imported any other sorts of goods into Great Britain were themselves almost self-supporting in food.

When we reflect on the top of that on the complications which the problems of debts have imported into every international question, of the delays which they have caused in the settlement of every difficulty, of the enormous share of the struggle for markets in the responsibility for the wars of the world, of the swollen armaments which it has been necessary to maintain for the support of the foreign investor in every quarter of the globe, when we reflect how small is the proportion of those debts that has ever been, or will ever be, repaid, can we hesitate in assenting to the apparent paradox that the world would have been the happier and we would have been the richer, had every penny which we exported on loan from Great Britain in the nineteenth century been exported frankly as a gift ? As even Sir George Paish, one of the strongest defenders of international lending, admits,[1] " Were every possible assistance and facility given to the debtor nations, to whom so much

[1] *Lloyd's Bank Monthly Review* (December, 1930).

credit has been granted or upon whom has been placed the duty of making reparations, to perform their tasks, the difficulty of meeting their obligations would still be exceedingly great." "Under conditions now imposed," he continues, "these tasks are quite impossible of performance."

In 1880 Disraeli's rule came to an end. He lingered on for a year, but then died in 1881. The sober pages of Monypenny and Buckle record all that is known, and indeed all that is probable, of the stories of his death-bed. Yet it is a proof of the strange power which this man of mystery exercised over the imaginations of Englishmen that there still linger upon the lips of gossips two striking stories, which bear witness not perhaps how he died but at least how men thought such an artist should have died.

According to the one story there came to his death-bed a priest of the Catholic Church, and he was there received a member of that enduring Body to which in his lifetime he had paid every tribute except that of submission—in *Sybil* the tributes of honour and understanding and respect, in *Lothair* the tributes of anger and misrepresentation. According to the other—artistically perhaps the more probable—the watchers bent low over the dying man. They heard strange murmuring in an unknown tongue. It was the ancient Hebrew "*Shaman Israel Israel Adonai Ehod*", "Hear, Israel, God, your God, is one God"—the oldest of all the professions of his race.[1] God was gracious, for at last to him it had been granted to bring the day of recompense. He, a member of the despised and Chosen Race, had imposed himself as the ruler of the navies of the proudest of Christian Empires, the creator of a Christian Empress, the friend of a Christian Queen, the mocker of Christian things, and the teacher of them to a proud and ignorant generation. He had made himself the first figure of that which in *Tancred* he had called with a splendid insolence "the intellectual colony of Arabia, once called Christendom".

In the *Recollections* of Princess Radziwill there is a story in which we come perhaps as near to a vision of that enigmatic soul as it is possible to get. At the height of the triumph of Berlin there was a party one evening. The statesmen and the diplomats of Europe were present at

[1] For this story I am indebted to Mr. G. K. Chesterton.

it. Lord Beaconsfield came in a little late, and, as his name was announced, the buzz of every conversation ceased and all Christian eyes were turned upon him. He stood near the door, looking round on the company with lazy pride. " What are you thinking of ? " the Princess whispered to him. " I am not thinking at all," he answered. " I am enjoying myself." [1]

[1] English ed., 1900, p. 149.

CHAPTER XV

IRELAND

The closing years of Beaconsfield saw the first appearance in parliamentary politics of a new and strange force of incalculable importance. It has been argued that party government is only possible when both the parties are substantially in agreement, and up till this time all the parliamentary politicians of consequence, whatever else their differences, were at least united in their desire that the system should work. In the last years of the 1870's there appeared in politics Charles Steuart Parnell—a man who differed profoundly from the leading politicians, who saw clearly that his difference would make the system unworkable, who intended to make the system unworkable.

" What is the Irish question ? " Disraeli had asked [1] some forty years before, and he had answered with truth and cynicism, " One said it was a physical question another a spiritual ; now it was the absence of the aristocracy, then the absence of railways. It was the Pope one day, potatoes the next." In all the answers there was truth. But, overriding them all, predominant over them all, was the greater truth that Berkeley had seen—the truth that the Irish question was the question of usury.

Between the time of Bishop Berkeley and that of Parnell there was a large increase in the productivity of agriculture. The population, which had risen throughout the eighteenth century, had sunk after the emigrations of the middle of the nineteenth. Ireland in the nineteenth century was free of the tyranny of the commercial code by which she was shackled in the eighteenth. By Parnel's time the problem of tithes was in some measure settled. And yet it is a curious, and not sufficiently noted, truth that, miserable as was the condition of the Irish peasantry in the eighteenth century, there were in that century no famines so utterly devastating

[1] Quoted by Raymond, *Disraeli, the Alien Patriot.*

as those of 1847 and 1879. In spite of the country's increased productivity the condition of the people had got not better but worse. Nor, in spite of the cry of over-population, did matters improve with the population's decline. In 1880 General Gordon reported [1] from personal observation that the condition of the people of Ireland was " worse than that of any people in the world, let alone Europe ". They were " lying on the verge of starvation in places where we would not keep cattle ".

Why was this ? It was because in Ireland, as in England, the landlord had only been able to keep his land through the Napoleonic Wars by going into debt to the London money-lender—a debt which in the nature of things could never be repaid since the money-lender was himself the issuer of money and only issued it as a further loan. In 1793, before the war, the Irish National Debt was £2,250,000 ; in 1797 it was £6,500,000 ; by 1800 it was £28,500,000, swelled by £6,000,000 for English troops for put down the Irish rebellion of 1798 and £1,500,000 to pay the bribes by which the Act of Union was passed. By 1815 it was £80,000,000.[2] In Ireland, unlike England, the holder of the debt was resident out of the country. The provision of the interest on this debt was a crushing burden on the Irish taxpayer. According to the British Treasury's own figures between 1820 and 1870 £287,000,000 were raised from Ireland by taxation and only £92,000,000 of public money spent there.[3]

The landlord was only able to furnish such taxes by mortgaging his lands. The rent which he wrung out of the impoverished peasant he in turn handed over to the unflinching money-lender. The peasant had, as a rule, to give one-half his year's labour in order to earn his rent and, as the figures of a previous page have shown, a million starved in the Hungry Forties while food for four million was being exported from the country.[4] The books tell us that Ireland was " overpopulated ".[5] (In the eighteenth century, when

[1] *Parnell*, St. John Ervine, p. 159.
[2] *History of Ireland*, S. Gwynn, pp. 418, 424.
[3] Ibid., p. 428.
[4] See Chapter 10, p. 116.
[5] *England since Waterloo*, 171 et seq.

they starved, the Irish used to be told the reason was that their country was " underpopulated ".) It was only over-populated if we admit that the primary and most unchallengeable of obligations is that of satisfying the demands of usury.

This aspect of the Irish problem was not vividly present to O'Connell, interested as he was in the obtaining of Catholic Emancipation and himself a landlord, and by no means an exemplary one. To him tithes even were to be fought not because they were a part of a system of usury but because they were a symbol of Catholic subordination to Protestant. Neither the Republicans of Young Ireland nor the staid and gentlemanly Repealers who followed Isaac Butt saw more clearly than O'Connell. One of the largest and worst of Irish landlords, Lord Palmerston, Prime Minister of England, was so busily engaged in supporting the claim of the Sicilians to self-government that he was compelled to dismiss the problem of his starving tenants with the sufficient witticism that " Tenant's right is landlord's wrong ".[1] Nor was the problem one that naturally presented itself even to Parnell.

Parnell, himself a landlord, had but little natural sympathy with agrarian reform. The burning passion of his soul was pride. He felt that he, as an Irishman, was despised because he was an Irishman and therefore determined to earn the respect of mankind for his country and for himself by holding up the whole machinery of the British Empire. To achieve this purpose, it was necessary that the Irish members should separate themselves from all other members of Parliament and should make impossible the transaction by whatever government of any other business until Irish grievances were remedied. It was necessary also that he should unite behind him all Irishmen. It was this second necessity of Parnell which gave his opportunity to the man who understood far more clearly than he the nature of the Irish agrarian problem. Michael Davitt was born in County Mayo in the year of 1846, a child of the famine. When he was 6 years old, his father, a peasant, was evicted from his home and driven from his country to find refuge in Lancashire. There Davitt

[1] *Palmerston*, Guedalla, p. 455.

grew up. He was sent to work in a cotton mill. When he was but 11 years old, since eleven-year-olds were cheaper, he was set to mind some machinery to which no one under 18 was supposed to be appointed. There was an accident which resulted in the amputation of his right arm. In his later teens he joined the Fenians and by the time that he was 24 he had earned for himself a sentence of fifteen years for treason-felony. He served for seven years, and those seven years of seclusion gave him the opportunity to shape his ideas into a coherent form. He emerged from prison to found the Land League and to devote his life to agrarian reform as the prime solution for the troubles of his country.

Up till this time Irish nationalists had fallen into two groups—the constitutional, moderate, Parliamentary party and the extreme revolutionary Fenians. Davitt was able to show Parnell that he had no chance of success unless he was prepared, whether he liked it or not, to advocate a strong agrarian policy so as to capture the support of those who would otherwise be violent revolutionaries. It was Davitt who first, it seems, of all students of Irish land conditions saw clearly that the rent which the tenant paid to the landlord, the landlord paid on as interest to the banker and that, since the money with which this rent and interest could be paid only came into existence by the issue from the banks of further loans, the breaking of the vicious circle was a mathematical impossibility. The penalty for non-payment of the rent, according to the orthodox economists, was eviction and the substitution of a tenant who would pay. This penalty between 1869 and 1886 was suffered by 129,708 fathers of families,[1] or, if we reckon an average of five persons to a family, by about 600,000 people, including incidentally, as we have said, Davitt's own father. A large landless class made it always possible for the landlords to find new tenants to attempt the miserable and impossible task at which the old had failed.

It is absurd to make the landlords the villains of the piece. There was hardly a landlord in Ireland at any time after the middle of the nineteenth century who would not have been only too glad to sell his land if only he could have

[1] *History of Ireland.* Sir James O'Connor, ii, 55.

found a buyer. But, until he found a buyer, he had to continue to exact his rents because of his debts. The alternative would be his own bankruptcy. Davitt's solution was a double one. First, let the tenants force the issue to a crisis by refusing to pay more than a fair rent. For an individual, who refused, the penalty would of course have been eviction. But, if there was a collective refusal of all tenants, a refusal by the landless to take the land of the evicted, a plan of campaign, a policy of boycott, the system would have to be reformed. Second, since it was not to be expected that any private person would buy out the landlords, the State must buy them out.

That was Davitt's policy. It had a curious history. Popular attention has been mainly focussed upon the sad atrocities with which its enforcement was sometimes attended or on the bad manners of the Parnellite policy of obstruction. That story has been too often told. It is enough here to point out that unfortunately it was necessary to bring some sort of pressure to bear on English politicians. The whole history of Ireland, and in particular the futile career of Butt, had proved that. Save only during the short and noble rule of Thomas Drummond, Melbourne's Under-Secretary for Ireland, there are all too few exceptions to the melancholy generalization that no reasonable concession was ever made to Ireland unless it was demanded by threats of violence. As Gladstone frankly confessed,[1] "It has only been since the termination of the American War and the appearance of Fenianism that the mind of this country has been greatly turned to the consideration of Irish affairs." Pressure there had to be. The contribution of Parnell and Davitt was to invent forms of pressure that were not bloody. It is unfair to blame Davitt because the policy of boycott occasionally led to bloody accidents. If it had not been for Davitt, there would not have been peace, as stupid Englishmen sometimes maintained; there would have been nothing but blood.

Davitt's notions were taken up by Parnell who neither greatly understood them nor greatly cared about them. Parnell's only interest was to compel the British Parliament

[1] House of Commons, 30th March, 1868.

to concede Home Rule. In order to obtain Home Rule, first it was, he thought, necessary to unite the Irish and therefore it was necessary to have a programme of agrarian reform. Secondly, it was necessary by a policy of obstruction to make the whole machinery of the British Parliament unworkable. Few British politicians cared anything at all for the problems of Irish land. On the other hand they cared greatly, for reasons which ranged from those of highest patriotism to those of selfish ease, that the Parliamentary machine should work. Therefore, as Parnell had foreseen would happen, while there was loud and pompous language about a refusal to be diverted from their course by hooliganism, in point of fact Parnell had only to persist in his tactics to obtain a remedy for Irish grievances. It was only his own quarrel with his own followers over the O'Shea divorce case which prevented Ireland from obtaining that remedy many years earlier than she did. In particular, the tenants had only to persist in their refusal to pay rents in order to convert the bankers to State purchase. For the last thing that the bankers wanted was to see the landlords go bankrupt, since it would do the bankers no good to have on their hands the quite unrealizable title-deeds of the landlords' lands.

At first the Liberals took up land reform, hoping thus to kill by kindness the demand for Home Rule, and the Irish got the Gladstonian Land Act of 1881, conceding the three F's of Fair Rent, Free Sale, and Fixity of Tenure. The Conservatives, hoping to outbid the Liberals, passed the Ashbourne Act of 1885, which commited the State to the principle of buying out the landlords, the tenants to repay the State by annuities over a period of years. When the Liberals took up Home Rule, it was doubly important for the Conservatives to take up agrarian reform, and by the Wyndham Act of 1903 the State agreed to pay to the landlord a bonus of 12 per cent in addition to the purchase price to be recovered out of the tenant. That is to say, Parnell took up land reform in order to unite the Irish in support of Home Rule, and the English politicians took it up in order to dish Home Rule by proving to the Irish that they would do better from a Westminster than from a Dublin Parliament.

It is important to see just how much Davitt's policy achieved—for Davitt's policy it was, although, since it happened to be brought in by the opposite political party, he had, according to the conventions of the game, to pick holes in it and denounce it. It was by no means a direct frontal attack on usury. The bankers did not lose a penny out of it. Had they stood to lose, we may be sure that they would not have supported it. All that they did was to lend the money to the State with which the State bought out the landlords who with the purchase money repaid their debt to the banks. The bankers became creditors of the State—which was a good debtor—whereas previously they had been creditors of the landlords—who were becoming increasingly bad debtors. On the other hand the peasant's position was enormously improved. He was, to begin with, given fixity of tenure, which made it for the first time worth his while to improve his land. Secondly, the burden on the land was immediately reduced, since the annuity which he had to pay to the Government was by the Ashbourne Act 4 per cent and by the Wyndham Act $3\frac{3}{4}$ per cent of the purchase price. As the land was always sold for less than twenty years' purchase, this meant that the new annuity was substantially less than the old rent, while after a period of years the annuity would be extinguished altogether. The consequence was that a large class of the community was freed from debt and put into a position where it was not compelled to go into debt again. It was a class, a high proportion of which had the enormous advantage of being for all practical purposes illiterate and therefore superior to the suggestions of the finance-controlled press.

The immediate result was a very great increase in prosperity, and the thirty years which elapsed between Parnell's adoption of the policy of obstruction and Lord Carson's reintroduction into Irish politics of the appeal to violence were certainly incomparably the most prosperous in Irish history. The further result has been to erect a State whose policy cannot be controlled by the manœuvres of central banks. One of the most interesting discoveries of recent years has been that of the complete failure of the money power to overturn, or indeed even to weaken, the position of Mr. de Valera.

CHAPTER XVI

MACHINE RUNNING DOWN

After Beaconsfield's fall in 1880 Gladstone came back to power. Throughout his rule the steady fall in prices continued, as it was to continue almost for the rest of the century. In Beaconsfield's last year, wholesale prices had, it is true, taken an exceptional jump-up from 1879's 98 to 1880's 103. But from 1880 onwards they fell gradually and steadily to 1898's 75. Wages, on the other hand, during that period were slightly but steadily on the rise. According to the Ministry of Labour's figures, in 1880 they stood at 77 to 1914's 100. By 1898 they had risen to 86. From that point of view the period was one of considerable and steady improvement, though even after all this improvement Charles Booth still found that in London "a million and a quarter persons fell habitually below the poverty line". "32 per cent of the whole population of London (in some large districts over 60 per cent) were found to be living in a state of chronic poverty, which precluded not only the elementary conditions of civilization and citizenship but was incompatible with physical health or industrial efficiency."[1]

The story which the unemployment statistics tell is a less simple one. On Gladstone's accession to power the percentage of Trades Unionists unemployed was very low—only 3·5 per cent in 1881. Throughout his rule it rose steadily until in 1886 it reached 10·2 per cent. There were probably more unemployed in 1879, when official statistics were not yet kept, but this is the highest percentage ever touched between 1880, when the statistics were first kept, and our present post-war years. It was the year of the Trafalgar Square riots and of the trial of Hyndman, Burns, and the Socialist leaders. The cause of the unemployment, in so far as the alternation of slump and boom was not

[1] *History of Trade Unionism*, Webb, p. 381.

merely inevitable under the double-money system, was the very rapid growth of the limited liability company, the establishment of large factories or stores, which produced the same quantity of goods or rendered the same services as had previously been produced by a number of small competitors,[1] and employed less labour in doing so. In fact, the cause of it was, surprising as it still is to this day to many people, that labour-saving devices save labour. That "rationalization", as we should call it, was favoured by the financial interests for the following reason. Lord Grey, the bimetallist, son of the Prime Minister of the Reform Bill, demonstrated at the time quite convincingly that, in the years immediately before 1886, the country's productivity was increasing more rapidly than its gold supply.[2] Therefore, unless people were suddenly to change their monetary habits, a fall in prices was necessary if that increased productivity was to be sold, and, as we have seen, prices were in fact steadily falling throughout all the early years of the 1880's. 103, 100, 99, 96, 89, 85, 81, run the price-indexes of the years from 1880 to 1886. This meant that every debtor had to repay to his creditor a principal considerably larger than that which he had originally borrowed. He could only pay more in debts to the creditor, if he paid less in wages to the employee. Trades Unions were now strong enough to make wage reductions difficult. Therefore the only alternative was to economize in the quantity of labour—to create unemployment. Therefore the banks, seeing that if they did not do so they might never get repaid, foreclosed on the small man, who was in debt to them, and sold up his business to large combine factories or multiple stores.

The readjustment was made, and in 1887 unemployment was down to 7·6 per cent, in 1888 to 4·9 per cent, and in 1889 to 2·1 per cent. In the next year there was the Baring crisis, caused by the excessive investment of the House of Baring in unrealizable South American securities. Owing to "the over-borrowing of the new" countries, there was, according to Sir George Paish,[3] a "partial breakdown of

[1] *Growth of Modern England*, Slater, pp. 511–13.

[2] See Nicholson's *Money and Monetary Problems*.

[3] *The Road to Prosperity*.

credit ", which " lasted for seven years from 1890 to 1897 and was felt by every country. The price of food fell to a level which reduced the farmers of all nations to poverty. Cotton, wool, and other raw materials became so cheap that those who produced them had scarcely enough to live upon ". This completed the ruin of British agriculture, but, on the other hand, the urban worker, as has been shown, steadily improved his position. The shortage of gold would have probably brought victory to the bimetallists in the currency controversy had not the situation been altered by the appearance on the market of South African gold in the years from 1893 onwards. Unemployment never again touched the 1886 figures.

If it is true that the smooth working of the party system demands essential agreement between the two parties, then it clearly follows that a statesman of vigorous personality, who imposes a policy on his own party, inevitably imposes it also on the other party as well. This was eminently true of Disraeli and his Imperialism. No one could have been by natural taste more antipathetic to Imperialism than Gladstone. Yet Disraeli's policy left to him a set of problems which caused him to be inevitably involved in the affairs of Egypt, Afghanistan, and the Transvaal, which were far from his interests. His Liberalism was strong enough to compel him to bungle these problems ; it was not strong enough to enable him to arrest the eventual advance of British Imperialism. After him the Liberal party passed under the leadership of a professed Imperialist, Lord Rosebery, from which it was only rescued at the price of excluding itself from office.

We come thus to the beginning of the twentieth century. Before considering its developments, it is important to recall to mind the generalizations upon the condition of the poor which the statistics of the previous four hundred years have allowed us to form. Whatever disputes there may have been about the interpretation of the facts, there is no real dispute about the facts themselves. They are that for just short of three hundred years from the reign of Henry VIII, taking into account changes of prices and wages and the incidence of rent, the condition of the English poor was getting steadily worse. From about 1820 to about 1860 it remained substantially stationary. The last forty years of the nineteenth century were, in spite of their ups and downs, on the whole years of steady improvement. Whether wages increased as much as productivity may be debated, and debate would lead on to disputes about the exact meaning of increased productivity. In any event the certain fact remains that wages did increase in their real values.

"To what purpose," it may be asked, "is all this history? We all know that horrible things were done in England in the early years of the last century. But nobody wants to return to those conditions. Do you seriously suggest that there is anybody who wants to return to them?" To this purpose. These conditions existed in the past not because our ancestors were ogres of wickedness but because they were driven along in spite of themselves by a remorseless system which they had come to believe to be a necessary system. If you had asked the Englishman of Henry VIII's time, he would have repudiated with horror the notion that the poor would ever be forced to live as they were forced to live in Cromwell's England, the Cromwellian Puritan would never have dreamed of the degradations of George II's England, the nobleman of 1688, little as were his illusions about the gloriousness of his revolution, at least was not so cynical as to believe that the conditions of the early factory system would come as its inevitable results. Under the rule of two men, Gladstone and Disraeli, there was a counter-attack, a regaining of some of the vast ground that had been lost. But these two men did not challenge the system at its roots. They merely took advantage of some fortuitously fortunate circumstances to shield the poor from some of the system's worst consequences. The fortuitous circumstances passed away; the system remained with money's great right to find its own level, and with the turn of the century and the passing of the circumstances the curve of the standard of living resumed its monotonous downward drop. It is true that you will never get wages down again to the level of the Hungry Forties, but it is also true that the working of the system inevitably demands that you shall get them down. And therefore, unless we smash the system, the attempt to make it work will inevitably smash us.

Because of the catastrophe in which they culminated, there is a great deal of nonsense talked about the first fourteen years of this century. Let us get clear the certain facts about them. With the turn of the century the rise in the real value of wages ceased. Instead they began to fall. In 1899 wages stood at 90; by 1913 they had risen to 100. In 1899, on the other hand, prices stood at 80 and by 1913 had risen to 100. To keep pace with the rise in prices wages should have risen to 112·5. It is a truism that to-day the financial system lies in ruins around us, and people of short memories often speak as if the years before 1914 were halcyon years and as if it was the War that smashed the system. It was not so. The War did not break down the system; the War was itself one of the consequences of the fact that the system was already breaking down. If any war smashed the system, it was not the European War but the Boer War.

Let us understand why.

Great Britain emerged from the Napoleonic Wars the naval mistress of the world, the possessor of all the important ports of call on all the great inter-continental trade-routes, the mistress of by far the greatest Empire of the world, the only country in a position to export capital on any considerable scale. Whatever unimportant overseas possessions other powers owned, they owned only, as it were, by the contemptuous permission of Great Britain. For practical purposes we may consider her in the early years of the century as the only Imperial power and the problems of the export of capital as purely British problems. The volume of British extra-European investments in the first years after Waterloo was kept within comparatively moderate bounds by a purely physical reason. Adam Smith shrewdly pointed out—as was undoubtedly the truth in the world that he knew—that, whatever the law might permit, whatever the dividends offered, most people would not be willing to invest their savings in concerns in distant countries because of the difficulty of keeping any control over their agents there and of getting any assurance that they were not being defrauded. "Every individual," he wrote,[1] "endeavours to employ his capital as near home as he can and consequently as much as he can in the support of domestic industry." The telegraph changed all that, making possible a communication between London and Bombay more rapid than previous communication had been between London and Birmingham and thus abolishing the bias in favour of domestic investment. Thanks to the telegraph there was a period of some fifty years of extensive British foreign investments. As yet, however—that is to say, up till the 1870's—no other country had developed its manufactures of capital goods sufficiently to be able seriously to challenge Britain's monopoly in that foreign investment market. The economic problems of the Continental countries were still predominantly internal problems and international conflicts were fought on issues that were genuinely nationalist and political.

After the Franco-Prussian War of 1870 however, a new situation began to emerge. The new German Empire was essentially a class Empire. Its peculiar strength required the preservation of the prestige of the ruling class—a prestige which was dependent—or so it was thought—upon the existence of wide inequalities of income. It was therefore important to keep German wages low. And, that being so, naturally enough, as Germany began to develop industrially, she found herself faced with the problem how she could sell her products, if she was unwilling to give to her people the money with which to buy them. It was clear that under such a circumstance they could only be sold abroad and the money with which to buy them must be lent to the foreign purchaser. For, if they were exchanged for foreign goods, there would, of course, still be the problem that the home market would be so highly stocked that increased wages would be necessary to get rid of its goods. Hence the emergence in the last quarter of the century of Germany as a large exporter of capital, the growth of the German colonial party, the Kaiser's demand for a "place in the sun", and the division of the continent of Africa between the European powers.

Yet it was not only into the German colonies that German

[1] *Wealth of Nations*, ed. Thorold Rogers, ii, 26.

capital penetrated. Large quantities went into Turkey, and larger quantities still, that were subscribed with the intention of their going to Turkey, went into the pockets of the promoting financiers both at the borrowing and the lending ends. Baron Hirsch, for instance, a member of that tribe, bought the bonds for the Orient Railway from the Turkish Government at 128·5 francs and sold them on to the public for 170 and 180.[1] Of the external debt which Turkey contracted between 1854 and 1875 "a bare 10 per cent", it is calculated,[2] was ever used for the country's economic development. Large quantities of German capital went also into the Transvaal. And therefore, naturally enough, the growth of an Imperial policy in Great Britain, leading to the Boer War and the annexation of the Transvaal, aroused furious anger in Germany. Germany did not intervene in favour of the Boers because it was impossible for her to do so owing to her not possessing an important fleet, but the lesson that she imagined the war to have taught her was the necessity of building such a fleet. The only alternative would have been to have raised wages at home. Without a fleet, she thought, all colonial possessions, all overseas investments were at the mercy of the British.

Hence the German naval programme, to which the British had to reply—the race in armaments. As a result, the cost of the British navy and army rose from £40 million in 1899 to £75 million in 1913, and labour was diverted from the production of consumable to the production of non-consumable goods. Yet the amount of direct expenditure on British armaments was but a small item. A larger cause of expenditure was the redoubled, feverish eagerness to push British loans into every corner of the world so that every country might be dependent on those loans and grappled by them, as was fondly hoped, to British interests. Whereas from 1900 to 1904 the average annual export of capital of long-term or permanent character had been only £21·3 million, from 1904 to 1909 it jumped to £109·5 million and from 1910 to 1913 to £185 million.[3]

It is true that our income on foreign investments was

[1] *Corps de Droit Ottoman*, G. Young, vol. iv.
[2] *Europe, the World's Banker*, Feis, p. 313
[3] Ibid., p 11.

also on the increase but it was not increasing nearly so rapidly as were our new investments. In the 1890's we were able temporarily to make a substantial profit on foreign investments. We received about £100 million a year in dividends and only sent out about £25 million in long-term investments and a trifle more on short-term loans. By 1913 we were receiving £210 million, but we were sending out £185 million on long-term investments and on short term a sufficient sum to make us substantial losers on the bargain.[1] Before the German menace we no longer dared to make use even of the profits of our usury. They must be stored against the day of war. It is true that, when war came, they were of use to us for the purchase of munitions in America and other services. But would it not have been a better plan not to have had a war?

At loggerheads with Germany, it appeared the obvious plan for Great Britain to seek the friendship of France. But that friendship was not so easily come by. France, defeated and robbed of Alsace-Lorraine, was anxious for revenge on Germany. Bismarck, from the German side, so long as he was in power, had seen that, in order to prevent this war of revenge, it was necessary to prevent France from gaining any important ally. He therefore cultivated friendly German relations with the two other Continental Great Powers, Austria and Russia, forming with them the *Dreikaiserbund*. Great Britain at that date was still content with her position of " splendid isolation ".

Unfortunately for Germany the ambitions of Austria and Russia were in direct antagonism with one another in the Balkans. And, after Bismarck's instruction to the Reichsbank to refuse to accept Russian bonds as collateral security for loans in 1887 and the accession of the Emperor Wilhelm II in 1888, Germany found it necessary to choose between the friendship of Austria and that of Russia. She chose Austria, and Russia was thus thrown into the arms of France. Now all that the Germans had wanted of Russia had been an assurance that she would not make common cause with France. So long as that was assured, they had no great wish to see her militarily efficient. The 1,200 million roubles of German capital that had found their

[1] *Export of Capital*, Hobson.

way into Russia had therefore been investments for the genuine industrial development of the country. France's interest in Russia was wholly different. She wanted Russia to be an efficient military ally when the war of revenge came. Now militarily Russia's strength was her enormous man-power and the impossibility for an enemy of conquering so vast a territory. Her weakness was her lack of railways and of the scientific equipment which would make possible the conduct of offensive operations against such a power as Germany. With every year that passed, with every advance in scientific technique, a mere superiority in numbers came to be of less and less value. France's strength, on the other hand, was that, of all the Continental countries, she was at this date industrially the most developed. She alone was in a position to export capital goods on a serious scale. A Danish financier, called Hoskier, saw his opportunity and acted as the underwriter for a series of loans by which the French investors were induced to subscribe their savings in order to equip Russia as a first-class military power.

There is no reason to think that Hoskier was not a man of honour. Yet it was, in the nature of things, nothing to him whether the Franco-Russian alliance proved political wisdom or political folly. Why should it have been? It was nothing to him even whether the Russians paid their debts or whether they did not. His only concern was that they should look like paying their debts for long enough for him to be able to induce the French public to take up the loans at a higher figure than that at which he had subscribed them. In this he was successful. But, when it came to the remission of the dividends, the situation was a difficult one. The loans had not been used to any large extent for genuine development of the country's resources; they had been used rather for such things as the building of strategic railways. According to Count Witte, the Russian minister, 37 per cent of the Russian railways were built for military rather than for economic reasons.[1] As a result the country's foreign indebtedness had increased out of proportion to any increase in its productivity and therefore, had the dividends been genuinely paid, a larger quantity

[1] Op. cit., Feis, p. 211.

of the country's products would have had to have been exported abroad, and indeed during Alexander III's reign, which lasted from 1881 to 1894, taxation was increased by 29 per cent and the allotments of the peasants were drastically cut down.[1] But it was impossible to lay hands on any great quantity of the country's products precisely because they were in the hands of the peasants, and it is physically impossible to extract from peasants an important proportion of their products. Therefore the French were only able to get paid by the Russians by the time-honoured absurdity of lending them some more money to pay with, while the Russians on their side, according to no less an authority than Raymond Poincaré,[2] spent a proportion of their old loans in bribing the French press to advocate the granting to them of new loans. Thus up to the War Russia used to borrow from abroad some 200 million roubles, or £20 million, every year, mostly from France. However, this was not sufficient to pay the interest which she owed on a debt which by 1914 had mounted up to between 7,000 million and 8,000 million roubles. Therefore the only solution lay in territorial expansion. The Russians knew from experience that attempts at expansion either in the direction of Constantinople or in that of India would lead to complications as a result of which they were unlikely to be financially profitable. They therefore turned their eyes to the Far East, making it their policy to step in to prevent Japan from seizing the Liao-Tung Peninsula, the reward which she proposed to herself for her victory over China in 1895. As the note which the Russians submitted jointly with France and Germany put it, " they would give a new proof of their sincere friendship for the Government of His Majesty the Emperor of Japan by advising him to renounce the definite possession of the Peninsula of Liao-Tung." [3]

In place of the Peninsula the Japanese were to receive from China an indemnity. This indemnity China was in no position to pay, and the Russians, therefore, lent them at 4 per cent 400,000,000 francs, which they had themselves

[1] See article on Russia in *Encyclopædia Britannica.*
[2] *Au Service de la France,* iii, 97.
[3] *Modern Japan,* Inayo Nitobe, p. 130.

borrowed on the Paris market. The condition of the loan was the establishment of the Russo-Chinese Bank, endowed with a lien on Chinese taxes, Imperial and local, and the profits of Chinese railways and telegraphs. By further treaties the Russians established themselves as virtually the masters of Northern China. The Germans acquiesced on the condition of their being allowed to seize Kiao-Chau; the British seized Wei-hei-wei. Then in its turn, to quote Vladimir, the Russian author, the German seizure of Kiao-Chau "forced" Russia "to claim some equivalent compensation", and therefore she occupied Port Arthur, the ice-free terminus of the Trans-Siberian railway, whose occupation by Japan she had forbidden five years before on the ground that it would be destructive to the integrity of China.[1]

There seemed every sign that the Far East was going the way of Africa and that but a few years would be required for its partitioning up among the European powers. So doubtless it would have been but for the rise of Japan. While French capitalists had been pouring their money into Russia, British capitalists had been pouring their money into Japan. If the expansion of Russia was necessary so that the French investor might get his dividends, the expansion of Japan was equally necessary so that the British investor might get his dividends. Hence the Russo-Japanese War—or at least one of the main causes of it—and the acquisition by Japan of those rights in China which the Russian Government had secured from China. Beggars cannot be choosers, and before the menace of the German army and the German navy the Governments of Great Britain and France had to sink their differences and make friends. France had to agree to see her ally baulked of any opportunity for territorial expansion and to bid her collect her dividends from her ancient territory as best she could. The result was an attempt to extract dividends by driving down the standard of living of the Russian poor—an attempt which led to consequences with which we are all familiar.

Thus came on the mad years. There was nowhere in the world so distant, so barren, so God-forsaken, but that

[1] Ibid.

some capitalists had some interest there, which any foreign movement must threaten. Day after day we were woken from our beds to hear that some foreigners had occupied some uncouth hovel, of which we had previously never heard but the possession of which by a foreigner was, we were told, a dreadful menace to all English life. In the old days it had been the Russians in Merv and the French in Fashoda. Now the Russians and the French were our friends, so we did not say so much about them. Instead it was the Austrians in Bosnia, the Germans in Morocco, Walfisch Bay, Zanzibar, Heligoland—the Lord knows where. The Japanese were sometimes our gallant allies and at other times a Yellow Peril, who any day might be found landing on our Eastern shores. It was a mad time, the madness of which was only not understood because people did not understand that the age was really an age of plenty—that there was really ample for all. Gentle reader of tender years, do not believe your admirable parents when they tell you of the staid and halcyon years before the War. They were years of lunacy, years of a breaking age, of a Heartbreak House, years in which only a few people were happy, and they because they were very stupid.

The truth is simple and can be stated in terms of a general proposition. The financial system can only work so long as there is in the world only a single important base for foreign lending. Had the Continental countries which started to export capital been only such countries as Holland, Belgium, or Switzerland, the system might have worked, for the financiers of those countries, seeing the feebleness of the Governments which they controlled, would doubtless have been willing to work within the system which operated from London. Up till the Boer War there was even a possibility that the German financiers would be willing to operate through the London system. The Boer War, as they thought, showed that they could not hope for fair treatment from such a system. From that moment the unity of the money-power was broken and the breakdown of its rule certain. The only question was whether it would be succeeded by chaos or by another system—a question that is not even yet certainly answered.

As a result of the confusion of the financial system, of

the necessity for this vast increase in foreign investments, there was in these first fourteen years of the century no longer an increasing sum to be distributed in wages. The difficulty of working the system caused discontent, and discontent in its turn made it yet more difficult to work the system. The world was no longer the world in which Castlereagh had lived and against which Cobbett had thundered. Gladstone and Disraeli had given to the poor a distant vision of better things, and under universal suffrage it was necessary that politicians should pretend that they had some benefits to distribute to those who had voted for them. But what was there to be done? We did not dare to reduce the standard of living of the poor for fear of domestic revolution. We did not dare to check the flow of foreign investments for fear of foreign war. Luckily the influx of South African gold raised the price-level, and, therefore, it was possible by raising wages, but raising them less than prices, to pretend that you were increasing the standard of living of the poor when you were really decreasing it. But it was a mean and desperate game, nor did the governing class dare to dock the poor of the necessities of life. All that they dared to do was to economize a little by the substitution of payment in kind for payment in cash. Therefore, while reducing real wages, they made up the balance by giving them back the goods of which they had been deprived through the social services which the Government undertook under the inspiration of Mr. Lloyd George.

Yet the trick manifestly did not work. Discontent was on the increase, so much so that, as we can see from Lord Riddell's *Diaries*, shrewd observers were speculating which war would come first—the international or the social. Indeed, it is perhaps at first sight hard to see why it was that the system did not collapse, why in these years of "increasing misery" there was indeed so little serious effort even to understand what was the system which was bringing this misery to mankind. The answer, I have little doubt, is that suggested by Mr. H. G. Wells in his chapters on the Fabian Society in his *Experiment in Autobiography*. The answer was that the Socialists had succeeded in establishing themselves in the public mind as the alternatives to capitalism. And, as Mr. Wells shows, and as indeed all subsequent history has shown, the Socialists neither understood nor wished to understand the workings of the monetary machine. Of the credit system they had no criticism to make save the meaningless palaver that in the Socialist State it would be worked in the interest of the community. They had no notion of the Disraelian doctrine of credit as " the exceptional auxiliary ". The international financier could always say to the international Socialist, as Charles II is alleged to have said to his brother James, " No one would be such a damned fool as to kill me to make you king." The retired spinster and the aged colonel might tremble in their beds at the thought that the wicked Socialists would seize their savings if they got the chance, but the masters of the system knew very well that there was someone a great deal nearer than Moscow who was prepared to seize those savings and that the colonel and the spinster would lose them any way when the inevitable collapse of foreign lending should come. They were content enough that there should be Socialists about, on whom the loss could be conveniently blamed, as indeed it was in 1931.

There is in Mr. Feis's book [1] a pleasant sentence on Greek finance, which is the epitome of so much of modern history. " This debt burden was plainly beyond Greek capacity, and Greek currency was falling in value, but the banks, in return for large commissions and extensive pledges, found loyal investors to furnish the funds to pay interest on all old debts." Loyal to whom ?

[1] Op. cit., Feis, p. 285.

Chapter XVII

AMERICA

It will inevitably occur to the objector to say, " Of the capital goods that went abroad from England, it may be true that a proportion went into the low-wage native countries. But others went into the new countries, where the white worker notoriously receives a higher wage than he receives in Europe. On the formula of money finding its own level, how was it possible for these new countries to borrow at all ? "

In order to find an answer let us return to the history of the most important of them, the United States of America, taking it up again where we left it in a previous chapter. It will be remembered that the question was there raised how far pre-revolutionary America was a high-wage country, supplied, as it was, by black slave labour and white forced labour, that was virtually slave labour. It was also argued that the desire for financial freedom was prominent among the causes of the American revolt.

As soon as Independence had been won from Great Britain, the decks were clear for a second fight. That fight, as is usually found after a successful revolution, was the fight to decide whether independence was to be true independence or whether, after the change of names, the financial system was to re-establish over the new government that same control which it had exercised over the old. The protagonist of plutocracy, a surprisingly frank protagonist, was Alexander Hamilton. Among his proposals was one astonishing in its impudence even for the antagonist of such a cause. The Germans in our own day have carried to a fine art the technique of first defaulting on the interest of their loans and then, when as a result the bonds have slumped, buying them up at a fraction of their par value and thus getting rid of their debts for perhaps a quarter of what they originally borrowed. Things were not very different in Alexander Hamilton's America. In order to fight the war, Congress had raised certain loans and then had subsequently defaulted on their interest. As a result, of course, they stood very low and were only sellable at a fourth or a fifth part of their par value. Alexander Hamilton, the Secretary of the Treasury, gave private information to his financial friends, who therefore bought up the loan at its low market figure. He then announced that the Government would redeem it by paying off the present holders at par plus accrued interest, with the price-level considerably lower than that of the time of the contraction of the debt. In order to pay them off, he raised a new loan from the New York bankers, thus saddling the new country with a permanent National Debt, which he confessed to thinking necessary in order that finance's mastery of its policies should be unshakable.[1] "He wishes it never to be paid," explained Jefferson [2] at the time, "but always to be a thing wherewith to corrupt and manage the legislature." He thus bound, as Calhoun afterwards put it,[3] "more strongly to the Government that already powerful class by giving them, through its agency, increased profit and a decided control over the currency, exchanges and the business transactions of the country." The interest on the new loan was to be raised by import duties.

Alexander Hamilton's great opponent was Thomas Jefferson. Hamilton spoke for the city interests, Jefferson for the agriculturists. It was Jefferson's belief that "our government will remain virtuous . . . as long as they are agricultural. When they get piled upon one another in large cities, as in Europe, they will become corrupt as in Europe." [4] It was this love of the broad acres which caused him, when he was President, to welcome the opportunity of extending the territory of the United States by purchasing from Napoleon France's vast western American Louisiana territory. In this purchase Jefferson saw two advantages. First, he would be freeing the United

[1] *Rise of American Civilization*, Beard, i, 341, et seq.
[2] Letter to President Washington, 9th September, 1792.
[3] Op. cit., Beard, i, 674.
[4] *Notes on Virginia*, see *Thomas Jefferson*, F. W. Hirst, pp. 195, 196.

States from the embarrassment of a strong neighbour over the frontier. Second, by adding good agricultural land to its territory he would be strengthening the agricultural as against the city interests.

His purchase had further consequences than he had foreseen. Had the United States remained a small country, hemmed into the sea by the Alleghany Mountains, it is not possible confidently to prophesy on which side victory would have lain in the controversy between the Jeffersonians and the Hamiltonians. But at least it would have been possible for the little country to have lived out a simple agricultural life, without the complications either of large foreign loans or of large immigration. By the Louisiana purchase she became a vast country; she also became an empty country. The temper of her inhabitants was one of hurry. They were not willing—perhaps in the circumstances it was not possible—to leave the country to fill up by the slow process of natural increase and only to develop its resources as natural increase created a demand for development.

Granted a sparsely populated country anxious for quick development, certain consequences inevitably followed. First, they could only develop by foreign loans, for they had not as yet got the surplus of goods to exchange against the foreign goods which they needed. Secondly, they could only develop if they consented to recruit their labour-supply by immigration. Either the immigrants had to go direct to the West or else, if the West was to be colonized from the East, then the immigrants had to be imported into the East to fill the vacant jobs there. Now the temper of the times forebade the importation of further black slaves. Therefore the new immigrants must be white. Therefore, while the black population was only growing by natural increase, the white population was growing both by natural increase and by immigration.

Now that the United States were independent, it was impossible for them to obtain European immigrants except by genuine persuasion, nor could they persuade anybody to cross the sea to them unless they offered him a higher standard of living than he could obtain in his old home. Therefore while, had things been different, slavery might have maintained itself for many years in its old home, it was certain that, whatever the laws might say, it would never really obtain a hold in the new states carved out of the Louisiana territory. Slavery would not obtain a hold simply because there were not enough slaves to do the manual labour. As those states developed, they would inevitably have come to rely more and more on white labour, and, as inevitably, the white labourer would have demanded the expulsion of the negro slave as the price of his labour. For the presence of the slave would have both destroyed the prestige and lowered the price of manual labour. Therefore there is little doubt that, even had there been no Civil War, slavery would soon have been abolished by the states themselves in all the new states south of the Mason-Dixon line. They would have followed California in the blunt battle-cry of "No niggers, slave or free." The Abolitionists had already all but won in Texas.

From the day of the Louisiana purchase the days of the domination of the Union by the old slave-owning states of the south-east were then certainly numbered. Indeed it was really certain that the days of the whole doctrine of state sovereignty were numbered. For it was inevitable that sooner or later the centre of gravity of the states must shift to the west. And, whereas the eastern state was a true unit, senior to the Union and the master of its citizens' loyalty, the western state was nothing but an artificially created administrative area, the object of no man's primary loyalty. If the Union was to survive at all, it was inevitable that in the end the West would conquer the East, the men of no state would conquer the men of a state. Had the south-easterners been wiser in their foresight, they would perhaps have made up their minds from the very time of the Louisiana purchase either to accept the inevitable or alternatively to leave the Union while they would still have been allowed to leave it peacefully. They did neither. They continued the experiment of the Union. The English capital poured into New York and from New York it was redistributed for the development of the country. On balance there was of course as yet no question of repaying the London loans. Every year London sent over in new loans far more than she received on the interest of the old.

It was not till 1873 that the tide turned and American exports began to exceed her imports. Yet, even in the early years of the century, she had to have some exports—she had to have something to offer which would seem to promise to the London lender a prospect of repayment of his loans. What could she offer?

She clearly had no manufactured goods to export. The cornfields of the west were not yet developed, nor indeed was England as yet willing to accept large quantities of imported food. The only thing that she could offer was cotton. Now cotton could only be produced in the slave states of the South. This fact had two consequences. On the one hand it made it of vital importance both to the English money-lender and to his New York jackal that the Union should be preserved and therefore there grew up a school of thought which denied that right of secession which had at first been universally taken for granted, which three states—New York herself, Rhode Island, and Virginia—had specifically affirmed as the condition of their entry into the Union, which had been taught as the generally accepted doctrine in such places as, for instance, the official military academy at Crown Point. This school of thought was, when the appropriate time came, to be launched upon the country as the Republican Party. On the other hand, it made it necessary not only that the south should produce cotton but that it should produce as much cotton as possible. Writers—the present writer among them [1]—have sometimes spoken of the life of the South before the Civil War as static and conservative. Such language is false. The two generations between Washington and Lincoln saw a profound revolution in southern life. In Washington's day the south-eastern planters were a race of subsistence farmers producing a variety of crops—rice, indigo, tobacco, corn. By the time of the Civil War all other crops than cotton had been as far as possible ruthlessly destroyed, while the cotton crop, which consisted of two million pounds at the time of Washington's inauguration, had risen by 1860 to more than two billion pounds—had increased by over 1,000 times.[2]

[1] In *The American Heresy.*
[2] Op. cit., Beard, i, 655.

How was this transformation effected?

In America there was no educational system to close the mind, such as the English public school and university system. What education existed was in somewhat slavish copy of English models, but fortunately for America there was not very much of it. As a consequence truths, that in England were only recognized by such men as Cobbett, were in America universally self-evident. The strength of the money-power was everywhere recognized; Alexander Hamilton had been frank and explicit in his proclamation of a purpose of making it strong. Yet, though strong and recognized to be strong, it was violently unpopular. Andrew Jackson from the frontiers of the West had in the 1820's made himself the leader of the battle against it. He denounced it as "more formidable and dangerous than the naval and military power of an enemy." [1] A great wave of public enthusiasm carried him into the White House in 1828 and he was triumphantly re-elected in 1832. His years were filled with his great warfare against the United States Bank—the central bank whose charter he refused to renew.

The bank fought him with those weapons which it is the habit of the money-power to use. It controlled the press, as it always can, since newspapers cannot be run without overdrafts and without advertising. It won to itself a majority in Congress by issuing loans to Congressmen on specially cheap terms on the plea that "it was in the public interest that such persons should have practical instruction in the principles of banking." [2] Daniel Webster, the great patriotic orator, the master of the Senate, was, as we now know, in its pay. The publication of the letters of Nicholas Biddle, the Bank's President, has revealed one in which Webster explains how he has refused to undertake a case against the Bank and adds, "I believe my retainer has not been renewed or refreshed as usual. If it be wished that my relation to the Bank should be continued, it may be as well to send me the usual retainers." [3]

Yet the money-power judged rightly that mere bribery of

[1] Ibid., i, 554, et seq.
[2] *History of the United States*, Cecil Chesterton, p. 103.
[3] Op. cit., Beard, i, 567.

politicians would not be sufficient. " Nothing but the evidence of suffering abroad will produce any effect in Congress," thought Biddle. And Webster agreed that " this discipline, it appears to me, must have very great effects on the general question of the chartering of the Bank." [1] As long as Jackson was in power, it was useless to do anything, but Jackson's successor, Van Buren, from New York and not from the West, was, it was hoped, of less stern stuff. Van Buren succeeded in March, 1837, the Bank's charter lapsed, and at once " this discipline " was duly applied—drastic deflation, imposed really by the money-power but ascribed to the loss of " confidence " owing to Jackson's " wild-cat finance "—and the usual result of a fall in prices and consequent ruin, bankruptcy, starvation, and unemployment. And naturally enough, when the next election came, the Democrats, Jackson's party, went down to defeat, and the Whigs, the party of the money-power, ruled in their stead. Concerning the money-power's candidate, General Harrison, Biddle gave instructions " Let him not say one single work about his principles, or his creed—let him say nothing—promise nothing. Let no Committee, no convention—no town meeting ever extract from him a single word about what he thinks now or will do hereafter. Let the use of pen and ink be wholly forbidden ! " [2]

The truth was that money had always the final ace. The West was always vulnerable because it was always in a hurry. It wanted loans for its rapid development, and the true source of those loans was not New York, which it could perhaps conquer, but London, which it could not reach. If the piper would not dance to his master's tune, the master would not pay at all. Thus the money-power of New York was able to dictate the development both of the West and of the South. We have spoken in another chapter of the system under which development is dependent upon loans of bank-created money which have to be repaid long before the goods for whose manufacture they were issued come on the market. It is of the essence of such a system, it was argued, that the issuers of money can control the pockets into which it goes and can therefore control

[1] Ibid., i, 568. [2] Ibid., i, 576.

the productive life of their country. As Calhoun put [1] it with moderation, the system gave them " a decided control over the currency, exchanges and the business transactions of the country ". There was only one strong limitation to that control. Wages had to be high to attract immigrants and to compete with the alternative of pioneer farming in the West and, if wages were high, then Americans could only manufacture if they were protected by a tariff against the competition of the lower-wage manufacturing countries.

But, if the producer for the home market must have a high standard of living, there was no reason why the producer for the foreign market, the cotton-grower, should share that high standard. For cotton's labour, fortunately for finance, was not dependent upon immigration. It was on the other hand desirable that its price should be kept as low as possible so that Lancashire might buy as much as possible and thus the London money-lender be persuaded that America's exports were large enough to give him a promise of larger dividends. Now the wages of labour in the South could not be reduced since the labourer, being a slave, did not get any wages—though there is indeed some reason to think that conditions for the slave became worse in the generation before the Civil War. On the other hand, the profits of the planter could be reduced, and they were being reduced all through the generation that preceded the Civil War. They were reduced in this way. The effect of the tariff was to raise the prices of all articles in the home market—of everything, that is, that the planter bought whether as machinery for his business or as comfort for his private life. On the other hand the price of cotton was a price in the world market, settled by the demand of Lancashire. Had the planter raised the price, the masses of the world would not have used cotton as they did. Therefore throughout the whole pre-war generation the southern planter was paying more for everything that he bought and receiving the same for everything that he sold. It is possible for us, as it was not possible for his contemporaries, side by side with Calhoun's great speeches on the unconstitutional nature of the tariff, on the high principles of freedom, on the undying nature of patriotism, to set the

[1] Ibid., i, 674.

account-books of the Calhoun estate with their sorry record of ever-mounting costs and ever-mounting debt. And in those books is the secret of what was happening to the South throughout that generation. Owing to the tariff the whole South was going into debt. We must never forget the important statistic which Horace Greeley, who had good sources of information, gave at the outbreak of the Civil War, that southern debtors owed at least $200,000,000 to money-lenders in New York City alone.[1]

Why to New York, it may be asked. With their philosophy of state rights, with their Jacksonian tradition of opposition to central banking, why did they not borrow from their local banks? Because, under the system, a large bank can always lend more liberally than a small bank. Suppose it to be a general truth that people only demand one-tenth of their deposits in cash. A large bank can count with confidence on the habits of its depositors corresponding to the general habits of the country. There may be one man here who demands more than one-tenth, but there is certain to be another, to balance him, who is content with less. A small bank cannot be sure. It may be indeed that its depositors on the whole demand considerably less than one-tenth, but it may equally be that they demand more. And, in face of this latter possibility, the small bank can never lend so large a multiple of its cash holdings as the large one. Also the large bank has clients engaged in every variety of business and therefore needing their cash at every different period of the year. It is probable that a high proportion of the clients of the small bank will be all engaged on the same business—the predominant local business—and therefore their demands for cash will all tend to fall in at the same period of the year. It may be argued that these considerations seem to prove the absolute superiority of large banks over small banks; it may be argued that they but prove that, if you are going to have a swindle, you had better have a gigantic swindle—for it is the whole system of double-money that is in debate. However that may be, they at least show how it was that the southern planters owed their debts to New York.

This southern debt to New York is the explanation of

[1] Ibid., ii, 64.

much. The debts were bank-debts. They were short-term debts. They had to be repaid, and yet they never really could be repaid. They could only be nominally repaid by further borrowings. And the price of the borrowings was the acceptance of the lender's terms. It is common enough for the books to describe to us how the area of cotton-cultivation spread in the years before the war. But cotton no more spreads of itself than gold flows into a country unasked. The area of cotton spread because the banks lent money to those who would grow cotton and forced into bankruptcy those who refused.

It was not difficult for any Southerner to see that here was a system that was steadily driving his country to ruin. Against that system he had two weapons. He had the weapon of the threat of secession, to prevent which most Northerners were prepared to make to him very considerable concessions. He had the alliance of the Jacksonian West, which cared indeed but little for states' rights, the feeling of which was on the whole settling against slavery but which shared with the South its detestation of the money-power. The somewhat incongruous coalition of the South and West, helped by some northern supporters, made up the Democratic Party, which on the whole ruled America from Jackson's time to the Civil War. It was an anti-financial party. Yet everything costs money—even attacking the money-power. And, as is the invariable way with political parties, with the passage of the years its living faith tended to sink down into the mere repetition of conventional formulae.

The cotton-planters were inconvenient debtors because they were possessed of a high pride and, under the leadership of such men as Calhoun and Hammond, of an inconveniently accurate understanding of the confidence-tricks of credit. If their banker-creditors pressed too hard, such men were always ready to answer with a threat to expose throughout the North the trick by which "the white slave" was kept the obedient servant of finance. As John Randolph threatened,[1] "Northern gentlemen think to govern us by our black slaves; but, let me tell them, we intend to govern them by their white slaves." Or, as Senator Hammond put it in a trifle greater detail,[2] "In all social

[1] Ibid., i, 693. [2] Ibid.

systems there must be a class to do the mean duties, to perform the drudgery of life. . . . The difference between us is that our slaves are hired for life and well compensated; there is no starvation, no begging, no want of employment among our people, nor too much employment either. Yours are hired by the day, not cared for and scantily compensated, which may be proved in the most deplorable manner any hour in any street of your large towns. . . . If they knew the tremendous secret that the ballot box is stronger than any army with bayonets, and could combine, where would you be? Your society would be reconstructed, your government reconstructed, your property divided. . . . How would you like for us to send lecturers or agitators North to teach these people this, to aid and assist them in combining and to lead them?"

The waning power of the southern planters, it became evident by the middle of the century, would be broken the day that the uneasy coalition of the South with the West was broken. At the Presidential Election of 1860 the southern Democrats made the fatal error of quarrelling with their fellow Democrats outside the slave states over the question of slavery in the new territories recently acquired by the Mexican War and the extension of the country westwards. Their split enabled the new party—the Republican Party—to win the election with a minority vote for their candidate, Abraham Lincoln.

The Republican Party was New York's bid to detach the West from the South. Before the nominating convention its most prominent member had been Seward, the representative of New York finance, "a believer," as was said, "in the adage that it is money that makes the mare go." The main plank of the party was that of high tariffs but, in order to attract western votes, it had added the plank of "free homesteads" for those who would settle in the West. "Vote yourself a farm," was the election cry throughout the West. As little as possible was said about the slavery question, for, as a Republican paper in Philadelphia pointed out, Frémont, the Republican candidate of four years before, "had tried running on the slavery issue and lost." [1]

[1] *National Intelligencer.*

The Republican tactics succeeded, if not so far as to give Lincoln a majority, at least so far as to make him President. He polled 1,857,000 votes against 2,804,000 for his opponents, but their divisions enabled him to carry a majority of the states. What followed is familiar to all. The south, led by South Carolina, seceded. Lincoln refused to accept their secession, and there followed the war, ending finally in southern defeat. The war was in no way a war against slavery. Before its outbreak Lincoln, in order to quiet southern fears, had been willing to give them a constitutional amendment specifically guaranteeing to them the continuance of slavery. Slavery was only abolished by accident and as a manœuvre of war. Nor in spite of the Gettysburg speech was it in any sense a war for "government of the people for the people and by the people". By an accident of the constitution Lincoln was the President of his country, but he had not the support of the majority of its citizens. It was, as he throughout most frankly recognized, a war for the preservation of the Union—preservation of it for a variety of reasons, noble and ignoble, ranging from those of high Imperialism to those of the lowest usury, according to the breasts that entertained them—but nevertheless always for the preservation of the Union.

Legend, skilfully directed for somewhat obvious purposes, has sought to make of Lincoln an almost superhuman figure. For there have been many to whom it was convenient that the origins of the Republican Party should be enveloped in a mist of almost Arthurian romance. It is therefore hard to say anything moderate or balanced about him without appearing to be engaged in an exercise of the odious art of debunking. But, while much can be said in praise of his engaging, colourful, and humorous personality, while he proved himself a great master of the diplomacy of war, the sane verdict on his political career cannot be other than this. He was put forward by the moneyed interest as an "available" candidate who would attract the votes of the West but who was never for an instant intended to be the master of his own policy. It was the stalest and most regular trick of American politics. He was put forward exactly in the spirit in which the Whigs had put forward General Harrison and General

Taylor. Whether he would have been pliable to his master's voice or whether he would have turned and fought the money-power, as Andrew Jackson, that other great leader from the western frontiers, fought it, can never be known, for he was killed before he had the chance to show.

One thing is very certain, and that is that, had he fought it, his place in the polite textbooks of history would have been to-day a different one from what it is. He had not fought it during the war. For, as in similar circumstances in England, the rich who supported the war refused to pay for it. In his first year of office Lincoln borrowed $8·52 for every dollar that he could raise by taxation, and even by the end of the war the ratio between loan and tax was still 3 to 1. The national debt, which at the time of his accession was $74,985,000 had risen by his death to $2,846,000,000. Prices, owing to inflation, had multiplied by three, but the patriots who lent their money lent on condition that they were paid their interest in gold. They lent the current money of the moment, but they were to be repaid in gold. If then one was a banker in the closing years of the war, lending to the Government was a profitable business. You said that you lent the Government $100 at 7 per cent. In fact, you wrote the Government a cheque on yourself for $100, of which, according to the usual proportion, the Government only demanded $10 in cash. On that $10 of Greenbacks, as the notes were called, you received interest of $7 in gold, which was at the rate of exchange about $21 of greenbacks. Therefore Lincoln's Government, instead of the mere 50 per cent per annum which the British Government paid to its bankers in the last War, was paying 210 per cent—a considerable rate. Jay Cooke, the most prominent of the War financiers, retired from the War a very rich man, but, as Mr. Beard truly says, he " did not escape criticism ".[1]

Lincoln, after his murder, was succeeded by his Vice-President, Andrew Johnson, a man from Tennessee, the only President to have come from that state except Jackson. He had unfortunate faults of personality which made him ill-suited for fighting the great battle which Jackson fought and which Lincoln perhaps would

[1] Op. cit., Beard, ii, 71.

have fought. President only by accident, he could bring to his task none of the prestige which Lincoln would have brought to it. He was not fitted for success and he did not meet with it. Yet both in the North and in the South he fought for the permanent appetites of mankind—for justice and for mercy and for honest government. Whatever may be said against him, there is this to be said for him. The men who hounded at him—Sumner, Thaddeus Stevens with his mulatto mistress, Benjamin Butler, the blackmailer—were perhaps as vile a crew as ever dabbled anywhere in the trade of politics. I know not where to find the likes of them unless perhaps among those who made the English Revolution of 1688. It is a certain title to honour to have been hated by such men. Of these men and of their policy during the years of reconstruction it is not unfair to say that they destroyed every good thing for which Jefferson Davis fought in the South and every good thing for which Lincoln fought in the North, and that under their rule " government of the people for the people and by the people " perished utterly from such portions of the earth as they were able to control.

The phrase is important, for the effect of the Civil War and the reconstruction was virtually to transfer the Government of the United States to the professional politicians of the Republican Party, whose nominees held the Presidency save only during Cleveland's terms of office, from the Civil War until 1912. And of that Republican Government, whether it was a good government or a bad government, at least this can be said in no spirit of wanton paradox, that it was probably the least democratic government that ever flourished in any great country in the whole history of European man.

The Republican party was the party of the money-power. In Lincoln's day it had made a bid for, and had captured, western support by its promises of free land to those who would settle there. It had kept its promise, and it still, as a general rule, allowed some citizen of a western state to be the holder of the nominally supreme power. But the masters of the credit machinery could always get back what they had given away by putting the owners of land into debts which it was impossible for them to pay and then foreclosing on their land. The policy of the 1870's was one of drastic deflation, owing to the return from greenbacks to gold and owing to the stoppage of silver coinage, a deflation which caused a fall in the price of wheat from over $2 a bushel in 1865 to under $1 a bushel in the subsequent decade. It was therefore obviously quite impossible for the farmer to get out of debt. Thus under the Republican rule of the last quarter of the century the land of the West was passing steadily into the hands of absentee landlords. In 1884 it was found that approximately 20,000,000 acres had passed into alien hands. Lord Dunmore had 100,000 acres, Lord Dunraven 60,000, the Duke of Sutherland nearly 500,000, a syndicate headed by the Marquis of Tweedale 1,550,000. Two English syndicates owned over 7,000,000 acres in Texas and a German syndicate more than 1,000,000 acres. More than half the land in the Pacific and Mountain states was in the hands of absentee landlords.[1] An official commission appointed by President Theodore Roosevelt made itself responsible for the strong judgment that " hardly a single great western estate held a title untainted by fraud ".[2]

There was as a rule little to choose between the official Democrats and the Republicans in the readiness of their service to usury. Yet there were individuals who saw what was happening and raised their protest against it. One at least, though his protest was a failure, yet made of himself a national figure—William Jennings Bryan, a man of some eccentricity, yet entirely undeserving of the absurd legend that he was little better than a half-wit, which the intelligentsia and the money-power combined to foist on him because of his hatred of usury and sincere belief in the Christian religion. (For the " parlour Bolsheviks " in the United States, with their mid-Victorian agnosticism have always been convenient instruments for playing usury's game and have fallen, like great fish, into every trap that it has laid for them.)

The dominating factor in the economic and political situation was that the country still needed foreign loans and, so long as that factor remained, so long the ultimate seat of American Government was neither Washington nor New

[1] Ibid., ii, 151. [2] Ibid., ii, 199.

York but London. If the capital goods were to continue to flow to America, she must be able to provide exports with which to offer the investor the prospect of dividends. What could she offer? Even after the Civil War there was still cotton, and Republican politicians, who fought secession, who clamoured for the humiliation of the planter, who loudly proclaimed the negro's right to a vote, were careful not to demand for him higher wages. Yet, as the volume of investments grew, cotton was no longer enough. What else could the Americans provide? There was corn in the West, and the English foreign investor in the 1870's, by destroying his own domestic agriculture, made it possible for payments to be made to him by importation of corn. Yet, if the western farmers were to sell their corn on the London market, they must put it there at the same price as competing exporters from Canada or from the Crimea. How could that be done? There were two ways. They could, as the American manufacturers did, sell a portion of their crop at a high price to the American consumer and the rest at the world price to the English consumer. But, had they done so, the price of bread in America would have risen. Wages would have had to be raised, and with more paid out in wages there would have been less to be paid out in dividends. Therefore, to prevent the farmers from doing this, the politicians, acting of course for their masters, while giving protection to every American industry, allowed no tariff on corn, and thus they could prevent any attempt of the American farmer to sell his corn at home at a high price by importing corn from Canada or elsewhere to undersell him.

The only remedy then was for the farmer to produce more cheaply than his competitor by making a freer use of the latest labour-saving devices. This he did, and was thus able to maintain a standard of living, which, though lower than that of his fellow countryman in the town, was higher than that of the farmer in other countries. But inevitably every invention was soon copied by the competitor and it was a hard race to keep always ahead. Once that for one instant he lost his lead, he had no alternative but to accept a yet lower standard of living and to go into debt. Once that he was in debt, his creditors could dictate his policy, could compel him to concentrate on the production of crops for the export market, just as they had compelled the southern planters to concentrate on cotton.

Yet the whole century was, though few understood it, a transitional century. For the first three-quarters of it American imports every year exceeded her exports. That is to say, every year she received more in new investments than she paid out in interest on the old investments. Then 1873 was the turning year. Thenceforward exports every year exceeded imports. She was paying more in interest than she was receiving in new investments. Yet, if she was to pay her interest, she still needed new investments. By the end of the century a third stage was reached. By then so large was the surplus of exports over imports that she could, had she wished, have paid her interest without accepting any further foreign capital.

Until recently the whole question of America's trade balances was rapt in much obscurity owing to paucity of data. There is still much to be made clear but the whole situation has been enormously illuminated by the statistics recently prepared for and submitted to President Roosevelt by Mr. George N. Peek, his special adviser on foreign trade. According to Mr. Peek's figures, between 1896 and 1914 the United States exported $31,033 million and imported $21,180 million. She had invisible exports of $86 million shipping charges and $652 million other miscellaneous items, making a total of goods and services exported of $31,771 million. Her invisible imports were $727 million paid to foreign shippers, $3,230 million, spent by American tourists abroad, $2,850 million sent abroad in charity or by way of immigrant's remittances, and $570 million miscellaneous items making a total of goods and services imported of $29,557 million. She had therefore a "favourable" balance of a little over $2,000 million. On the other hand she had to remit as interest on foreign investments in the United States $3,800 million, while she only received as interest on American investments abroad $760 million. She had to pay out therefore on balance $3,000 million. She only had a "favourable" balance of $2,000 million to pay it from. Therefore she had to borrow another $1,000 million. But, formidable as such a sum may sound, yet, spread over a period of eighteen years and a population of some 100,000,000, it only means about 50 cents per person per annum. There was little doubt from the turn of the century that every person in America could, if need arose, have been induced either to consume 50 cents a year less or to produce 50 cents a year more. Foreign capital was no longer a necessity to the United States.

She did not however during these years merely borrow $1,000 million from abroad. She borrowed $2,000 million and lent $1,000 million. That is to say, rather than get the country out of debt, her financiers preferred to start foreign lending themselves. Thus in 1899 J. P. Morgan floated the first important American foreign loan on behalf of the Mexican Government. In 1901 he lent $50 million to the British Government to fight the Boer War. Further loans followed to Japan and China. But it was mainly into the countries of Spanish America that American capital found its way. Some of it went there for those countries' economic development; other loans were political. For these latter there were almost a regular formula. It would be suggested to General X that he should raise a revolution against President A. Money would be lent to him to make the revolution and to President A to suppress it. For a time the loans would be so controlled as to keep the rival fighting forces roughly equal. Then, when it appeared that no more could be squeezed out of the country, one of the combatants would be offered far more liberal loans than his rival on the condition that, when successful, he made himself responsible for his rival's debt as well as his own. The Church would be either pillaged or reinstated according to whether it had been found the more convenient to make the liberals or the conservatives win. By a formula of which this is not an unfair description a solution was found for the problem of Santo Domingo in 1905, for that of Cuba in 1906, for that of Nicaragua in 1907, for that of Honduras in 1911. It was used by Woodrow Wilson to establish in power the anti-clerical régime of Madero in Mexico and to depose President Sam from the Presidency of Haiti.[1] Whether it was a better or a worse policy than the policy of frank annexation of the European powers is debatable.

Yet the important truth is that, even in spite of the American

[1] Ibid., ii, 501 et seq.

export of capital, with the twentieth century she no longer had any absolute need to import capital. This made a most remarkable and almost immediate difference to American political life. London ceased to be the capital of the United States. In the nineteenth century every serious political candidate for high office (with the exception of Bryan who was always defeated) had always been at pains to denounce "radical policies" and to deny—what every single person in America knew perfectly well to be true—the overriding influence of the money-power over politics. In 1893 Andrew Carnegie, who was allowed to hire private assassins from Pinkerton's to shoot down his workmen, had the impudence to write in his *Democracy Triumphant*,[1] "There is not one shred of privilege to be met with anywhere in all the laws. One man's right is every man's right. The flag is the guarantor and symbol of equality. There is no party in the state that suggests or which would not oppose any fundamental change in the general laws. These are held to be perfect."

In 1911 a member of the plutocracy, Frederick Townshend Martin, wrote a most remarkable book called *The Passing of the Idle Rich*, in which he frankly explained the ideals of his class and the methods by which for the past half-century it had ruled America through the politicians.[2] "We," he wrote of the plutocracy, "care absolutely nothing about statehood bills, pension agitation, waterway appropriations, 'pork barrels,' state rights, or any other political question, save inasmuch as it threatens or fortifies existing conditions. Touch the question of the tariff, touch the issue of the income tax, touch the problem of railroad regulation, or touch the most vital of all business matters, the question of general federal regulation of industrial corporations, and the people amongst whom I live my life become immediately rabid partisans. . . . It matters not one iota what political party is in power or what President holds the reins of office. We are not politicians or public thinkers; we are the rich; we own America; we got it, God knows how, but we intend to keep it if we can by throwing all the tremendous weight of our support, our influence, our money, our political connections, our purchased senators, our hungry congressmen,

[1] Ibid., ii, 209. [2] Ibid., ii, 303.

our public-speaking demagogues into the scale against any political platform, any presidential campaign that threatens the integrity of our estate . . . The class I represent cares nothing for politics. In a single season a plutocratic leader hurled his influence and his money into the scale to elect a Republican governor on the Pacific coast and a Democratic governor on the Atlantic coast."

In the next year there was a remarkable proof of the revolution in American life which her freedom from the need for English capital had brought. There was a Presidential election. The three important candidates were Wilson for the Democrats, Roosevelt for the Progressives, and Taft for the Republicans. Martin's thesis, the thesis for which twelve years before Bryan had been denounced as an anarchist and a lunatic, was now only not an election issue because it had passed beyond being an election issue. It was accepted by all the candidates. " Suppose you go to Washington," wrote Wilson [1] in the *New Freedom*, " and try to get at your government. You will always find that, while you are politely listened to, the men really consulted are the men who have the biggest stake—the big bankers, the big manufacturers, the big masters of commerce, the heads of railroad corporations and of steamship corporations. The Government of the United States is at present a foster-child of the special interests." " Behind the ostensible Government," ran Roosevelt's policy [2] " sits enthroned an invisible government owning no allegiance and acknowledging no responsibility to the people. To destroy this invisible government, to dissolve the unholy alliance between corrupt business and corrupt politics, is the first task of the statesmanship of the day." Taft was by far the most conservative of the three, but he, fresh from the experience of the Presidency, admitted that things " seem to have crystallized into a rigid control of all by the great business combinations. . . . That the occasion for the general alarm was justified, no one who had studied the situation can deny ".[3] At about the same time Elihu Root, the veteran and most distinguished of American lawyers and statesmen, in sight of the end of his long career, recorded that " the ruler of the State (of New York) during the greater

[1] Ibid., ii, 592. [2] Ibid. [3] Ibid.

part of the forty years of my acquaintance with the State Government has not been any man authorized by the constitution or by law ".[1] With that very un-English directness of speech which the Americans have, he gave the name of that ruler ; it was Mr. Platt, a usurer.

That was the situation when there burst upon America and the world the War of 1914. She was still on balance a debtor country, and her whole past history had been profoundly modified by that indebtedness. During the War the need of the Allies caused them to sell their debts to American investors in exchange for munitions of war. They needed more munitions still and, unable to give goods in their exchange, in their turn borrowed from the Americans. The Americans emerged from the War a creditor nation and by consequence the inheritors of a set of problems wholly different from those which had troubled their ancestors. As one looks back, it is not difficult to see how profoundly their policy had been dominated for a hundred years by this burden of the foreign debt. Yet the United States, a country of 100 million people, had in 1914 a foreign debt of some $1,000 million. The foreign money-lender never had over her the hold which he has over the British Dominions to-day—Australia with a population of 6¼ million and a foreign debt equal to that of America in 1914, Canada with a population of 10 million and a debt to London equal to the total American foreign debt of 1914 with a debt in addition of some £700 million more to New York.[2]

[1] Ibid., ii, 592–3.

[2] *A Main Cause of Unemployment*, Loftus, p. 34.

Chapter XVIII

THE 1920's

It is a platitude that an old world came to an end when the guns spoke in the summer of 1914. From time to time one hears sincere, if sentimental, plans for a return to that halcyon world before the death. But, even though the historian may debate whether those years were in truth good or bad, the practical politician cannot but record that the dead, whatever were their virtues, are dead. The world of Edward VII has passed away as completely as the world of Richard Cœur de Lion.

Let us explain.

Sir Charles Morgan-Webb in his admirably lucid *Rise and Fall of the Gold Standard* has shown most clearly the enormous confusion that has been introduced by the vague use of the phrase, "the gold standard," for any system in which the amount of money in circulation is in any way regulated by the country's holdings of gold. There have been in the last 120 years, he very clearly shows, four quite distinct "gold standards", bearing but little relation to one another and at times even in open conflict with one another. The system that ruled in England, when it was not suspended, during the nineteenth century, he calls "the sterling standard". The essence of that system was that gold should have monetary value in every country, at least to the extent that an increase in that country's gold holdings would cause an increase in its monetary supply, a decrease in its gold holdings a decrease in that supply. Its claim was that, so long as each country allowed its gold to have its full monetary effect, no change other than a temporary change in the distribution of gold between the various countries was possible. The virtue of the gold standard was that it prevented trade from being in gold. Thus suppose that the British want some wine from the French but have not at the moment any convenient commodity to exchange for it. The British pay in gold. As a result there is rather more money in France and rather less in England. Every price in France therefore goes up a little and every price in England comes down a little. Therefore Englishmen, finding French goods dearer, buy less of them, and Frenchmen, finding English goods cheaper, buy more of them. Therefore the French cannot export to England, and, to make up the balance, they have to send back the gold which they had originally received for their wine.

Therefore the first requisite of the sterling standard is that every country should allow its gold to have its full monetary effect. As the Macmillan Report put it,[1] "Countries which are losing gold must be prepared to act on a policy which will have the effect of lowering prices, and countries which are receiving gold must be prepared to act on a policy which will have the effect of raising prices." The second requisite is that the world should contain large undeveloped areas, whose inhabitants cannot as yet exchange goods for the goods of the developed countries which they require, and who are therefore desirous of loans. It is a system therefore which can of its nature only work for a short time. For, if the borrowing country will never be in a position to have a favourable balance of trade, it is folly to lend to it, while, when it comes to have such a favourable balance, it no longer wishes to borrow. It was inevitable from the first that, one by one, the new countries would emerge from the borrowing stage until there must be no one left in that stage. It is only a calamity such as that of war or disruption—a calamity such as that which fell on Central Europe in 1918—which can reduce to borrowing a country which has once risen above the necessity for it. The third requisite is that the important creditor should be a free-trade country, willing to accept the payment of its dividends in whatever goods its debtors choose to offer.

We have seen how in the years between the Boer War and the European War the system was already with every year growing increasingly difficult to work owing to the challenge to the primacy in the world's foreign lending of Free Trade Britain by Protectionist France and Germany.

[1] Quoted by Morgan-Webb, *Rise and Fall of the Gold Standard*, p. 84.

The world that emerged from the European War was a world unrecognizably different from that of 1914. It was now Great Britain who had an inconvertible currency, the United States who were " on gold ". Great Britain was indeed still on balance a creditor country and still prepared to export large quantities of capital, but the major creditor country, the greatest exporter of capital, was now the United States. Great Britain was in debt to the United States.

If by some miracle the nations of the post-War world could have been induced to work the nineteenth century monetary system, there can be little doubt what the consequence must have been. When the nineteenth century financiers of the European countries were competing against one another to find extra-European destinations for their loans, they assumed always that the non-European was a convenient creature—just intelligent enough to use machines and tools, not intelligent enough to use them for his own advantage. They took for granted the continuing domination of the white race over every portion of the world in which he cared to exercise it. That dream of confidence has been quickly shattered, and few would to-day be willing to prophesy how large a portion of the world will be under white man's government by the time that this century comes to an end. Meanwhile one non-European country at any rate—Japan—has proved itself fully capable of handling all the tools and machinery of Western industrialism. Only half a century ago Gilbert, desiring some completely comic country for his fantastic songs, chose Japan and gave us the *Mikado*. To-day it is the Japanese who have the laugh. According to the Huskissonian formula, the basic formula of the nineteenth century, that money should be allowed to find its own level, British money at the end of the last century and at the beginning of this flowed out from London to Japan. The exact figures of British investments there it was, and is, to the common interest of British financiers and the Japanese to conceal. The present writer once made inquiries of an eminent cotton statistician concerning the proportion of British money behind the Japanese cotton trade and received the answer, " No one knows except the Japs and they won't tell." But there is little doubt that substantially the original capital was entirely British and that to-day through the Hong-Kong and Shanghai Bank and other channels British capital is still pouring into Japan. As Mr. Feis puts it,[1] "The technical knowledge and equipment of the world were drawn upon, but the capital came mainly from Great Britain. By virtue of that capital no less than through its political alliance Great Britain may be said to have made a Great Power of Japan. . . . In London the capital was chiefly found to develop those agencies with which the Japanese Government exerted itself to create a strong modern industrial system."

Japanese industrialism is then the creature of the City of London, the industrialism of a people who do not produce in order that they may consume but to whom low costs of production are a weapon to be used for the overthrow of the white man's hegemony. Under the conditions of Cobdenite competition Japan's victory over the industry of Lancashire or of any other place in Europe is merely inevitable. As that most important Polish economist, M. Otto Bankwitz, wrote [2] in his report to the International Cotton Congress in August, 1933, "the European industry is powerless." He noted as the most important factor in post-War industry "the migration of industry from Europe and the United States to Asia". Before many years, if we continue to live our lives according to the canons of sound finance, we shall be faced with a situation unparalleled since Christendom began—with the situation that the centre of gravity of civilization has passed to a country in whose making the Christian tradition has played no part at all. Are we prepared to accept such a situation? Sentimentalists sometimes tell us that our troubles are due to the fact that, what with tariffs and quotas and restrictions, the old pre-War system is not allowed to function properly. Tariffs and quotas and restrictions are not in themselves lovely things, yet it is clear enough in truth that the only reason why we have survived at all is that the old pre-War system has not been allowed to function properly. Had it functioned properly we would have had no defence at all against the attack from Japan.

[1] *Europe, The World's Banker*, Feis, p. 422.

[2] Quoted by Jeffrey Mark, *The Modern Idolatry*, pp. 158, 159.

Most fortunately the United States, the greatest lending country of the post-War world, refused to play the game. The United States, in contrast to the Great Britain of before the War, was a highly protectionist country. Therefore foreign goods could not obtain admission there. Therefore, when the time came for her debtors to pay their debts, prevented from paying in goods, they could not but pay in gold. During the years between 1914 and 1922, to quote again from Mr. Peek's analysis, American exports exceeded their imports by so gigantic a figure that, though the Americans took over from foreigners investments in the United States to the value of $2,422 million, though they lent to foreigners no less than $17,083 million there still remained owing to them from abroad another $1,746 million which they could not but take in gold—about a sixth of the total monetary gold of the world.

Now, had the American gold standard of these years been the British gold standard of the nineteenth century, "the sterling standard," such a country as the United States would not have been protectionist at all. She would have been Free Trade and would have taken payments of her debts in goods. Had the exigencies of war prevented its debtors from paying in goods and compelled them to pay in gold, then she would have allowed that gold to have had its full monetary effect on the domestic market. She would have put it into circulation, thus causing an enormous domestic inflation and consequent rise in the American domestic price-level. Prices would have risen so high that, even in spite of the tariff, foreign goods would have come into America and undersold the native product, and the gold would then of course have flowed out again in payment for those foreign goods.

But the Americans, though they said that they were "on gold", neither used nor ever had any intention of using gold as the British had used it in the nineteenth century. Their concern was with a stable domestic price-level, and, therefore, when they found that gold was coming into their country so rapidly that, if allowed its monetary effect, it would drive up prices, they refused to allow it to have its monetary effect. They "sterilized" it. As a result, so far from the gold flowing out of America, during the remaining years of the 1920's more gold flowed into that country. Between 1923 and 1929 the United States increased her gold holdings by another $175 million. She only did not increase it by very much more because she only accepted payments on vastly the greater part of her debts by the time-honoured dodge of lending her debtors the money to pay with. On balance her foreign investments during these same years increased by $2,572 million.

Sir Robert Kindersley in his evidence before the Macmillan Commission said,[1] " America went on her bended knees, almost, to the rest of the world to adopt the gold standard—but no sooner had she got them to adopt it than she refused to allow it to work," and " Although New York professed to be on the gold standard she never really allowed the gold standard to work properly." But really little purpose is served by using such question-begging words as ' properly '. As the Federation of British Industries report to the same commission more sensibly put it,[2] " So far as the U.S.A. is concerned, the Federal Reserve Board, as far back as 1923, openly proclaimed its deliberate abandonment of the automatic pre-War gold standard with its regulation of the volume of credit by gold, and the substitution of a system of credit control designed primarily to promote the ' national ' industrial and commercial development of the United States." That is to say, the Americans never pretended that they were going to play according to the rules of the nineteenth century system and, if anybody expected them to do so, he had only his own folly to blame.

What then did they want the gold for at all ? What was the point of saying that you were " on gold " if your true policy was simply one of price stabilization ? One is tempted to say that there was no point, and indeed there is some truth in such an answer. The main reason why the Americans insisted on this curious arrangement was a psychological and not a financial one. No American politician was willing to take the responsibility of advocating cancellation of America's foreign debts. At the same time no economist was willing to answer for the disruptive consequences on American life, if they were truly paid—that is, paid by the import of foreign goods. Therefore some trick had to be

[1] Op. cit., Morgan-Webb, p. 83. [2] Ibid., p. 82.

discovered by which they could be paid—both paid and not paid at the same time. The trick by which they should be paid in gold and the gold then buried under the earth was as good as another.

The present writer has been warned by one who holds a very distinguished position in the banking world that there is no more fatal error in the interpretation of financial history than to imagine that financiers have any far-sighted motives for their actions. The explanation of by far the greater part of the important financial decisions of recent years is quite certainly that those who have taken them have had but a small acquaintance with history, with psychology, or with economics, to say nothing of the laws of simple arithmetic. Yet there was a reason for American policy—a reason but little understood in England. That portion of popular opinion in America which at all understood what was happening favoured it for this reason. Among the masses of the Middle West there was but little feeling of cousinly love for the English. The Americans had in the end come into the War not because they liked the English but because they disliked the Germans. But, even when the necessities of co-operation in arms made it inconvenient to say so, their private opinion remained very much that which President Wilson expressed in the War's first days, when he said that there was not much to choose between the two combatants. To Middle Western opinion the Treaty of Versailles seemed a confirmation of President Wilson's judgment.

On the other hand, what the Western farmer did feel about England was that owing to her command of the machinery of credit she had been able to deprive Americans of the reality of independence for some 130 years after that independence had been won in arms. It is true that they did not draw a sufficient distinction between the City of London and the people of England, and talked about "English policy" in the same way that people in England were talking in equally preposterous generalizations about the "aims of Germany" or the "ambitions of Japan", but men always exaggerate the single-mindedness of distant countries of which they are ignorant.

The Great War had at last put America out of debt.

For her it had indeed been a war of freedom, but it was not only from Potsdam that she had won her freedom. She had won it also from London. The main determination of wise Americans was never again to submit to the humiliation of being in foreign debt. Now the stage property with which London had played its confidence trick was gold. The pretence by which Governments were induced to prefer the bankers' paper to paper of their own printing was the pretence that the bankers' paper was a mere symbol for gold. Therefore the one certain way of preventing the City of London from reasserting its claim to dominate the world was to drain it of gold, or alternatively to compel it to repudiate.

The system established by the Americans in the years after the War must eventually have worked to this end. For not only did the English have to pay English debts to America; they had to pay the debts of other countries, too. For those countries, not possessing sufficient gold, were in no position to pay their debts in gold. They could only pay in goods. Now America, it is true, being a protectionist country, would not take their goods, but Great Britain, being still Free Trade, would take them. Therefore the policy of all the nations of the Continent was to dump all their cheap goods in Great Britain and to pay to America the British gold which they received in exchange for them. This suited the Americans well enough, for it made impossible the reassertion by the City of London of its historic claims. But the very fact that such was their objective proves that the American gold standard of the twentieth century, so far from being the same as the British gold standard of the nineteenth century, only existed at all for the purpose of making impossible the return of the British gold standard.

Now it was the boast of the nineteenth century sterling standard that, since it had erected a delicate machinery to prevent large fluctuations in the amount of gold in the country, it was able, while keeping the foreign exchange value of the pound stable, at the same time to give a reasonable stability of prices. How far the boast was justified has been discussed in previous chapters, but at any rate that was the boast—that was the argument for the nineteenth century sterling standard, and there was no other argument for it. If then we made Great Britain's monetary supply dependent on her gold-holdings at a time when there was a steady drain of gold to America, which the Americans were not allowing to have its monetary effect, then the gold standard, instead of giving the stability which under other circumstances it at least professed to give, would impose upon the country a necessary instability. It was not a question of balancing the advantages of a return to gold against the disadvantages; there were no advantages. Politicians made speeches about the pound being able at last to look the dollar in the face again; and it is true that the return to gold did, of course, fix the pound-dollar exchange rate. But what advantage was there in that when it was accompanied by a complete disorganization of the British internal price-level. The advantage of fixed exchanges is that our foreign customers will be the more ready to do business with us if they can calculate in certainty how much of their money will be required in order to obtain a given quantity of our money. But what advantage was it to an American customer to be completely certain how many English pounds he could get for his dollars if he had no notion at all how many English goods he could buy with his pounds?

It is indeed true that it would have been a grave disaster to Great Britain had her pound collapsed completely in the 1920's and gone the way of the German mark. But there was not the remotest prospect of that happening. Experience had completely shown that the stability of the pound was not in the least dependent on its pretended convertibility into gold. On the other hand, while there were no advantages in the return to gold under the circumstances of 1925, there were the very gravest disadvantages. It was inevitable that the next years must see a drain of gold from Great Britain to America, and, with the pound tied to gold, that drain must have a deflationary effect at home and produce the misery which invariably accompanies deflation. It is of course easy to be wise after the event, but the politicians cannot here plead that they were not forewarned of the consequences of their policy. For in July, 1924, the Federation of British Industries presented to the Cunliffe Commission a memorandum,[1] in which it claimed that the return to

[1] Ibid., pp. 91–2.

the gold standard and the consequent "immediate return to parity with the dollar . . . would represent for us a measure of drastic deflation ". It would, it said, raise the real value of our money by 10 per cent and the consequences of that would be :—

"(*a*) Serious temporary dislocation of trade and a probable increase in unemployment due to the effect of the certainty of a period of falling prices on producers, traders, and buyers.

"(*b*) A severe fall in British prices involving serious loss to all holders of stocks and commodities and on all who trade on borrowed money.

"(*c*) A serious industrial dislocation due to the necessity of reducing money wages by 10 per cent, which would in present circumstances seriously increase the difficulty of maintaining industrial peace.

"(*d*) A strong probability that a severe check would be administered to export trade since the improvement in the exchange value of sterling would be likely to precede and to move faster than the adjustment of internal prices.

"(*e*) An increase in the real burden of the National Debt as a result of revenue falling with prices, while interest charges would remain unaltered."

Mr. Baldwin, as Chancellor of the Exchequer under Mr. Bonar Law, had been responsible for the American debt settlement which made inevitable the drain of gold from Great Britain to America. As Prime Minister, he was responsible for restoring the country to the gold standard. Mr. Winston Churchill was the Chancellor of the Exchequer. The Governor of the Bank of England was the newly appointed Mr. Montague Norman, until recently associated with Brown, Shipley and Co., a City firm with American affiliations. The prediction of the Federation of British Industries was fulfilled in every detail. The return to gold was, as Mr. Keynes describes it in his *Treatise on Money*, "a rapid and cold-blooded deflation." As Mr. Montague Norman himself confessed before the Macmillan Commission "so far as the international position is concerned, we have been continuously under the harrow." At a time when science was clamouring as it had never clamoured before for the opportunity to enrich mankind by the exploitation of its inventions, the Bank of England put the Bank rate at 5½ per cent lest people should demand too much credit and thus make the gold standard insecure. As the depression deepened, the Bank replied in September, 1929, by moving the bank rate up to 6½ per cent.

By such methods of what one can only call desperate lunacy the British were able for a time to borrow back from the Americans the gold which they had paid to them, and throughout the 1920's the physical stock of the country's gold reserves did not vary greatly. They remained at round about £150 million. Yet with the increased quantity of goods even a constant gold reserve was not sufficient to keep prices stable, and from 1921 to 1929 British internal prices, taking 1913 as 100, ran, 197, 159, 159, 166, 159, 148, 142, 140, 137, whereas the American prices for the same years ran 140, 139, 144, 141, 148, 143, 137, 140, 138.[1] The British index moved sixty points while the American moved two. Nor was the effect of living on American loans any other than to make the British crash more sudden, and therefore worse, when it came. These loans could not in the nature of things be repaid so long as America had a high tariff. It was inevitable that the lenders would find this out sooner or later and recall their gold. They found it out after the slump of 1929, when the American gold reserve jumped from $4,284 million to $4,593 million. For a year the British were able to keep up their reserve by borrowing from France what they lost to America. Then owing to the Austrian troubles France got frightened and refused to lend any more. The British gold reserve sank from £148 million in 1930 to £121 million in 1931. Wholesale prices fell from 120 to 104, a National Government had to be formed and the gold standard to be suspended.

Naturally the result of these falling prices was exactly what the Federation of British Industries had prophesied that it would be. The Macmillan Report tells us that "Great Britain established a gold parity which meant that her existing level of sterling incomes and costs was relatively too high in terms of gold, so that, failing a downward adjustment, those of her industries which are subject

[1] *Intelligent Man's Guide Through World Chaos*, G. D. H. Cole, p. 194.

to foreign competition were put at an artificial disadvantage ". That is to say, to put the point in somewhat blunter language, the working-classes were offered their choice between lower wages or unemployment. In an earlier age, when trades unionism was less strong, advantage would have been taken of the dilemma to smash down their wages and to rob them of that advance in their standard of living which the necessity of rapidly attracting workers into munitions had gained for them. As it was, they resisted wage-reductions with the strike weapon—the General Strike and a number of particular strikes. Mr. Winston Churchill claimed that the return to gold was no more responsible for the troubles in the mining industry than was the Gulf Stream. But all serious students agreed with Mr. Keynes in dismissing the argument as " feather-brained ".[1] And, while other Conservative politicians who had the good fortune to be ignorant of the laws of simple economics were able to assure their constituents that there was no intention of a general attack on wages, Lord Hugh Cecil, possessed of a brain and of a University constituency, pointed out the truism that there was no conceivable sense in going back to gold if there was not going to be such a general attack. The gold standard could not conceivably be made to work without lower wages, any more than the proverbial quart could be got into the pint pot. Public opinion was opposed to the General Strike but, in spite of the efforts of the finance controlled press, it remained unconvinced that in a world of rapidly increasing productivity drastic reduction of wages was the solution of the country's troubles. The dole made impossible any such reductions on a large scale, for it is not possible to pay the employed man less than the unemployed. Therefore the working class, while suffering a certain reduction of wages, received the greater part of their punishment in increased unemployment.

Yet a British deflation is much more than a domestic blunder ; it is a world calamity. For Great Britain is by far the largest importer of food in the world, so that the world price of foodstuffs is settled by the price that can be paid on the London market. Now in a deflationary fall of prices the price of foodstuffs always falls much more

[1] *Essays in Persuasion*, Keynes, p. 246.

steeply than those of manufactured goods, for the manufacturer can adjust his supply to the effective demand from week to week, but the farmer has to make his calculations a year before when he does not yet know how much purchasing power will be available to buy his products by the time that they come to the market. It is extremely difficult also to get co-operative action between all the farmers of the world to restrict production. And thus it is that a British deflation not only spreads unemployment throughout Great Britain. It spreads ruin throughout all the great food exporting countries of the world. This the policy of the British Government did.

CHAPTER XIX

CRISIS AND THE COUNTER ATTACK

The City of London made no serious attempt to prevent the Socialists from succeeding the Conservatives in office in accordance with the regular routine in 1929. Of the members of the previous Socialist Cabinet, one alone, Colonel Wedgwood, had indulged in any radical criticisms of the financial system. He was omitted from the new ministry. There returned to the Treasury Mr. Philip Snowden (as he then was) a man hardly balanced in the fanaticism of his devotion to the gold standard or in his utter inability to understand what that standard was.

Meanwhile the return of Great Britain to gold had been followed by a period of high prosperity in the United States. Great as her prosperity was during those years, it was in no way artificial ; there was no reason why it should not have been permanent, and indeed it would be very easy to argue that the standard of living of the American people was below rather than above what it should have been. For every year the United States was exporting large quantities of goods on loan and receiving for them no equivalent import. There was no reason why she should not have made her foreign debtors supply the keep of her tourists abroad and remittances of her emigrants and have cut down her exports so as to balance her imports, using the extra goods thus saved for the benefit of her own citizens or alternatively, if it was preferred, giving increased leisure to those who were, as it was, employed on production for this profitless export market.

What was the reason why the Americans continued to export more than they imported? Two quite different classes of Americans were engaged on the task of breaking the mastery of the City of London. On the one hand, were the manufacturers and the working classes who asked only for freedom from a tyranny and for prosperity. On the other hand were the gentlemen of Wall Street who wanted to prevent the City of London from playing the game of the world's usurer only in order that they might play that game themselves.

For a time the conflict between these two classes could be concealed. It could be concealed so long as the question of the repayment of foreign loans had not yet arisen. But it was inevitable that sooner or later foreign investors would begin to ask, " How can we be repaid so long as there is a high tariff which prevents foreigners from sending us their goods ? " Payment in gold was really only a trick—a trick moreover that could only be played so long as the debtors had some gold to give. That would not be for long, for such gold as was not already in the vaults of New York was steadily pouring into the other great creditor of the world, France. Throughout the latter half of the 1920's her reserves of gold were increasing with a quite intolerable rapidity. In 1926 she held 20,425 million francs, in 1928 31,838 million, in 1929 41,622 million, in 1930 53,563 million, in 1931 66,863 million, in 1932 78,291 million.[1] In addition M. George Bonnet, then Minister of Finance, estimated that on 5th January, 1934, there were 30,000 million francs hoarded throughout France.[2]

Now France, like Great Britain and the United States, was " on gold ". But her gold standard was a third standard, utterly different from either the American or the British. All demonstrations that French policy is an obstacle to the prosperity whether of France or of the world are, to a Frenchman, an irrelevancy. The object of French policy is not, it must be understood, prosperity ; its object is security. Its first concern is to see to it that Frenchmen consume less than they produce. In that, thanks to the frugal habits of the nation, it has been successful. Its second concern has been to discover some means by which the equivalent of that surplus can be made available in the time of crisis. The first attempt to solve that problem was, in the years before the War, by foreign investment—mainly in Russia—but this experiment turned out so disastrously that the French are unwilling to repeat it. Reluctant to

[1] *Intelligent Man's Guide to World Chaos*, G. D. H. Cole, p. 240.

[2] *Rise and Fall of the Gold Standard*, Morgan-Webb, p. 129.

invest abroad at all, they positively refuse to invest save in short-term loans. They prefer rather to return to the principles of the old mercantilist philosophy of the seventeenth century, to receive the balance of their payments in gold and to hoard the gold against the day of crisis, when they will bring it out to buy the necessities of war. The French Government therefore hoards because it does not trust the foreigner, and the French peasant hoards because he does not trust the Government.

Therefore as a result of French policy there was no gold with which the debts to America could be paid. If they were to be paid, they had to be paid in goods and it was not possible to persuade further investors to send out more loans unless they could be persuaded that there was at least a prospect of foreign goods being admitted in repayment of them. President Hoover might argue,[1] " I believe we have to-day an equipment and a skill in production that yield us a surplus of commodities beyond any compensation we can usefully take by way of imported commodities. To me there is only one remedy, and that is by the systematic, permanent investment of our surplus production in reproductive works abroad. We thus reduce the return we must receive to a return of interest and profit." But permanent lending is a contradiction in terms, and the number of people who understood that this was merely a roundabout way of saying that the debts would never be paid at all was on the increase. Messrs. Foster and Catchings commented on the President's argument in their *Profits*,[2] " What does this mean ? It seems to mean that if we work very hard, we can send more wealth abroad, and thus acquire more capital abroad, and thus possibly receive more interest and dividends from abroad, wherewith to acquire still more capital abroad, and so on, generation after generation, without finding any way whereby we or our children or our children's children can ever benefit greatly by our increased productivity. According to this theory our own standard of living must remain the same as though we had never produced all this surplus wealth."

Mr. John Foster Dulles, counsel to the American

[1] *A Main Cause of Unemployment*, Loftus, p. 37.
[2] Ibid., pp. 38–9.

Commission to Negotiate Peace, said,[1] at about the same time, " So long as we have a national policy of promoting exports, of protecting our industry by a high tariff, of full collection of debts—so long as we have such a policy and the basic economic conditions remain substantially as they are to-day—so long must we finance our exports very largely through the medium of loaning foreigners the money wherewith to pay for them." Strange as it may seem, this argument was intended by Mr. Dulles to be an argument for foreign loans, for it never occurred to him to ask whether a " national policy of promoting exports " was not a very silly policy. But, after he had done defending foreign loans, there was hardly anything to be added to the case against them.

It became clear that the debts could only be paid if the tariff was lowered so that foreign goods could come into America. But under conditions of free trade or conditions even approximating to free trade the foreign goods could always undersell the American goods because of the lower wages by which they were produced. Therefore, with the tariff reduced, American goods would only be able to hold their own in the American market if American wages were lowered. The American working man, like the English working man, would have to choose between low wages and unemployment.

It was this conflict between employers and their workmen on the one side and the financiers on the other that led America to her catastrophe. The issue was not clearly defined, for the financiers were astute enough to see that their victory was only possible if they spread as widely through the country as they could the habit of speculation. Therefore the banks lent wildly and assisted in the forcing up of securities to impossible heights by themselves investing their invented money on a prodigious scale. On 30th June, 1921, according to the Report of the President's Research Committee on Recent Social Trends in the United States, the investments of banks who were members of the Federal Reserve Board stood at $6,002 million. By 30th June, 1928, they had risen to $10,758 million.

How far the financiers foresaw the consequences of their policy, how far they did not foresee only because they

[1] *America Self-Contained*, Samuel Crowther, pp. 130, 131.

preferred not to look ahead, how far they were genuinely blind, it is impossible to say. One can but describe the facts. Certainly the policy pursued was, at a time when the productivity of American industry was increasing with unexampled rapidity, to see to it that there should be no increase in the purchasing power of those who wanted the mass-produced articles which that industry was throwing on to the market. There was no such increase in purchasing power for two reasons. First, because there was no appreciable rise in the wages of the factory worker. While the output of industry rose between 1923 and 1929 from $25,850 million to $31,900 million, the sum total paid out in wages rose from $11,009 million to $11,684 million.[1] The one increased by 25 per cent while the other only increased by 5 per cent. Secondly, there was a sharp decline in the purchasing power of those engaged in the two great export businesses of cotton and corn. For the price received for these articles is the world price, that is to say, the price on the London market. That price, as has already been explained, fell heavily owing to the British policy of deflation.

On the other hand, the profits of the well-to-do, the non-wage earner, in America had everywhere increased. The result of the bank's investment policy was to force up the value of securities and, with the prospects of a continuing rise, those with money to spare spent it on buying securities instead of on buying commodities. Even foreign countries, who were still telling the Americans that they were too poor to pay their debts and who had borrowed from America large sums in order to preserve themselves from chaos, were able to lend back to America out of their bankruptcy no less than $2,131 million in long term investments and $2,437 milliion in short-term.[2] In 1929 the United States, though on balance enormously a creditor country, was yet at the same time probably more heavily in debt than she ever been before in her history.

The banks, having thus caused the speculation boom (whether they intended to cause it or not) now announced that it was their duty to step in and save the country by deflationary measures. Throughout 1928 and 1929 they

[1] *Speculation and Collapse in Wall Street*, R. G. Hawtrey.
[2] From Mr. Peek's report to President Roosevelt.

pushed up the discount rate from 3½ per cent to 4 per cent, to 4½ per cent, to 5 per cent, and finally to 6 per cent. The effect of this was indeed to stop speculation, but only as Mr. Hawtrey fairly says, in his *Art of Central Banking*, " by stopping prosperity." And, if one is to pay the bankers the compliment of assuming that they had any knowledge of the ABC of their own business, one can only conclude that their true purpose was not to stop speculation but to stop prosperity. Either the financial affairs of the nation were in the hands of men who simply did not know that if everybody bought securities the price of them rose, or alternatively the bankers purposely created the speculation in order that, under the excuse of killing it, they might kill the prosperity. Thus it might be possible to win the consent of the American people to free trade and its necessary consequence of low wages by making it appear that that collapse was the inevitable result of the high tariff. It is in all soberness hard to see how there is any third explanation of what happened.

I do not say that there was any secret document, signed by the masters of the credit machinery, in which they pledged themselves to work for such an end. But there was that very real, if tacit, agreement which comes from the breathing of the same ambient air. As Thomas W. Lamont of J. P. Morgan put it in his comments on the American Power Trust, " I wouldn't say, if I were you, that there was anything in the nature of a Trust. There isn't anything like that at all ; what I would say is just simply that we and the banks and certain other companies interested in Power are all standing around in a co-operative frame of mind."

The Wall Street crash did not bring about an immediate collapse of the American tariff. The first result of it was that Americans, thinking that they had learnt in time of the folly of speculation, began to recall the gold that they had lent to Great Britain. Great Britain found that her gold reserves were vanishing away. The Labour Government was in power in Great Britain. But no member of it betrayed one inkling of understanding of what was happening. They inherited the gold standard from their so-called opponents and, as the country's gold holdings decreased, they obediently decreased its monetary supply, thinking apparently that the two were related by a law as inevitable as that of the multiplication table. The effects were of course those which the Federation of British Industries had predicted. Distress and unemployment increased with horrible rapidity. Utterly without a notion of the disease from which the country was suffering, its governors, who on the election platform a year or two before had announced that they alone had a remedy for unemployment and that, if they were returned to power, the sufferings of the poor would at last have an end—these men in their desperation appointed a committee which should investigate and report and tell them how to govern the country.

The Committee—the famous May Committee—issued its report in the summer of 1931. The medicine which it prescribed to the country was that of drastic economy. We were spending more than we could afford and, in order to balance our budget, we must reduce expenditure. As the numbers of the unemployed were rising with rapidity, factories at the same time were either working half-time or not working at all and our foreign customers were destroying their food because we refused to produce manufactured goods to exchange for it, the diagnosis was manifestly a false one. It was true that the nation was consuming more than it was producing, but it was consuming enormously less then it could produce. To seek to reduce consumption to actual production was about as sensible as it would be to cut a number of people's heads off because there were not enough hats to go round. What was wanted was not a reduction but an increase of purchasing power. But, *if the country's currency was to remain tied to gold*, then the May Committee was manifestly right. As gold left the country, the monetary supply must be reduced and such reduction could only be effected by a reduction of expenditure.

The Labour Cabinet, according to Mr. G. D. H. Cole,[1] never even debated the possibility of suspending the gold standard. They agreed to maintain it and to carry through the economies demanded by its maintenance and, since Great Britain was herself denuded of gold, they agreed to maintain it by borrowing gold from its only two substantial possessors—the financiers of New York and of Paris. Now

[1] *Intelligent Man's Guide Through World Chaos*, G. D. H. Cole, p. 100.

the financiers of New York were anxious to compel a reduction in the dole paid to the British unemployed. For the reduction of wages is much easier when there is no dole for unemployment and, if the English dole were reduced, it would be easier to resist the demand for a dole in America. If the crisis did not make possible the reduction of American wages, there was, from the American financier's point of view, hardly any point in having it at all. Therefore they made the reduction of the English dole a condition of their granting of the loan of gold to the Bank of England.

Before this demand the majority of the Labour Cabinet, to their credit, revolted, though, as they still demanded the balancing of the budget and the maintenance of the gold standard, and had no coherent proposals how the budget could be balanced without the reduction of the dole, their revolt was a singularly futile one. The minority of the Labour Cabinet did not even revolt at this humiliation. They accepted the terms of the American financiers. It is true that Mr. Ramsay MacDonald, as a general rule, pretended that it was not American dictation which was responsible for the reduction of the dole, but in a moment of forgetfulness he admitted that it was so in the House of Commons in answer to a question from Mr. Frank Owen.[1] There was no limit to the sacrifices, which in the opinion of this minority, must be made to the sacred cause of gold. The Conservative and Liberal politicians agreed with them. The pretence that there was any difference between the parties was abandoned, and all joined together in a great National Government for the defence of gold.

Yet all was in vain. The gold still continued to flow out of the country. And one September Sunday we woke up to hear that the gold standard had been suspended. A banker has told the present writer how he went to his bank the next Monday expecting to find a queue of angry men demanding their deposits. There was nobody there. There was no queue

[1] See *Hansard*, vol. 256, col. 1272 (21st Sept., 1931). Mr. Owen asked: "In view of the falling value of the pound and the fact that every other class singled out for a reduction has been granted a concession, will the Prime Minister now consider granting a concession to the unemployed?"

Mr. Ramsay MacDonald answered: ". . . The handling of the unemployment cuts was necessitated by special conditions of borrowing, and they must remain."

anywhere in all England. The bankers and politicians had held over our heads the threat that, if the link with gold was snapped, the price-level would rocket up to the skies and the pound go the way of the post-War mark. The threat was found to be the purest moonshine. Not only did the price-level not get out of control; there was never the remotest chance of it getting out of control. Indeed the difficulty was to raise prices enough. Instead everything got a little better. Employment improved. Exports were easier. The beginnings of returning prosperity began to appear. It was as if a runner who had ploughed along with a heavy burden on his back had at last been able to throw that burden off and now ran free.

For years we had been told by the bankers that our troubles were due to our own laziness and stupidity and out-of-date equipment. We found that it was not so, that they were due rather to the standard which the bankers had themselves imposed upon us. " The game was played up to the limits of quixotry," wrote Mr. Keynes,[1] " even at the risk of driving British trade to a standstill." And then, when at last the game was of perforce abandoned and when the wheels of industry as a consequence began slowly to move again, we opened our newspapers and found to our amazement that it was the bankers who were taking to themselves the credit for having guided the country through its crisis. Their creatures, the politicians, made speeches in praise of their masters. It is impossible to withhold a certain tribute of admiration for the very impudence of the claim.

Yet I think that history will have to record that they made a false move, exaggerating a little the gullibility of the public. The important authority of Mr. R. G. Hawtrey[2] has spoken of " central banks proceeding from their position of complacent detachment to generate depression, unemployment, bankruptcy, budget defaults, with all the resulting political and social convulsions, while Government after Government is broken because it can neither stem the flood of ruin, nor even provide tolerable palliatives to alleviate the consequences ". And I think and hope that Sir Charles Morgan-Webb is right when he tells us, " The

[1] Op. cit., Morgan-Webb, p. 107.
[2] *Art of Central Banking*, 127.

contemptuous references to the incompetence of the British manufacturer and to the laziness and greed of the British workman, as being responsible for disasters now known to have been due to the gold standard, have not been forgotten. There is an unshakable conviction in the minds of the leaders of industry and of the workers alike that the seven years of depression and humiliation from 1924 to 1931 were artificially induced, and artificially prolonged, by the Bank of England and the Treasury in order to restore and maintain the gold standard."[1]

Yet, if our monetary supply was not to be regulated by gold, there arose the question, "How then was it to be regulated?" To that question there was but one sane answer. "Go right back to the teaching of Bishop Berkeley and return to the ancient standard of Christendom, to the stable price-level." That policy had already been recommended by the Macmillan Report,[2] which said, "The ultimate aim should be the stability of the international price-level, meaning by this the composite price at wholesale of the principal foodstuffs and raw materials entering into international trade as measured by the best known wholesale index numbers." Such a declaration was eagerly welcomed in the British Dominions, whose whole economic life had been thrown into chaos by the British deflation and consequent collapse of the London prices of primary products. And therefore at the Ottawa Conference of 1932 the new policy was formally adopted. The *Economist* index was taken as the guide of British financial policy.

In that same year of 1932 there was a Presidential election in the United States. The Republicans with their high tariffs had by now served the purposes of finance. It was no longer desired to attract immigrants. What was now wanted was to attract goods from Europe for the payment of dividends. And, if the goods were to come in, the tariffs must come down. Therefore Mr. Hoover, the Republican, was defeated, and Mr. Roosevelt, the Democrat, was elected. Mr. Roosevelt was to enter upon his office in March, 1933. It is not, I hope, too cynical to imagine that it was not wholly a matter of chance that his inauguration happened to coincide with an enormous financial crisis and the whole

[1] Op. cit., Morgan-Webb, p. 127. [2] Ibid., p. 163.

country trembling upon the verge of chaos. In such a crisis it might reasonably be expected that the new President, terrified of his responsibility, would go on his knees to the masters of finance and beg them to save the country from final ruin. The price that they would have exacted would have been the reduction of the tariff. It would doubtless have been recommended to the people with some unctuous generalities about free trade and international comity, and they would have been offered the choice between employment at European wages and no employment at all.

If such were its calculations, then Wall Street had utterly misjudged its man. They had put into power a man who did not flinch in his courage, and who used the very magnitude of the crisis, which the financiers had created, for the financiers' undoing. He proclaimed his faith in two things—strange and unrelated to one who has not given his mind to such matters, intimately and necessarily interlinked to their student. He proclaimed the reality of his religious faith and his intention of establishing a stable price-level—" a commodity dollar." " The United States," he wrote to the World Economic Conference, " seeks the kind of dollar which a generation hence will have the same purchasing and debt-paying power as the dollar value we hope to attain in the near future."

In his inaugural address on 4th March, 1933, he denounced without flinching the philosophy which had brought his country and the world to ruin and proclaimed without flinching the philosophy which alone could break that ruin. The world's troubles, he said, were " primarily . . . because the rulers of the exchanges of mankind's goods have failed through their own stubbornness and their own incompetence, have admitted their failure and have abdicated. Practices of the unscrupulous money-changers stand indicted in the court of public opinion, rejected by the hearts and minds of men . . . The money-changers have fled from their high seats in the temple of civilization. We may now restore that temple to the ancient truths. . . . In this dedication of a nation we humbly ask the blessing of God ". It was the death-sentence of an economic system. But it was far more than that. It was the deliberate repudiation of a heresy that has cursed and warped the story of mankind for five hundred years—the gigantic heresy that Man is sufficient to himself and that it is possible to organize a human society apart from God.

In Dante's great vision of Hell, among the false Gods that have deceived mankind to none is there given a more shameful place than to Plutus. He is the most cowardly of them all. He alone is dumb, for Greed dare not honestly preach its gospel, since it is a gospel that can only be accepted when it is misunderstood. Before the words of a brave man it collapses, Dante tells us, "as the sails swollen with the wind fall when the mast breaks."[1] So it proved six hundred years after Dante died. If anything be certain of our times, it is certain that that day, 4th of March, 1933, will be remembered for ever as one of the great turning days in the history of mankind. And it is permissible to believe that there stood with the President that morning the spirits of those men throughout the ages who have fought for mankind the eternal battle against usury. Aristotle and Moses were there, who stand at the fundament of all Christian thought, and all the saints and doctors who have built upon their teaching, the prophets of every great religion that has ever made claim to the large allegiance of mankind, Dante and Shakespeare, Sir Thomas More, martyr for an even nobler cause, Charles II who was such an unconscionable time in dying and Charles I whom they killed so swiftly, Dryden, who earned by his immortal verse those guineas which he refused to earn by raising his tenants' rents, Bishop Berkeley, to whose ample vision the whole panorama of folly lay manifest, the great Napoleon who challenged the evil Thing in arms, Cobbett, "the horseman of apocalypse," who fought it with scorn, Shaftesbury, the lover of the poor, Jackson, to whom "these truths" were "self-evident", and Ruskin, driven to frenzy by the callousness of the world. There stood the spirits of this strange and ill-assorted company—men differing from one another in every taste and in every characteristic, united only in the unison with which they bear witness against the eternal lie of Shylock. "Or is your gold and silver ewes and rams?" asks Antonio. "I cannot tell," answers Shylock, lying. "I make it breed as fast."[2] Two years before, in

[1] Quoted by Ruskin, *Unto This Last*, 74 n. [2] *Merchant of Venice*, I, iii, 96–7.

1931, the great Pope had sent forth his lamentation. "None dare breathe against their will." [1] Across the Atlantic there came the answer from the man who dared to breathe against their will.

If the price-level is kept stable, then the power of the moneyed interest must inevitably be broken. For no longer can the money power create by deflation a situation where there simply is not the money in existence with which to repay to it its debts. So long as the policy is one of keeping stable the price-level, then, as fast as the banks withdraw money from circulation, the Government issues out new money to take its place. Under the old system the banks lent out $100 million to the producers of the nation and demanded $105 million in repayment. But, as no money came into existence except as a loan, the extra $5 million did not anywhere exist. However efficient the producers, however great the increase of their productivity, it was mathematically impossible for them as a body to get out of debt or for any individual among them to get out of debt save by plunging some colleague yet more deeply into debt. The bankers protested that they were only too willing to lend if only they could find any credit-worthy borrowers. But it was their own system which made it mathematically impossible for borrowers to be credit-worthy. But under President Roosevelt's system an increased monetary supply, issued by the Government, is put out to purchase an increased quantity of goods. There is therefore, say, $150 million in circulation throughout the nation. The producers can repay their debts of $105 million and still have $45 million in their pockets. If you make two blades of grass grow where one grew before, you can, under President Roosevelt, sell for two pence what it only cost you a penny to produce. Under the old system all that happened was that the price of blades of grass fell to a halfpenny and you had to pay back to the money-lender twice as much, in terms of goods, as you had borrowed.

So long as the price-level is kept stable, it does not even greatly matter if, for political reasons, the Government should at first borrow its new money from the banks. For it can always break the money-power at whatever moment

[1] *Quadragesimo Anno.*

suits its purposes by demanding that the banks pay out their loans in cash, which, since they have promised to pay ten times more than they possess, they will be unable to do. The banks will then have no alternative but to ask the Government to guarantee their deposits, which the Government will do on condition that a dollar's debt is crossed off for every dollar guaranteed. Thus all money will become Government-issued money, and double-money will no longer exist. With the price-level stable inevitably the people will soon begin to get out of debt and the stranglehold of usury will be broken.

The policy to which President Roosevelt had committed himself was the policy to which the British National Government was already pledged at Ottawa. It was forced thus to pledge itself by the Dominions who, being exporters of foodstuffs which they sold on the London market, had, as has been said, suffered cruelly from the collapse of prices of primary products owing to British deflation. It is hardly too much to say that the condition of the continuance of the Empire was a guarantee that there would never again be another such collapse. President Roosevelt had therefore reason to think that on this high programme the ancient discord of the two countries could at last be forgotten. With this hope he agreed to send an American delegation to the World Economic Conference at London, agreeing that "the Conference must establish order in the place of the present chaos by the stabilization of currency." [1]

Now it is clear that by "stabilization" he meant stabilization of the price-level. And it is clear, too, that if all the nations agreed to keep stable their internal price-levels, the exchange values of their currencies, one against another, could not in nature oscillate very greatly. But it is clear also that, if they all agree to keep their exchange-values stable without any guarantee that internal price-levels will be kept stable and if one country is determined to force down its price-level, then all other countries will have to force down their price-levels too. Now France was a nervous creditor country with a mercantilist mentality. The lower the world price-level, the greater the value of the gold which she received. The lower the domestic price-level

[1] Quoted from the speech of Mr. Neville Chamberlain, 10th July, 1933.

the less the amount of gold that would be required to back her domestic currency, the larger the amount that could be hoarded for foreign purchases in the day of the calamity of war.

President Roosevelt therefore meant by "stabilization" stabilization of price-level; the French meant stabilization of exchange-values. Remembering the policy to which they had already committed themselves at Ottawa, the President was entitled to expect that the British would be on his side. However in face of the rising German menace the British did not dare quarrel with the French. It is the strange, the incredible part of the business that London had itself created that menace by which it was terrified. For the money-lender must for ever go on lending. He will lend money to his mortal enemies to enable them to buy the guns to blow him to bits, sooner than not lend it at all—and that is precisely what the London financiers have done to Herr Hitler. "She has gone on buying wool, cotton, nickel, rubber, and petrol," writes the *Stock Exchange Gazette* of 3rd May, 1935, "until her requirements were fulfilled, and the financing has been done directly or indirectly through London." Yet the British, in spite of having created the power of Nazi Germany, were nevertheless terrified of it. Mr. Neville Chamberlain therefore affected not to understand the distinction between the two senses in which the word "stabilization" was used and, caring only that it should collapse, allowed the Americans to bear the odium of the Conference's collapse. As he put it, "President Roosevelt said that the Conference must establish order in the place of the present chaos by the stabilization of currency," and "as to the desirability of some permanent stabilization and ultimate stabilization he did not think that there could have been any difference among the delegates. The quotation he had already read showed what an important place it took in the mind of Mr. Roosevelt only a short time ago,"[1]—two statements which bear the marks of having been worded with some care so as to prevent the possibility of their having any meaning.

As soon as the Conference was safely dead, the British Empire delegates met and issued their Currency Manifesto.

[1] Op. cit., Morgan-Webb, p. 131.

They demanded, first, the raising of the price-level to a figure that would cause debts to be repaid in money of the same value as that in which they were contracted. Then they resolved—" That the movement of price-levels towards the stabilization point must be measured by a Price Index, not by gold. That the stabilization of the exchanges depends on stabilization of prices. That stabilization of the exchanges is only possible with those countries adopting a common policy in regard to stabilization of prices. . . . That stabilization of prices and exchanges within the Empire must not be jeopardized by exchange commitments with any countries not pursuing the same price policy." [1]

It was the end of the old world.

[1] Summary by Morgan-Webb, op. cit., pp. 143, 144.

EPILOGUE

Across one of the meanest of London's slum streets at the time of the Jubilee of King George V there hung a streamer on which was inscribed, "To hell with the Capitalists. God Save the King." I do not claim that there was any deep or accurate philosophy behind the first of these sentences. Yet they are, I think, expressive of a new, and yet old, faith that is alive in the world. The old-fashioned Swinburnian radical who saw in the priest and the king the two enemies of the people is dying fast. The true enemy is he whom Mr. H. G. Wells so happily calls the "smart Alec",[1] the man to whom the whole end of life is the extraction of money from the pockets of his fellow-citizens by a variety of tricks. Priests and kings may have had their faults, but at least they are symbols of a power that is not of this world; they are reminders of values that the "smart Alec" has never known. And with all his pomposity what is the high financier but a "smart Alec" in a top-hat? It is intolerable that the high culture of Christendom should be thrown into jeopardy to provide a platform for the tricks of these empty men.

Nor is it only by their follies and their incompetence that they throw us into jeopardy. There is a more subtle danger. They set up their standards of what life is, and weary, simple souls answer that, if that is all that life is, then it is not worth living. It is to that conclusion of futility that the Western world has been gradually coming under the tyranny of "smart Alec's" rule. There is no materialistic reason at all why our civilization should be in danger of dissolution. The material damage of the last War was tiny. The new inventions which its necessities called forth were sufficient to replace all that was destroyed again and again. The danger to our civilization is a spiritual danger—the danger that a race is growing up which is unable to see any point in life, which merely does not care to survive. The

[1] *Experiment in Autobiography*, H. G. Wells.

poetry of Baudelaire, M. Paul Valery tells us, is " la poésie même de la modernité ".[1] Statistics do not carry us very far in the demonstration of this danger, but, in so far as a statistic is relevant, it is not that of material productivity but of the falling birth-rate.

In any newspaper that one picks up one can find raging the eternal controversy whether people should be permitted to use contraceptive devices. But it is extraordinary how rarely one hears the comment, " What an amazing thing it is that people should not want to have children ! " And it is extraordinary, too, among all the welter of statistics, how rarely attention is called to the exact and grim coincidence between the fall in the birth-rate and the rise in the suicide-rate.[2] Yet it is our sorry privilege to belong to the generation which reproduces itself less frequently and which blows its brains out more frequently than any generation since Christendom began.

It is not easy to find arguments against the use of contraceptives, where for medical reasons, the woman is unable to bear a child. The Christian indeed must refrain because he believes that the sexual gift is a very special gift of God, and it is only legitimate for him to use God's gifts in the way which God ordains. But, if he be asked what is his evidence that God has so ordained, the only utterly convincing answer is that the Church, which is the voice of God, says so. It is therefore unreasonable to expect those who do not recognize in the Church the voice of God necessarily to accept its ordinance. But what is interesting is that in the modern world the use of contraceptives is, more often than not, defended not as an exceptional expedient where child-bearing is impossible but as a general habit to prevent child-bearing. The argument used is the economic argument. Now this argument is not only a false argument ; it does not begin to make sense at any point whatsoever. If there is unemployment to-day, the reason for it is that there are not enough consumers. Never has there been a time when the world could more easily produce the necessities for a population vastly greater than it possesses. And the true reason for the fall in the birth-rate

[1] *Do What you Will*, Aldous Huxley. Essay on Baudelaire.
[2] See the present writer's *Breakdown of Money*, pp. 198–210.

is beyond question not an economic but a psychopathic one. People are ceasing to have children because they are ceasing to want children ; they are ceasing to want children because they are ceasing to want anything ; they are ceasing to want anything because they are ceasing to believe in anything. To them

> *πᾶντα γέλως, καὶ πᾶντα κονίς, καὶ πᾶντα τὸ μηδὲν.*
> *πᾶντα γαρ ἐξ ἀλόγου ἐστι τὰ γιγνόμενα.*[1]

The ultimate punishment then which usury exacts is a spiritual punishment—the destruction of joy. It is the great cheater. It cheats the few, the lenders, with the vain hope of living for ever upon their breeding metals and a permanent, independent income, they and their families plastered round with their mechanical amusements, bored while they have them and terrified lest they lose them. It keeps the many, the borrowers, under the continual tyranny of a debt that is irrepayable, though the failure to repay it is a deadly sin. To Voltaire, the high prophet of the faith of Mammon, the London Stock Exchange was a holy place, for there they asked no one for his religious faith "*et ne donnent le nom d'infidéles qu'à ceux qui font banqueroute*".[2] The mocking sceptic thought that he was putting forward a humorous plea for tolerance. But he did not foresee that the turn of time would give to his words an irony more terrible than any of which even he was ever master. He did not foresee that a whole world would come to hold his faith and that the whole world would be driven into bankruptcy. For under usury life withers, and the worship of the sterile metals spreads sterility over the whole life of society.

Now the deepest strength of President Roosevelt's appeal, as we can see from such a book as Mr. Cornelius Vanderbilt's *Farewell to Fifth Avenue*, is that it is at bottom a spiritual remedy for a spiritual disease. Both he and his ministers have perhaps made mistakes in detail and will perhaps make still more mistakes. But such mistakes can never blur the mighty truth that his appeal has not been

[1] "All is laughter, all is dust, all is nothing; everything is born of unreason." Glycon, ed., *Greek Anthology*, Mackail, 12, 34.

[2] Quoted by Amintore Fanfani, *Catholicism, Protestantism, and Capitalism*, p. 98.

to one class against another class. His appeal has been to a people and a world, sick to death of the division of the Two Nations and the meanness of class war, an appeal to the noble soul against the petty soul in every man of every class, an invitation to destroy class divisions in the transcendent unity. It has been, as he himself has put it with courage and with simplicity, an appeal " to restore . . . the *ancient* truths ".[1]

[1] From his Inaugural Address.

INDEX

Printed in Great Britain by Stephen Austin & Sons, Ltd., Hertford.

www.ingramcontent.com/pod-product-compliance
Lightning Source LLC
LaVergne TN
LVHW011121300926
849160LV00008B/467
9781138865372